Fighting for the Dream

ALSO BY RW JOHNSON

How Long Will South Africa Survive? (1977)

The Long March of the French Left (1981)

Shootdown: the Verdict on KAL 007 (1983)

The Politics of Recession (1985)

Heroes and Villains: Selected Essays (1990)

Launching Democracy in South Africa: The First Open Election, April 1994
(ed. with Lawrence Schlemmer) (1996)

Ironic Victory: Liberalism in Post-Liberation South Africa
(ed. with David Welsh) (1998)

South Africa: The First Man, the Last Nation (2004)

African Perspectives (ed. with Christopher Allen) (2008)

*South Africa's Brave New World: The Beloved Country since the
End of Apartheid* (2010)

*The African University? The Critical Case of South Africa and the
Tragedy at the UKZN* (2012)

Look Back in Laughter: Oxford's Post-War Golden Age (2015)

How Long Will South Africa Survive? The Crisis Continues
(first edition 2015; second edition 2017)

RW Johnson

Fighting for the Dream

Jonathan Ball Publishers

JOHANNESBURG & CAPE TOWN

Published in South Africa in 2019 by
JONATHAN BALL PUBLISHERS
A division of Media24 (Pty) Ltd
PO Box 33977
Jeppestown
2043

ISBN 978-1-86842-957-8
ebook ISBN 978-1-86842-958-5

Twitter: www.twitter.com/JonathanBallPub
Facebook: www.facebook.com/JonathanBallPublishers
Blog: http://jonathanball.bookslive.co.za/

Cover photograph: Opposition parties and civil society groups
march against President Jacob Zuma in Tshwane, 7 April 2017
(Gallo Images/Alet Pretorius)

Cover by publicide
Design and typesetting by Triple M Design
Set in 11/16 pt Plantin Light

For Barbara

Contents

Abbreviations and acronyms

AGOA	Africa Growth and Opportunity Act
ANC	African National Congress
ANCWL	ANC Women's League
ANCYL	ANC Youth League
ATC	African Transformation Congress
AU	African Union
BEE	black economic empowerment
BLF	Black First Land First
Brics	Brazil, Russia, India, China, South Africa
CDE	Centre for Development and Enterprise
Codesa	Convention for a Democratic South Africa
Cope	Congress of the People
Cosatu	Congress of South African Trade Unions
DA	Democratic Alliance
EFF	Economic Freedom Fighters
EWC	expropriation without compensation
FNS	Friedrich-Naumann-Stiftung
Gear	Growth, Employment and Redistribution
GNU	government of national unity
HSF	Helen Suzman Foundation
IMF	International Monetary Fund

MEC	Member of the Executive Council (provincial cabinet minister)
MK	Umkhonto we Sizwe
MKMVA	Umkhonto we Sizwe Military Veterans' Association
Nafupa	National Funeral Practitioners Association of South Africa
MP	Member of Parliament
NDP	National Development Plan
NDR	National Democratic Revolution
NEC	National Executive Committee
Nepad	New Partnership for Africa's Development
NGO	non-governmental organisation
NHI	National Health Insurance
NPA	National Prosecuting Authority
Numsa	National Union of Metalworkers of South Africa
OAU	Organization of African Unity
OBE	outcomes-based education
PIC	Public Investment Corporation
Prasa	Passenger Rail Agency of South Africa
RDP	Reconstruction and Development Programme
SAA	South African Airways
SABC	South African Broadcasting Corporation
SACP	South African Communist Party
Sadtu	South African Democratic Teachers' Union
SAIRR	South African Institute of Race Relations
SAPS	South African Police Service
SARS	South African Revenue Service
SIU	Special Investigating Unit
SME	small to medium enterprise
SOE	state-owned enterprise
UDF	United Democratic Front
UN	United Nations

Foreword

When I returned to South Africa permanently in 1995, I did so with the intention of helping the liberal current in the country as far as possible. It seemed to me then – it seems to me now – that with the country in transition from one authoritarian nationalism to another, nothing could be more important than to keep the liberal spirit and tradition alive.

I left Oxford in order to take up the post of director of the Helen Suzman Foundation (HSF) at the invitation of the Friedrich-Naumann-Stiftung (FNS), which has played an admirable role in promoting the liberal cause in South Africa for many decades now. Although one of the smaller German political foundations, it has probably had more impact than any other. The Democratic Alliance (DA), which it has supported, has multiplied its vote more than 13-fold since 1994 and the HSF and the South African Institute of Race Relations (SAIRR), which it also supports, are without doubt the country's two leading political NGOs.

I enjoyed working with the FNS's small but dedicated staff, and over time I came to have a strong friendship with Count Otto von Lambsdorff (then world president of the FNS) and his wife, Countess Alexandra. Otto and Alexandra were always wonderfully well-informed about world affairs as well as analytically shrewd; besides which they were just warm, good friends. My wife and I mourned Otto's death in 2009, and to this day his photo occupies an important place in our house.

Those were difficult times. The African National Congress (ANC) was utterly dominant and very hostile to the liberal cause. Fundraising was next to impossible. Running the HSF then meant extreme unpopularity and sometimes being under threat. The real divide was between the few people with the backbone to stand up – and the rest. One relearns old lessons in such a situation. As Pericles put it over 2 500 years ago, 'The secret of happiness is liberty, the secret of liberty is courage.' The friends you made in such a situation really counted.

Of that little group of HSF and FNS staff that I worked with in Johannesburg in those years only one person remains today, Barbara Groeblinghoff. Barbara has worked indefatigably to assist liberal parties and NGOs throughout southern Africa for a quarter of a century. Her contribution has been immense, and although she and I have ploughed different furrows, I have always been conscious of her working away in rough parallel with myself. A wide variety of organisations owe Barbara a great deal, and she has always worked unobtrusively with efficiency, energy and charm. I have little doubt that Otto and Alexandra would understand and applaud the fact that this book is dedicated to Barbara. Naturally, neither she nor anyone else carries any responsibility for the opinions in this book. Both they and all the mistakes are my own.

RW Johnson
Cape Town, February 2019

Chapter One

Moment of truth

17 December 2017. A moment of high political theatre in the Nasrec conference centre in Johannesburg. For years, things had been building up to this, the election of a new president of the ANC, who would, almost automatically, become the new president of South Africa.

Jacob Zuma, the sitting president, had won power by defeating Thabo Mbeki at the ANC's Polokwane conference in 2007. Mbeki had fallen for that besetting sin of African presidents: he wasn't willing to give up power. Since he had really run the country under Nelson Mandela's presidency and then had two terms of his own, by 2007 he had held power for 13 years but still couldn't bear to walk away. And whereas the state presidency was limited to two terms, the ANC presidency could be held indefinitely, so Mbeki decided he would run again and use that position to continue pulling the strings of government. But he had antagonised too many people and was decisively voted down by the conference.

Ten years later, Zuma found himself possessed of an equally strong wish to retain power beyond his allotted two terms. His gambit was to run his former wife, Dr Nkosazana Dlamini-Zuma, in his place – with exactly the same intention of pulling the strings of government and ruling through her as a virtual puppet. The evidence suggested that Zuma was immensely corrupt and had made both his family and himself extremely rich in office, while virtually handing the country over to the control of his friends, the Gupta family. Zuma was naturally keen to maintain this lucrative arrangement, but he also had reason to fear that if he lost office he might face losing everything and going to jail.

It was not difficult to find ANC old-stagers who were horrified at the thought that Zuma might be followed by another Zuma, that South Africa should succumb to the same dynastic rule that had destroyed Angola and the Congo. And they could point to Zimbabwe where, only a month before, Robert Mugabe's attempt to arrange for his wife, Grace, to succeed him had provoked a military coup and the end of the Mugabe regime.

The truth was that there was a grossness to Zuma. It showed not only in his corruption, indeed his virtual treason in handing over the state to the Guptas, but also in the completely blatant way it was conducted and his cheerful dismissal of any criticism of it as 'racist' or even as 'persecution'. It showed, too, in his propensity, even well into his seventies, to father further love children here and there – most recently with Nokuthula, daughter of Ben Ngubane, the former board chair of Eskom and the South African Broadcasting Corporation (SABC).[1] This side of Zuma drove many South Africans almost to despair, for Zuma's appetites seemingly had no limit. He adopted the style of a 19th-century Zulu king, with his own 'royal kraal'; had as many wives and as many children as possible; and pride of place was given to his large herd of cattle. Indeed, Zuma benefited from gifts of cattle from several ANC premiers, who allegedly scooped up the money allocated to help poor black farmers and spent it on Zuma's herd instead.[2]

This grossness showed in Zuma's political methods too. It was not just that he was tempting fate by trying to prolong his power beyond his two terms as ANC president, after having denounced Mbeki for attempting the same thing. He was shrewd, knowledgeable and effective, but his style was that of Tony Soprano. He was only too happy to work through corrupt provincial bosses; they were at home with his methods, knew who to bribe or bully, and knew how to get things done for themselves and their boss. Committees were rigged, caucuses were packed, key actors and gatekeepers were paid off, and sometimes, especially in Zuma's home province of KwaZulu-Natal, those who made difficulties were assassinated. Above all, Zuma, the one-time head of ANC Intelligence, made full use of the security services, ANC security and the crime intelligence division of the South African Police Service (SAPS), all of which he packed with loyal Zulus. ANC politicians, knowing that Zuma's spies were ubiquitous and always listening, were careful to take the batteries out of their cellphones before talking to each other.[3]

Enter Ramaphosa

The man who stood between Zuma and the realisation of his ambitions was Cyril Ramaphosa, the former trade unionist and multimillionaire businessman whom Zuma had drafted into his regime in 2012. In part Zuma had done this because his government's image was suffering under the weight of his and the Guptas' corruption. Ramaphosa was the man who had negotiated the Constitution, who had been secretary-general of the ANC, and he had clean hands. Ramaphosa knew he was joining a thoroughly rotten regime but his earlier career had been thwarted by a rivalrous Mbeki, and he knew that if he ever wanted to get to the top he had to do so from the position of deputy president, the position which had traditionally served as the launch pad to the presidency. Even so, sources close to Ramaphosa say that, at first, used as he was to the more rational discussions of company boardrooms, he could hardly believe what he heard around the cabinet table, a forum where ignorance, incompetence and ideological blindness jostled to produce often extraordinary arguments and proposals.

However, Ramaphosa had not joined the regime in order to argue but in order to get along, so he held his tongue and went along.[4]

Zuma was not, though, a man to give away a post such as the ANC deputy presidency on general principle. He had first done a deal with Ramaphosa on a crucial matter, the expulsion of Julius Malema, the wildly populist head of the ANC Youth League (ANCYL), who had backed Zuma's rise to power but had by then turned against him. Zuma recognised in Malema an operator just as shrewd and ruthless as himself, and Malema too was determined to get to the top. He was not easily to be bribed or bullied into line, and both in his home province of Limpopo and in the ANCYL he had set afoot powerful organisations directly answerable to himself alone. In a word, he was a real threat, and when he began to denounce Zuma as a dictator, Zuma decided to act. But the ANC had always been squeamish about disciplining its own, so when the job had to be done it was invariably whites or Indians in the ANC who had to chair the disciplinary committee. In the case of Malema, the job was given to Derek Hanekom, an old white trusty, who duly found Malema guilty and sentenced him to five years' suspension from the party.[5]

Malema naturally appealed. He was an unbridled racial populist and it was clear that he would denounce Hanekom's verdict as 'white man's justice', so a senior black figure would have to be found to chair the appeals committee, a thoroughly dirty job because Malema would be bound to denounce any African who played such a role as a traitor and sell-out. But in April 2012 Ramaphosa agreed to accept the job and duly confirmed Malema's suspension. Zuma then happily agreed to fulfil his part of the bargain and back Ramaphosa for the party's deputy presidency at the Mangaung (Bloemfontein) conference in December 2012.

Ramaphosa had paid a considerable price. Zuma, having dispossessed Malema of his ANCYL base, now moved against Malema's Limpopo base. The provincial executive committee was thrown out and Malema supporters evicted right down to ward level in every town and village in a thorough act of extirpation.[6] But in July 2013 Malema launched his own party, the Economic Freedom Fighters (EFF), and it soon became clear that not only would he not lie down dead, but he would also be a considerable factor into the future. And Malema was not a man to forget a slight. From then on he viewed Zuma as a mortal enemy, with Ramaphosa close behind. Meanwhile, Zuma continued to hand dirty jobs on to Ramaphosa.

Zuma's downward slide

What Ramaphosa had not bargained for was the depth of the Zuma regime's corruption. As more and more evidence came to light, public opinion was appalled. The Constitutional Court found that Zuma had violated his oath of office. There were repeated motions of no confidence in Zuma mounted in Parliament. Every parliamentary appearance by Zuma was turned into a shambles by the EFF, whose members shouted 'Pay back the money!' until they were ejected by security officers. The justice system had become so rotten and compromised under Zuma that when his son Duduzane – one of the biggest beneficiaries of the regime's corruption – drove his Porsche into the rear of a minibus taxi, killing two women and injuring two others, a judicial inquest found that the deaths had been caused by negligent actions but the National Prosecuting Authority (NPA) nonetheless declined to prosecute.[7] With the NPA in the president's pocket, a Zuma could now literally get away with murder. It was only when an application was made by AfriForum to bring a private civil action that the NPA decided to charge Duduzane with culpable homicide[8] – and that was only when the public indignation against Zuma had risen to such heights that the NPA could sense the end was nigh.

Throughout this gathering mayhem, with Zuma's reputation plunging in the polls among all categories of South Africans, Ramaphosa maintained a cheerful public attitude of support for the president. He had decided that he must be able to campaign for the presidency from the platform of the deputy presidency, and that he could therefore not risk doing or saying anything that might allow Zuma to sack him.[9] But such silence did Ramaphosa's reputation no good. By the time the campaign for the party presidency got under way, the media clamour against Zuma had reached fever pitch and was echoed by many leading ANC stalwarts.[10] Even ordinary ANC members concluded that Zuma's corruption had brought the country low, and it was clear that Zuma's troubled reign was ending in complete disgrace. Inevitably, this undermined Nkosazana Dlamini-Zuma's campaign for the party presidency. Ramaphosa had strong media support and was now quite obviously a strong alternative candidate. Thus, Zuma found that he had lost control of events and that getting Dlamini-Zuma elected would be far more difficult than he had envisaged.

A bridge too far

The campaign itself was unprecedented. Traditionally the ANC leadership had been decided by a small cabal of senior party leaders who presented the party with a single candidate, who was then duly elected with unanimity. But now there were seven candidates openly competing for support, trying to put across their own personal manifestoes and implicitly criticising the previous (Zuma) administration. What could not be disguised was that this new openness was a sign of how divided the party had become.

Zuma had hardly given up, though. He knew that every possible sort of manipulation and vote-buying was possible in the election of delegates to the ANC conference – and he was allegedly a past master at it. Inevitably, this meant having to work through the great party bosses of the so-called Premier League – Ace Magashule (Free State), David Mabuza (Mpumalanga), Supra Mahumapelo (North

West) – as well as the pro-Zuma leadership of KwaZulu-Natal. In the other ANC-ruled provinces Zuma leaned strongly on the premiers to deliver their delegations, or, as in Limpopo, if the premier was hostile, he encouraged insurrection against him by ambitious rivals within the local ANC apparatus. On top of that, of course, Zuma knew that at the conference itself there would be extensive vote-buying. It was a measure of how far the ANC had changed that all the presidential contenders were now extremely wealthy men and women, so the conference would somewhat resemble an auction. But with the resources of the state at his disposal, backed up with funds from the Guptas and other major supporters, Zuma felt sure he could outbid all comers.

Ramaphosa knew what Zuma knew, which was why one key element of his campaign was asking white businesspeople for support. His business career had seen him move for years among the white business elite, and now these connections proved of great benefit both financially and in terms of shrewd advice. Under Zuma, business had lain in its bunker, distraught at the damage being done to the whole economic infrastructure but intimidated by the constant appeals for action against 'white monopoly capital', which made it quite clear that the state viewed business as the enemy. Speaking out would only make one a target for revenge action, so little was said publicly.

Privately, business was in despair. Fresh investment had largely ground to a halt in 2010–2011 and now the main preoccupation was to get as much money as possible out of the country. South African companies bought up foreign companies as fast as they could, often in a state of near panic. A lot of very poor purchases were made as a result, but at least the money was offshore. Naturally such businessmen grasped at Ramaphosa as a virtual saviour and opened their wallets for him. One prominent businessman asked Ramaphosa how much he wanted from him. When Ramaphosa said 'ten million rands', the man gave him thirty million.

Zuma's spies were following Ramaphosa's every move, so Zuma was fully aware of this. A rumour campaign was spread that Ramaphosa was a sight too friendly with white businessmen, especially Jews. This canard was widely seen as being aimed at Stephen Koseff, the head of Investec, which handles some of Ramaphosa's investments.

The mood in the Zuma camp was embattled. When under pressure, Zuma liked to depict himself as a victim being unjustly persecuted, a posture that is almost second nature for ANC activists with their history of struggle against white rule. Zuma had grown up in Nkandla, Zululand, listening to the stories of his elders about the Bhambatha Rebellion of 1906, during which Chief Bhambatha kaMancinza, head of the Zondi clan, had staged raids on the British colonial administration from his hiding place in the Nkandla forest. So, while the opinion surveys and focus groups carried out by eNCA, the independent TV network, made it clear that Zuma's unpopularity, even among ANC voters, was overwhelmingly due to his reputation for corruption, Zuma's own depiction of the situation was quite different. He was the modern Bhambatha fighting against the forces of imperialism and their agents and lackeys – such as Ramaphosa. This narrative was picked up and relayed by Zuma's supporters. Ramaphosa was cast as a tool of the imperialists (assumed to be local businessmen plus the British and Americans) and even as a CIA agent.[11]

The Mabuza switch

When the conference began, Zuma felt he had all the bases covered. Magashule and Mahumapelo had made sure their provinces would cast almost unanimous votes for Dlamini-Zuma (though popular opinion in both cases lay massively the other way). Both the ANC Women's League (ANCWL) and the ANCYL were securely in the hands of Zuma clients. Both these organisations were mere shells of what they once had been, but their bloc votes were still invaluable. (The ANCWL was in such a tattered state that its delegation to the conference actually included men.) Even in her home province of KwaZulu-Natal, Dlamini-Zuma had run only slightly ahead of Ramaphosa, but Zuma had made sure that the province's delegates would also be almost unanimously behind her. Limpopo was solid for Ramaphosa, as were Gauteng and the tiny Western Cape delegation. There had been pro-Ramaphosa insurrections in both the Northern and Eastern Cape, though Zuma still counted on a substantial fraction of the latter's delegates, and the Northern Cape delegation was also tiny. What this meant was that the contest would come down to what David Mabuza, the premier of Mpumalanga, would do.[12]

Until recently, Mabuza had been one of the most solid members of the pro-Zuma Premier League. He had come to power thanks to Zuma's patronage and had built his regime into an impregnable fiefdom. He was alleged to have looted endlessly – *The New York Times* was later to run a special feature on the extensive corruption and extremely rough methods of the Mabuza regime.[13] Mabuza had, as a result, become extremely rich, and any opponents who put their heads above the parapet were not likely to survive long. Zuma knew all this and had felt confident of Mabuza's support. It had therefore come as a very unpleasant surprise when Mabuza, in the run-up to the conference, had announced that he was sitting on the fence – clearly with the calculation that this could make him the kingmaker. Zuma's initial response to that had been fury: how could Mabuza be such an ingrate and traitor? Dire threats of wrath were made by the Zuma camp, but Zuma quickly realised that Mabuza was so well dug in that it was impossible to dislodge him or even encourage any significant opposition to him within his province. The only way to buy his votes was to offer him a king's ransom.

After endless politicking, on 17 December things finally came to a head. Zuma sat impassively, wearing an ANC golf shirt and baseball cap, as he heard the results read out: Dlamini-Zuma 2 261 votes, Ramaphosa 2 440 – a majority of 179. There was pandemonium in the hall. Zuma grimaced slightly but was otherwise stony-faced. In one second all his hopes had been dashed. It could only be due to treason. Quite obviously, Mabuza, on whom Zuma had counted, had switched sides at the last moment. A few moments later the results were announced for the deputy presidency: Lindiwe Sisulu 2 159, David Mabuza 2 538. The kingmaker strategy had worked.

Zuma's distress was so obvious to his family – outwardly impassive though he was – that a Zuma daughter got up, walked across and sat down next to her father to comfort him. For Zuma could already read the meaning of the result. President Ramaphosa. Zuma would be forced to resign. He would have to face the courts, with the whole country wanting to see him jailed. As Zuma was well aware, the Guptas had already fled the country. He had had that option too but he had turned it down.[14] He was simply too much the Zulu traditionalist to ever want to live in Dubai. He wanted to be in Nkandla, with his wives, his cattle and other Zulus all around him. He would stay and fight it out. When Mbeki had sacked him as deputy president in 2005, it had seemed that he was down and out, that he could never come back from that, but he had come all the way back and triumphed at Polokwane. Well, this Venda upstart, Ramaphosa, might think he could overthrow a big Zulu chief but we would see about that. Ramaphosa was soft. He could be pushed – and he had none of Zuma's grassroots political skills. He might think he'd won now. But the fight had only just begun.

★ ★ ★

Three months after Cyril Ramaphosa's accession to the presidency of South Africa, confidence had begun to slip. The wave of so-called Ramaphoria that had greeted his arrival in power had proved brief. Everywhere throughout the country there was civil strife – land invasions, conflicts between communities, shootings, endless protests and, within the ANC, factional division and assassinations of councillors and party officials. Ramaphosa had even had to fly back from the Commonwealth Heads of Government Meeting in London as a violent insurrection swept across the North West province following the removal of the corrupt ANC provincial structures.[15] Perhaps most worrying was the fact that, like the gleaners that followed a medieval army, robbing the dead and wounded on the battlefield, integral to all these disturbances were bands of looters who vandalised and pillaged without pity, always targeting shops owned by Somalis, Pakistanis or other foreigners.[16] Business confidence faltered and the value of the rand fell.

There had not been such widespread civil strife since the last days of apartheid – and in those days the army and police who had to deal with it were a far stronger and more disciplined body than they were by 2018. For a quarter-century of ANC rule had hollowed out almost every public institution, including the armed forces and police. The ANC still greatly honoured the struggle, when people had risen up to protest and take violent action against apartheid, but here were their descendants protesting and committing violence in the face of an ANC government. This had not been part of the script. The wave of protest seemed to equate the ANC government with the apartheid government, the ultimate embarrassment. When dozens of striking mineworkers were mowed down by police at Marikana in 2012, the ANC government had made a concerted attempt to prevent the media from speaking of this as the 'Marikana massacre', because a massacre was, definitionally, something that only the apartheid government would commit. But one could not but notice that the old ANC slogan of 'Power to the people! The people shall govern' was now seldom heard. The fact was that, although the ANC had always presented itself as the government of the people – so that an ANC government meant that 'the people' were in power – the people were now a problem.

Ramaphosa faced a crisis on nearly every front. There were now 9.6 million unemployed, and the figure kept rising. Real incomes had been falling for five years. The economy was stagnant and growing hardly at all. Already South Africa's bonds had been relegated to junk status by two out of three international credit-rating agencies, and if the third agency, Moody's, followed suit, the value of the rand would fall even more. Under Zuma the state had been captured by corrupt and frankly criminal elements, and now Zuma's corrupt placemen – and Zuma himself – resisted any change. They had stolen the country and did not want to hand it back. They had also virtually bankrupted the country. Investment had all but ceased and capital flight was endemic. Indeed, South Africa was now referred to by some investors not as a developing country but as 'a formerly developed country'.[17]

Against this Ramaphosa had not much to call upon. He came from a minority ethnic group and had only a small political base. He was hemmed in from every side by hostile factions and his command of the ANC was less than sure. Indeed, the ANC secretary-general, who presided over the party's headquarters, Luthuli House, was Ace Magashule, who continued to support Zuma quite publicly and was widely perceived as one of the most corrupt members of the *ancien regime*, closely tied to the Guptas.[18]

Yet what was clear was that if the original promise of Mandela and the rainbow nation was to be saved, it would now come down to Ramaphosa and his supporters. Many of these supporters were drawn from Ramaphosa's old comrades in the United Democratic Front (UDF) of the 1980s – Trevor Manuel, Pravin Gordhan, Popo Molefe and, for all that he was now leading another party, the Congress of the People (Cope), Mosiuoa Lekota. This was itself of great significance. Since 1994 South Africa had been ruled by the old ANC exiles. Now, at last, it was the turn of those who had stayed behind and fought apartheid on the home front. What was apparent to all of them was that if Ramaphosa failed it was unlikely that there would be another chance. And failure would also mean that the old white right had been vindicated in their predictions that black majority rule would end in chaos and disaster. If the Ramaphosa regime failed it was by no means clear that the country would hold together; it might just collapse in shambles under the weight of popular discontent and politicking, and it might even split up into its constituent units. This was always a potent threat in a country like South Africa – like Yugoslavia or Iraq – which had been cobbled together relatively recently out of separate national units. But it was tolerably clear that if the centre did not hold, power would devolve not to the old Boer republics but to the major metropoles, which were now the centres of national life.

This, then, is the drama that South Africa faces. For any liberal, communist or African nationalist, indeed for any democrat, the awful possibility now exists that majority rule – the goal so long fought for – will go down in history as a sad failure. That would not only give the verdict to the white right but it would also seem to invalidate, or at least to mock, the popular struggles of a whole century. Such a failure would not only have tragic repercussions for any sense of black pride or self-respect in South Africa; it would also have repercussions for black self-confidence and race relations right around the world. The stakes could hardly be higher. What this book is about is how it came to this. What are the real problems? And what will be necessary to fight for the dream?

Chapter Two

How did it come to this?[1]

Most South Africans look back to the Mandela and even the Mbeki presidencies as a time when things worked better than they do now – a sort of lost golden age. The truth is rather different.

Mandela: 'a vacuum at the centre of government'

When Nelson Mandela took office as president in May 1994 he was two months short of his 76th birthday. In his life he had been a student, a trainee lawyer, a political activist and a prisoner. He had no experience of administration or government whatsoever. The new constitution gave him considerable powers as president but he showed little interest in using them. Rather, he conceived of his role as mainly ceremonial and symbolic. He was at first mainly concerned with attempting to unite the nation – inasmuch as there was just one nation, something that was in some doubt and was, indeed, sharply contested by some. To this end he preached the gospel of racial reconciliation, which won him huge affection among the minorities but which, after a while, led to a certain amount of Africanist grumbling that he was being a sight too nice to the whites.

Mandela was also the New South Africa's ambassador to the world. The world's leading politicians, led by François Mitterrand and Bill

Clinton, flocked to meet him, as did an unending caravan of celebrities of every kind – film and sports stars, pop singers, models and a large number of business moguls. One and all were asked for substantial contributions to ANC funds or one of Mandela's charities. Some extremely dubious characters made the guest list, such as the former Liberian warlord, Charles Taylor, who was later sentenced to 50 years in jail at The Hague for 'terror, murder and rape', the judge observing that he had been responsible for 'some of the most heinous and brutal crimes recorded in human history'.[2] Taylor's presence at Mandela's house only came to light when supermodel Naomi Campbell caused a sensation by revealing that, in 1997, Taylor had given her three small diamonds – probably blood diamonds – which she had handed over to Jeremy Ractliffe, the head of the Nelson Mandela Children's Fund, who had pocketed them.[3] It then emerged that Taylor's presence was supposed to have been a secret, giving rise to speculation as to what other secret visitors Mandela may have had.

Mandela was also the ANC's chief fundraiser, travelling the world to tap up possible benefactors. These too included all manner of folk – Saudi royalty, Libyan strongman Muammar Gaddafi, dictators of various Third World countries, company directors and wealthy celebrities. When it was a question of paying for the ANC campaign for the 1994 election he was extremely successful – Winnie Mandela is said to have referred to him bitterly as 'the ANC's ATM' – but it was soon clear that once the ANC had won those elections, finding donors would be far harder for the next election, in 1999. This problem hung over the ANC like a sword.

Meanwhile Mandela played only a minor part in the actual running of the country. He didn't bother to chair the cabinet and would usually leave cabinet meetings long before the end. This left his deputy, Thabo Mbeki, to act as the de facto president, a role in which he was run off his feet. He too, like all the other ANC cabinet members, had no experience of governance or administration. It was thus in this period that cabinet coordination was lost, and most ministers simply did their own thing. It was also in this period that the policies of affirmative action and cadre deployment were introduced, rapidly ruining the civil service and rendering the state largely ineffective. And, with so many opportunities now open to it, elite corruption really began to take off. Mandela did nothing to stop any of these processes and even presided over the early retirement of thousands of the most experienced teachers, a blow from which the education system never recovered. Thus, while Mandela remained highly popular there was no doubt that South Africa's downward slide began under him.

In addition, of course, it was Mandela who insisted – very much against Mbeki's will – that Jacob Zuma should be made deputy president. This was a fateful choice, for Zuma could not otherwise have hoped to succeed as president. Later, when Zuma was campaigning against Mbeki, Mandela gave him a R1-million donation.[4] In that sense, then, Mandela was indirectly responsible for the disaster of the Zuma period. The best that can be said in his defence is that he didn't know what he was doing.

The best picture of the situation was given by the Centre for Development and Enterprise (CDE), an NGO, which carried out a searching investigation into how governance worked in this period.[5] 'Functionally there exists what many have described to us as a vacuum at the centre of government,' the CDE reported. 'Somewhere between the offices of the President and the Deputy President and between these and the departments lies a space ... The office of the President should be the core and apex of the whole system of government in South Africa. But currently it is not providing the necessary support required for the head of state or the effective running of government as a whole.'[6]

The CDE was too diplomatic to make the point any more plainly but the truth was that Mandela was at once too old and too inexperienced for the role of president. Mbeki was younger but also inexperienced and was simply overwhelmed by his responsibilities, and almost all the ANC ministers lacked administrative experience. The best hope would have been a true government of national unity (GNU) for a prolonged period so that the old National Party ministers could pass on more of their knowledge and skills, but that was something the ANC was determined to avoid. By 1996 the National Party had quit the government.

The creation of the bureaucratic bourgeoisie

The CDE report also noted that South Africa 'is among the world's biggest spenders on public-service salaries and wages' when compared to other middle-income countries. By 1998/99 public-service salaries already constituted 49.5 per cent of non-interest spending in the budget. If South Africa were to revert to the mean among middle-income countries, 320 000 of the country's 1.17 million public servants would have to be laid off, thus releasing an extra eight per cent of the budget every year for expenditure on capital projects.[7]

In light of this, the government made a commitment to 'right-sizing' the public service, but little was achieved. In practice there was huge pressure from within the ANC for more public-service jobs and in the end every ANC government gave ground to this pressure. Moreover, these cadres expected to be well rewarded: they had played their part in the struggle, had they not? The result was, according to the CDE report:

> Unlike many other developing countries, South Africa's public service personnel have not suffered salary and wage cuts due to the macro-economic pressures of the 1990s.[8] In fact, the reverse is true – public sector wages in real aggregate terms have increased well in advance of the GDP from 1996 onwards. This has been a deliberate policy choice. Initially, it was aimed at putting

public servants at ease during the amalgamation of the various administrations,[9] by guaranteeing their jobs and pay. A second reason was the government's commitment to uniform conditions of service within the public service ... A third ... reason for competitive public service wages was the government's determination to give public servants material incentives for increased loyalty, productivity and honesty.[10]

This is highly diplomatic language. What it means is that there was a general levelling up of wages to the highest level among the 11 administrations being amalgamated. Typically, this meant jumping up the salary of ill-qualified (black homeland) bureaucrats to the levels of well-qualified Afrikaners in the old public service. Another rationale was 'narrowing the wage gaps between public servants'; this always meant levelling up, not down. One can well imagine that this must have helped put public servants 'at ease', though as for rewarding increased productivity and honesty, it was quickly discovered that there were major problems in both directions, with much lower productivity and the early discovery of increased public-service corruption.

Other factors were also at work: 'Understandably, the ANC has appointed new senior public servants from within its loyal political ranks ... many provincial appointments have not been based on skill alone ... In national departments ... senior public service appointments ... generally reflected the ethnic or racial composition of the minister ... A rather more sinister but associated problem has arisen from some public officials' reluctance to unmask corrupt practices and misconduct amongst their colleagues ...'[11]

This was Mandela's most damaging legacy: an overlarge and massively overpaid and underskilled bureaucracy. In effect, the old civil service had been destroyed and the government was deprived of the key instrument with which to implement policy.

The ANC government had found itself facing a dilemma. On the one hand, it had an extremely ambitious programme of social and economic change to carry out and for this it needed the services of the most skilled and experienced civil service possible. On the other hand, it faced heavy pressures from within its own ranks to Africanise the public service as quickly as possible. There was never any doubt that it would choose the latter course, particularly since it nourished paranoid fears that the old civil service would deliberately sabotage the new government.

This was part of a larger gap in self-confidence. Essentially, the ANC had so convinced itself of the evil nature of its Nationalist opponents that it found it hard to believe that FW de Klerk really had put the national interest above that of his party and had offered the ANC power on a plate. It seemed too good to be true, and a great deal of energy was wasted on looking for hidden catches and, even more, the malign activities of a mysterious 'third force'. In general, anything that went wrong was immediately attributed to this third force – without the slightest evidence. This was very much the way that the ANC had operated in exile, throwing out evidence-free accusations that anyone who criticised it was actually a CIA or MI5 agent.[12] Similarly, for several years ANC activists continued with the refrain that their movement was 'in government but not in power'.

The sweeping Africanisation of the public service was a fateful move, for it led not only to a widespread de-skilling but also the loss of institutional memory, so that most of the new public servants had no idea how their departments had operated historically, what pitfalls to avoid, and so on. The situation was further worsened by the fact that many of the new recruits, finding themselves in well-paid jobs for the first time, tended to overspend, get themselves into debt and seek to remedy their situation by job-hopping. As will be seen, the creation of this bureaucratic bourgeoisie would have fateful implications for the ANC and for South Africa as a whole.

A government in search of a policy

In exile, the ANC had not thought much beyond 'the conquest of power'. Its vague utopian notions of a sweeping transition to socialism had been undermined by the collapse of the Soviet bloc, and there was considerable uncertainty over what it wanted to do. On the crucial subject of land reform it simply turned to the World Bank (which it reviled) for advice. The Bank suggested that a target of redistributing 30 per cent of the land in a decade might be reasonable, and so this target was adopted without more ado and with no consideration of how blacks were supposed to acquire the training and capital necessary to make a success of farming.

It was decided that the country must have a large Reconstruction and Development Programme (RDP), but such were the uncertainties that it went through draft after draft. In the end the RDP was simply a vast, unbudgeted wish list with no provision as to how it was supposed to relate to all the various ministries affected. After just two years the whole plan was effectively cancelled and replaced by Growth, Employment and Redistribution (Gear) – a plan of completely opposite intent. Where the RDP had envisaged a large Keynesian public-spending bonanza, Gear called for sharp cuts, budget balancing and privatisation.

The same switchback ride occurred elsewhere. Against the overwhelming advice of education experts the government decided to introduce outcomes-based education (OBE), an education theory then in vogue in several countries. The government had already taken the fatal step of encouraging most of its experienced teachers to take early retirement. The less-skilled remnant of the teaching profession could not cope with OBE and it eventually collapsed in shambles and had to be abandoned. Many educationalists felt that OBE had done as much damage as Bantu Education.[13]

The other factor was that from 1994 on South Africa saw large net outflows of skilled people – the first time such a thing had occurred since the Second World War. Mainly, though by no means exclusively, those leaving were whites.[14] This further accelerated the process of de-skilling and the resulting 'juniorisation' of many professions. The awkward (and generally unspoken) truth was that South Africa's main competitive advantage vis-à-vis many other emerging markets was its educated white population, containing most of its professional and managerial skills.

However, the government reacted to the consequent skills crisis with the completely perverse policy of strict controls on the entry of skilled people into South Africa, for this, of course, was what the black educated class – the rising bureaucratic bourgeoisie – demanded in order to maximise its own competitive position. Once again the demands of this class were given complete priority over the national interest. Indeed, time after time, the 'normal' development of the country was distorted in order to suit the interests of this group, such was its complete political dominance.

The ANC in these early years was aware that its own sociology was changing rapidly. In 1997, a report by the party's Department of Education and Training offered this snapshot view: '... the last few years have seen the rapid development of a new black, upper middle class. The gap between the richest ten per cent of blacks and the majority has grown very rapidly. Many of the ANC's leading cadres have benefited directly from these new realities.'[15] The party's 1997 Strategy and Tactics document continued in this vein: 'Other sections of the black middle strata are also benefiting directly and indirectly from opportunities created by government. Indeed, the rapid advance of these sections constitutes one of the most immediate and most visible consequences of democracy ... experience in other countries has taught us that, without vigilance, elements of these new capitalist classes can become witting or unwitting tools of monopoly interests, or parasites who thrive on corruption in public office.'[16]

In fact, by the time these words were written an extremely witting and corrupt arms deal (costing $4.8 billion in 1997 dollars) was already well in progress. As was to become only too clear from the way in which the military equipment acquired was barely used, the driving force behind the deal had been the corruption that it enabled.

The unending search for campaign finance

To this day it is difficult to be certain of the full list of the arms deal's beneficiaries. In the typical Third World arms deal, the chief beneficiaries are the minister of defence and the president or prime minister. In this case, there was widespread belief that the defence minister, Joe Modise, was a major beneficiary through a string of intermediaries.[17] Mandela was president when the deal went through, and it seems barely credible that he could have been ignorant of what was going on. However, he had by that stage so completely delegated his executive functions to Thabo Mbeki that it is, indeed, just possible that he didn't know what was going on. If that was really true it is a remarkable testament to Mandela's simple failure to do his job.

Mbeki was only too well aware of the frailties of ANC ministers, and, as a micro-manager himself, would have been well aware of what Modise was up to. Indeed, at various junctures Mbeki himself played a key role in forcing the deal through and in throttling discussion and parliamentary oversight of it. To this end he strong-armed the Speaker of Parliament, Frene Ginwala, who played her full part in preventing Parliament from investigating the matter properly.[18] Later, the (Johannesburg) *Sunday Times* ran a headline to the effect that Mbeki had also been a major beneficiary of the deal.[19] Through his office, Mbeki threatened to sue. There were recurrent reports that he had received $20 million. It is highly probable that a considerable cast of lesser characters received pay-offs and that the deal also paid for the ANC's election campaign in 1999, thus solving a major problem for Mbeki.

Thereafter the problem of how to finance the ANC's election campaigns was solved partly by putting a squeeze on the local business community but also by setting up the ANC's own investment company, Chancellor House, which then benefited from insider deals with state-owned enterprises (SOEs). Most notable of these was a deal with the local subsidiary of the Japanese company Hitachi, which was keenly interested in the $2-billion plan to build the new Medupi power station for Eskom. This highly profitable arrangement proceeded to the mutual satisfaction of both parties until, in 2015, the US Securities and Exchange Commission investigated the matter and accused Hitachi of making 'improper payments' and deliberately failing to record them properly in their accounts. Hitachi never denied or admitted to these charges but simply paid a fine of $19 million to make the whole case go away.[20]

For the ANC, this question of how to finance its election campaigns never really went away. Few of its members were able to contribute much, so the party depended on outside sources. There is little doubt that the vast amounts of money spent by government departments and SOEs in 'wasteful and irregular expenditure', noted every year by auditors, played a considerable role in funding the party, as well as filling many other private pockets. But, increasingly, the party atrophied. It became noticeable that it was only able to pull itself together once every five years to fight parliamentary elections: it never managed to pull out its vote properly in municipal elections, thus favouring the opposition DA, which was far better at this.

Even so, election campaigns depended increasingly on threats and on money. Time after time, the ANC dinned it into voters that if the DA got in it would bring back apartheid and cut off all the social grants on which a huge section of the electorate depended. Rural voters particularly were susceptible to these calumnies, for there was seldom a DA presence in rural areas. There was also the more muscular threat of traditional chiefs and their enforcers and of the

ANCYL. On the other hand, the party also spent enormous amounts on distributing free food and drink, food parcels and other gifts, as well as ubiquitous T-shirts. Urban voters were less susceptible to such tactics and gradually the party became more and more dependent on a shrinking rural core. All of which meant that money remained a perennial problem. At the party's December 2017 Nasrec conference, its treasurer-general, Zweli Mkhize, had once again to report that the party was effectively bankrupt.[21]

Mbeki: paranoia, grandiosity and denial

The Mbeki presidency was characterised by hugely ambitious schemes in foreign policy; by Aids denialism, which cost the lives of over 300 000 people;[22] and by Mbeki's own tendency to play the philosopher-king. That is to say, he was very much in the mould of the first generation of independent African leaders of the 1960s – Kwame Nkrumah, Sékou Touré or Julius Nyerere. In their time each of these leaders was lionised as his country's leading intellectual force, eliciting a good deal of slavish obsequiousness. Each tried to stamp his own philosophy on the country and each of them preached a passionate though impractical Pan-Africanism.

It was exactly the same with Mbeki. In his case he was instrumental in reshaping the discredited Organization of African Unity (OAU) into the African Union (AU) and setting up a (ludicrous) Pan-African Parliament, based permanently in South Africa. His watchword was the African Renaissance and, in concert with other African presidents, he devised the New Partnership for Africa's Development (Nepad), intended as a vast Marshall Plan for Africa, with the funding provided by Western donors, who would effectively pour their money into an institution in which Mbeki was the dominant influence. Clearly, if this came to pass Mbeki would in effect become president of Africa. To assuage Western concerns about African governance, he also set up the African Peer Review Mechanism, a toothless (and soon obsolete) scheme whereby African countries would monitor their own governance.[23] Beyond even that he presided over the 1998 summit of the Non-Aligned Movement, clearly with the aim of making himself the effective leader of the Third World as a whole.

These gargantuan schemes were a reflection of Mbeki's own grandiosity. For Mbeki had a complicated psychological make-up marked by an inflated sense of self and a belief in his own superiority. It was typical that he should think himself able to second-guess all manner of scientists and medics about the nature of Aids. But to this he added a strong streak of paranoia. It was a toxic mix that led to some very peculiar public performances. By the end not only had all these schemes ended in failure but he had also convinced most world leaders that it would not be safe to trust him with any international role once his presidency ended – something he craved.

By 1996 Mbeki had realised that effectively the ANC had no economic policy and that the country was drifting rather dangerously. Not only had capitalism easily survived apartheid but black capitalists were beginning to appear at some speed. In theory, the ANC remained committed to its old revolutionary goals, but these were at increasing variance with reality. Mbeki feared that this rudderlessness might end in a bail-out from the International Monetary Fund (IMF), something the ANC would not accept and would blame on him. Accordingly, he took the major gamble of launching Gear, which was essentially a package of the sort of pro-market reforms the IMF would have demanded as the price of a bail-out. Fatally, he dared not challenge the reigning ANC orthodoxy and therefore shrouded Gear in as much neo-Marxist rhetoric as possible, although Gear's clear aim was to accept the new normal of a multi-racial capitalist society with a growing black middle class. This earned Mbeki the undying hatred of the left. In fact, only part of Gear's reforms were carried out and the policy was thrown off course by the 1997 Asian banking crisis. Only after 2000 were its positive effects felt, greatly assisted by a prolonged commodity price boom.[24]

Mbeki was also uncomfortably aware that the ANC was changing fast under his feet. Although the ANC in exile had been no stranger to corruption, when it had returned home it began to put down roots, a process hugely assisted by its conquest of governmental power in 1994. Everywhere – in ANC-ruled provincial and municipal governments, in the SOEs, in government departments, in the schools and hospitals and public agencies of every kind – gatekeepers, middlemen and patronage barons began to appear, all of them with their own rackets. So-called tenderpreneurs became legion, the policy of black economic empowerment (BEE) was a hardly disguised form of crony capitalism, and rent-seeking was general.

In the exiled ANC all funding had flowed through the party leadership, thus making it the sole source of patronage and thus the singular power centre. Thus the most extreme, indeed Soviet, form of democratic centralism prevailed. Now, however, the multiplicity of sources of patronage and profit saw the growth of multiple power centres, which inevitably threatened democratic centralism. Mbeki, who was habituated to the old Soviet ways, sought to reassert the primacy of the party – and thus of himself – over these over-mighty subjects by effectively making all important positions, including provincial premiers and mayors, simple presidential appointments.[25]

Mbeki might even have got away with this had he not picked a fight with Jacob Zuma, his deputy president. Zuma put together an unbeatable coalition of the biggest ethnic group (Zulus), the trade union federation, the Congress of South African Trade Unions (Cosatu), and the ANC's two most powerful factions, the South African Communist Party (SACP) and the ANCYL. When this coalition swept Mbeki aside at the ANC's Polokwane conference in 2007, Mbeki claimed that this was an ANC he neither knew nor recognised. As well he might, for these were the powerful and opportunist new elements spawned by 13 years of ANC rule. They had, in presidential spokesperson Smuts Ngonyama's famous phrase, not joined the struggle to be poor,[26] and they correctly saw in Zuma a much better vehicle for their ambitions.

Zuma: descent to the depths

Zuma, far from resisting these trends, embraced them. Given that his principal objectives were to keep the law at bay over the 783 counts of fraud, corruption and money laundering he was facing and to enrich himself and his family, he was quite happy to work in tandem with all manner of local and regional bosses, and even with a whole raft of corrupt businessmen, including the notorious Gupta family. Under Zuma the state came to resemble a medieval kingdom in which the monarch (Zuma) stood at the apex of a huge pyramid of patronage that provided the sinews of the state. The monarch received tribute and military support from his barons in return for which he bestowed upon them their lands and allowed them to make exactions from the peasantry beneath them. Under Zuma the premiers and mayors were allowed to loot their provinces and towns, provided they furnished Zuma with occasional tribute and unstinting support. The key expression of this was the so-called Premier League – the premiers of KwaZulu-Natal, Free State, North West and Mpumalanga – who guaranteed Zuma re-election as party president, seeing off a challenge from Kgalema Motlanthe, at the Mangaung conference in 2012.

Under Zuma, corruption became all-pervasive. But it would be a mistake to personalise this too far. Zuma was able to get away with open law-breaking, breaking his oath of office, public attacks on the courts and flagrant corruption for three key reasons. First, the ANC backed him up whatever he did, just as it had never made the slightest effort to stop Mbeki's genocide against HIV/Aids sufferers. In the last analysis ANC members of Parliament (MPs) always preferred to keep their parliamentary salaries and privileges rather than risk annoying a president. Second, the great army of corrupt ministers, patronage bosses, tenderpreneurs and middlemen all naturally supported Zuma, for they had even more to lose. And, third, elements within the police, the security services and the national prosecution service were under the firm control of Zuma henchmen (almost always Zulus). Zuma had all the bases covered.

A useful micro-study of this period is provided by Crispian Olver's account of Nelson Mandela Bay (Port Elizabeth) in his book *How to Steal a City* (2017). Olver, a long-standing ANC activist, was tasked by his superiors in the party to attempt a civic clean-up because, notoriously, the ANC there was so riddled with corrupt functionaries and had so misgoverned the city that it was in danger of falling to the DA in the upcoming 2016 municipal elections. Given Port Elizabeth's role as the historic forcing ground of the ANC, this was a prospect not to be countenanced. Olver soon uncovered the horrific extent of the corruption but became uneasy as he found himself using some of the same patronage techniques to cement the 'good guys' in place that had been used to put their factional opposites in place beforehand.[27] Olver was too loyal an apparatchik to question the fact that only the risk of losing the city had caused the ANC to take any action at all. Clearly, the ANC leadership had no objection to corruption in itself, only to its political consequences.

By the book's end, Olver is driving thankfully away from the city with his job far less than completed. He has done his best but it is clear that the problem is endemic. Indeed, in a sense the corrupt factions are not a deviation from the norm for the city's ANC. Rather, they *are* the ANC, or, at least, what the party is bound to become given the scale of the opportunities for corruption presented by any large city budget. One can see forming in Olver's mind the uneasy question of why one should believe that the situation in Nelson Mandela Bay might be any different from that in any other town or city ruled by the

ANC. The forces in play are exactly the same everywhere, after all. In other words, the entire ANC may be a series of interconnected corrupt networks. Olver, an honest man himself, clearly does not wish to admit that he may have been wholly mistaken about the nature of the party to which he has given his loyalty. There is also the question of why any democrat should be working so hard to prevent the logical political outcome of such a situation, that the opposition party should come to power to clean the city up. Which is what duly happened in 2016.

As I have argued elsewhere,[28] it has been an iron law of South African history that no government can withstand a protracted investment strike. And this is what the Zuma regime soon produced, as both foreign and domestic investors recoiled from its toxic mix of corruption, lawlessness, state intervention and overregulation. Soon the paralysis fed upon itself, for the investment freeze caused economic growth to falter, a reason in itself not to invest. Zuma effectively paid no attention to such economic phenomena, but as unemployment and social distress rose his popularity inevitably fell. His response was to tack to the left, promising 'radical economic transformation' and attempting to throw all blame onto 'white monopoly capital'. The result was a populist downward spiral.

In May 2015, when my previous book first appeared,[29] I had argued that this downward spiral would see South Africa down-rated to junk status by the credit-rating agencies with the probable ultimate result being the necessity for an IMF bail-out. I suggested that this down-rating would take about two years. In fact, within 23 months both Fitch and Standard & Poor's had lowered their ratings to junk status, with the third agency, Moody's, hovering on the edge. Naturally, the Zuma forces attempted to dismiss the agencies as racist and imperialist, but there was no doubt in the public mind that the situation had reached a nadir.

As the ANC approached its five-yearly conference at Nasrec, Johannesburg, in December 2017, Zuma's primary focus lay on his determination to stay out of jail. Cyril Ramaphosa, for his part, was quite open in his condemnation of 'state capture', a barely disguised attack on the way Zuma had hocked the state out to the Gupta family and other corrupt fixers in return for personal gain. The scene was now set for an all-out contest.

Chapter Three

The contest

The ANC presidential contest of 2017 opened up a new era. It was more open and competitive than any previous contest, more like that in ordinary democratic parties. It also overthrew the old system within which Jacob Zuma had seemed invincible. To understand how he came to lose in 2017 we need to begin by looking back at the 2012 contest, when the Zuma machine was in its pomp.

The contest for the ANC presidency at the party's Mangaung conference in December 2012 was never really a race. Kgalema Motlanthe, who had been the country's interim president after Thabo Mbeki was forced out in September 2008, put his name forward but never mounted a proper campaign. Motlanthe was constrained by the fact that he was deputy president. As such he could hardly criticise the president, but it was no secret that he deeply disapproved of Jacob Zuma's behaviour.[1] So he had decided that, in principle at least, the party should have a choice. But the chief reason to look at this contest was that it gives us sight of the full cast and dynamics of the Zuma machine.

The Premier League

First, there were the members of the so-called Premier League – Zweli Mkhize, premier of KwaZulu-Natal, Ace Magashule, premier of the Free State, and David Mabuza, premier of Mpumalanga. After Mangaung, the three were joined by Supra Mahumapelo, the unchallengeable boss of the North West, which had already gained a reputation for corruption and poor service delivery.[2] The latter three were widely viewed as corrupt; indeed, Magashule was deeply involved with the Guptas and his two sons worked for them. Mahumapelo had similar links. These men, all clients within the Zuma patronage network, were themselves patrons within their provinces, pushing in their protégés as mayors of local towns or into other positions of interest, and receiving tribute in return.[3]

Most important, the Premier League had shown monolithic support for Zuma in the contest for the ANC presidency. KwaZulu-Natal, with the biggest ANC membership, had gone for Zuma by 858–0, Free State by 324–0, and Mpumalanga by 427–17. Thus, these three provinces had all but settled the contest on their own. But, in addition, Zuma could rely on the full support of the ANCWL, thanks to protégées and clients such as Bathabile Dlamini, Dudu Myeni, Baleka Mbete and Nomvula Mokonyane; on the SACP, whose leader, Blade Nzimande, was a younger Zulu, slipstreaming on Zuma's consolidation of a united Zulu bloc; on the Umkhonto we Sizwe Military Veterans' Association (MKMVA), run by the controversial Kebby Maphatsoe, who was greatly disliked by most genuine military veterans;[4] and finally on the ANCYL, which had had to be completely replaced once Julius Malema had led away the previous ANCYL leadership to become the nucleus of the Economic Freedom Fighters. The new ANCYL leaders, such as Collen Maine, who counted for nothing with the youth, were completely dependent on Zuma's patronage.[5]

Invisible behind this great machine were the key financial backers – particularly the Guptas and various other corrupt businessmen[6] – who made money available to oil the wheels, pay the bribes and 'manage' the conference in return for financial advantages, usually in the form of state contracts and tenders.

The central pillar of the Zuma machine was, of course, his native KwaZulu-Natal. Many of Zuma's key lieutenants, in the cabinet, the security forces and elsewhere, were Zulus, and he had the solid support of Zweli Mkhize. Mkhize had backed Zuma from the first days of his struggle against Mbeki, and once Zuma won, Mkhize had been rewarded with the premiership in 2009. But he was an enigmatic figure. Although there had been a financial scandal involving his wife, Mkhize himself – an educated man and a medical doctor – had a clean reputation and was a popular premier. There had been repeated rumours that he was no longer so close to Zuma, but in the event so unanimous was the KwaZulu-Natal vote for Zuma at Mangaung that there was considerable suspicion of rigging and vote-buying – for such practices were seen as normal enough at any ANC conference. At Mangaung, however, Mkhize was elected as ANC treasurer-general, which meant that he would need to stand down as premier.

Ironically, this was to be a key turning point, and the beginning of the fall of the Zuma machine. Mkhize tried to hold both posts for a while, but in August 2013 he finally stepped down as premier and was replaced by Senzo Mchunu. Mchunu, who lacked Mkhize's stature, faced an extremely difficult situation. Because the KwaZulu-Natal ANC had become the key bastion of Zuma's rule, competition was intense for positions within it, for it was assumed that these would bring not only local spoils but national power too. The fact that President Zuma was careful to ensure that Durban got far more than its fair share of big public events, and KwaZulu-Natal more than its share of public spending, only increased local expectations and appetites.

Within KwaZulu-Natal the pivot was the city of eThekwini (Durban), which, with an annual budget of over R40 billion, was by far the province's greatest centre of money, jobs and power. This had already led to ruthless infighting for positions within the ANC; in 2011, the ANC's regional secretary for eThekwini, S'bu Sibiya, was gunned down by a hitman apparently hired by rivals within the ANC.[7] The great prize at stake, of course, was the tenders and contracts of the eThekwini municipality.

The succession struggle begins

Already the leaders of the Premier League – in collaboration with President Zuma – had begun to plan the succession to Zuma. Just as Thabo Mbeki had sought to extend his power beyond the constitutional limit of two terms, so Zuma now looked to achieve something similar – an objective also much desired by the Premier League, for nothing would suit them better than being allowed to continue with their various lucrative rackets. Quite early on it was decided to nominate Zuma's ex-wife, Dr Nkosazana Dlamini-Zuma (then chairperson of the African Union Commission). Zuma was sure he could rely on her to keep him out of the dock and in general to allow him a large measure of influence.

The next step, naturally, was to get the new premier of KwaZulu-Natal to join the cabal. But, crucially, Senzo Mchunu refused to join. This could only mean that he was likely to favour the other leading candidate, Cyril Ramaphosa. Moreover, Mchunu followed up by making it clear that he would not countenance corruption of any kind.[8] This was a direct threat to the Zuma faction, which had always worked as a crony capitalist machine, cutting in business interests in return for their financial support.

This was shocking news not only for Zuma but also for the Premier League. The league was grouped around the central pillar of the KwaZulu-Natal ANC, the biggest ANC bloc in the country. If KwaZulu-Natal defected, the whole bloc might fall to pieces. It thus became a key objective for Zuma and his backers to get rid of Mchunu. But, as the Zuma bloc mobilised, it found there was a difficulty with the SACP. To be sure, the SACP had been firm backers of Zuma for many years and the SACP general secretary, Blade Nzimande, served in the cabinet – as minister of higher education and training – together with several other SACP ministers, such as Jeff Radebe, Rob Davies and Ebrahim Patel. But the endless succession of corruption scandals involving Zuma had taken its toll on the party. Many SACP members felt that as a matter of principle the party ought to be exposing and opposing all such corruption.

Nzimande's position in the cabinet made this a delicate matter, particularly since in traditional terms he was bound to show deference to Zuma as his elder. Soon, a substantial lobby formed within the SACP that wanted Nzimande replaced as leader by his far more outspoken deputy, Solly Mapaila. Nzimande's reluctance to criticise Zuma and his friends the Guptas earned him considerable scorn and accusations that he valued his ministerial perks more than any principles.[9] Worse still, the populist radicalism of Julius Malema's EFF had eaten deeply into the SACP's constituency, and the party had visibly lost a lot of ground.

Nonetheless, the party retained considerable relevance in KwaZulu-Natal. In the ANC's exile years Xhosas had dominated all the top positions and Zulus in the movement felt somewhat marginalised – there was much grumbling that most scholarships and top jobs went to Xhosas.[10] As a result the SACP acted as a sort of alternative hub for Zulus, particularly in those years (1979–1986) when Moses Mabhida, another Zulu, was its leader. This connection was maintained after the party's return from exile and further strengthened when Nzimande became leader in 1998 and enrolled large numbers of Zulu members.[11]

The significance of this was that when the Zuma forces began to mobilise to reassert their control over the province they quickly realised that the many well-placed communists were a problem. Many of them were bitterly critical of Zuma, even if the party's official line was still supportive of him, and there was little doubt that they would support Senzo Mchunu in the coming struggle. The result was an undeclared but savage war between the Zuma bloc and the SACP in KwaZulu-Natal.[12]

The battle for Durban (eThekwini)

The first and greatest battle was for control of eThekwini and its munificent budget. The mayor, James Nxumalo, was the chairman of the SACP in KwaZulu-Natal, and a known critic of Zuma. Accordingly, a long and bitter battle was fought to unseat him by dint of endless regional conferences of the ANC. No fewer than five of these were called, attempted and abandoned, until in December 2015 a rigged conference finally took place, boycotted by the Nxumalo faction, which elected his opponent, Zandile Gumede, as chairperson of the mayoral committee by a vote of 283–1. This victory gave the Zuma forces control over the province's main source of patronage and contracts, which enabled the Zuma faction to bring powerful business interests to its side. The conference outcome was declared unlawful by the High Court in Pietermaritzburg[13] but Gumede continued as mayor.

Only later, when the Moerane Commission was set up to inquire into the scores of political killings in KwaZulu-Natal, was a more revealing light shed on these events. At that commission Themba Mthembu, secretary of the KwaZulu-Natal ANC, testified with James Nxumalo sitting beside him. Nxumalo lived in Inchanga, on the outskirts of Durban, and, strange though it may seem, that was where a key battle for the future of South Africa was to be fought.

Nxumalo claimed in his testimony that the political killings in KwaZulu-Natal – and nearly 50 councillors and various others were assassinated in the 2012–2017 period – were all part of a 'grand plan' for the 'political takeover' of the eThekwini region by a faction composed of national politicians and local business interests. The assassination of S'bu Sibiya – gunned down at his home in Inanda in

2011 – had been carried out by these same forces within the ANC. Several other assassinations followed.[14]

Mthembu testified that 'these killings were seen as a precursor to the real build-up towards a fierce contestation of the eThekwini ANC region ... Understanding [this] power struggle helps to understand the national power struggle in the ANC, which is strongly believed to have a direct link. ... The belief among many structures on the ground is that any faction that heads eThekwini metro is also likely to have an influence on national politics and the national leadership.'[15]

Nxumalo carefully stopped short of naming the Zuma faction (to do so would have invited instant retribution) but his evidence clearly posed the question as to Jacob Zuma's ultimate responsibility for at least some of the killings.

Since Nxumalo was such a block to the ambitions of the Zuma faction, no holds were barred. As always happens, there was a local rival – who naturally attached himself to the Zuma faction. In this case it was one Dennis 'Boy' Shozi, who accordingly supported the mayoral candidacy of Zandile Gumede. According to Nxumalo, Shozi and his supporters blocked the Nxumalo supporters from gaining ANC membership in order to ensure the election of one of Shozi's men as councillor for Inchanga. Nxumalo's faction then consolidated within the local SACP branch. They then nominated one of Nxumalo's family, Malombo Nxumalo, to contest the ward. This led to a series of attacks by the Shozi faction. In the end 11 people died in the Inchanga area alone. At the time of the Moerane Commission several members of Shozi's family had been charged with murder. Nxumalo nonetheless won the ward. Here, then, is the peculiar reality of politics in KwaZulu-Natal, where ultimately some semblance of the democratic process allows a political battle to be won, though only after the 'facts on the ground' have been settled by a real military battle.

Nxumalo's testimony was corroborated by Themba Mthembu, the SACP secretary for KwaZulu-Natal, who also detailed other attacks on Nxumalo supporters at KwaNdengezi, near Pinetown where two ANC councillors and a hitman they had hired were sentenced for the murder of a local squatter leader. One of these was also charged with the murder of an Nxumalo supporter, Mobeni Khwela.[16]

This general picture was further supported by Senzo Mchunu, who gave a detailed account of how state and party resources were used and abused in order to settle ANC leadership contests. This manipulation went all the way down to branch level, with the creation of multiple fraudulent or 'ghost' memberships, the use of security companies and 'bouncers' to keep others out of branch meetings, and all manner of stratagems to ensure that meetings were only attended by one's own faction. The same sort of thing happened at regional and then at provincial level – it was 'a complicated rot'.[17]

Mchunu said the situation was actually far worse because the police's specialist priority-crime unit, the Hawks, and the intelligence services were all rotten too and effectively part of the Zuma faction. (It was noticeable that Zuma, the former head of ANC Intelligence, had always kept tight control of the security sector, with all-Zulu ministers reporting directly to him.) Just before Mchunu was toppled as premier, he had been accused of murder. Using a private investigator working from cellphone data, Mchunu identified a probable suspect within two days and he told the police. They failed to investigate, and even after Mchunu had intervened personally with the minister of police, the case was left unsolved – just as political murders were always unsolved, clearly because the police didn't want to solve them.[18]

The dominoes begin to fall

Once the Zuma faction gained the upper hand in eThekwini, Senzo Mchunu was effectively doomed as premier. Sure enough, in November 2015 Sihle Zikalala defeated Mchunu for the post of KwaZulu-Natal ANC chairman; his deputy, Willies Mchunu (no relation), was elected as deputy chairman; and Super Zuma (President Zuma's nephew) was elected as secretary. Senzo Mchunu was duly sacked in May 2016 and replaced by Willies Mchunu.[19]

Now that it was clear that the Zuma faction had won the struggle in KwaZulu-Natal, Zuma felt free to act nationally. Within days he had sacked the finance minister, Nhlanhla Nene, who had been obstructing the schemes of Zuma and the Guptas, notably with respect to a mammoth proposed nuclear deal with Russia and the financing of South African Airways (SAA). Zuma had been preparing the ground for this for several months. At the end of September 2015, he had plucked an obscure provincial MEC (Member of the Executive Council) from the Free State, Mosebenzi Zwane, and named him minister of mineral resources, thus displacing Ngoako Ramatlhodi, a senior figure who had also stood in the Guptas' way.[20] This astonishing appointment had clearly been cooked up by Zuma in consultation with the Free State premier, Ace Magashule, and the Guptas. Zwane, who was already embroiled in a corruption scam of his own,[21] had helped organise the notorious Gupta wedding at Sun City in 2013 (when state resources, including an air force base, had been put at the Guptas' disposal as if they were heads of state) and then, as MEC for agriculture, had introduced the R570-million Estina dairy-farm scheme, in which funds earmarked for small black farmers were diverted into the Gupta purse. Magashule had prepared the ground by having Zwane secretly flown to Cape Town to be sworn in as an MP. Then, when Nene was sacked, the unknown David van Rooyen was made finance minister.[22]

This appointment was so obviously tantamount to handing the National Treasury over to the Guptas that there was an immediate roar of outrage. The value of the rand plummeted, and up to R500 billion was wiped off the value of South African shares. The other members of the ANC's 'top six'[23] all told Zuma that they could not support this. Within days, Van Rooyen had been replaced by Pravin

Gordhan, a former finance minister who was no favourite of Zuma's. It was a landmark moment because Zweli Mkhize had now come out in open opposition to Zuma's machinations. So, no sooner had Zuma dealt with one Zulu upstart – Senzo Mchunu – than a far more powerful one emerged.

Only three months later the Constitutional Court came out with its judgment that Zuma had failed to uphold the Constitution and thus broken his oath of office – and that Parliament had also failed in its duty to hold him responsible.[24] The judgment related to Zuma's failure to implement the remedial action recommended by the public protector in her report on the Nkandla scandal, in 2014. Further disgraceful evidence of the effective capture of the state by Zuma's friends, the Guptas, continued to accumulate, leading to a motion of no confidence in Zuma mounted by the DA in November 2016. This was defeated, though only by 214–126. In the debate the DA leader, Mmusi Maimane, listed a number of ANC leaders who had already spoken out against Zuma – the chief whip, Jackson Mthembu, the health minister, Aaron Motsoaledi, the minister of public works, Thulas Nxesi, and Mathole Motshekga, a former chief whip. Such a public fraying of loyalty to an ANC leader was unprecedented.[25]

Zuma naturally attempted to *tomber à gauche* (fall to the left), insisting that his critics were motivated only by a racist wish to support an unjust status quo. (When those critics were African they were alleged to be sell-outs to the imperialists, CIA agents and the like.) Zuma found a passionate defender in the young minister of home affairs, Malusi Gigaba, who had already distinguished himself as a strong Gupta ally, even granting them passports en bloc. Addressing the National Assembly in November 2016, Gigaba said, 'The truth is that there's a bitter struggle in South Africa between the former oppressors and those whom they oppressed,'[26] and tried to insist that those who opposed Zuma were merely conspiring to hand over control of South Africa's mineral resources to foreign interests. This echoed almost word for word what the Afrikaner Nationalists had said in order to answer criticism of apartheid, though in their case the villains were Anglo-American big business and foreign communists.

Only days later the ANC minister Derek Hanekom proposed a motion of no confidence in Zuma at a meeting of the ANC's National Executive Committee (NEC). The motion failed, naturally, but it represented a new high-water mark of opposition.

In March 2017 Zuma carried out a major cabinet reshuffle (his eleventh), sacking Hanekom and also the finance minister, Pravin Gordhan, replacing him with the tame Gigaba. Once again it was clear that Zuma was intent on subordinating the Treasury to his and the Guptas' plans. Five of the top six were all against, and Ramaphosa publicly said that Gordhan's removal was 'totally, totally unacceptable'[27] – an open sign of revolt against Zuma.

Unabashed, Zuma continued with his theme of 'radical economic transformation' and raised the highly emotive notion of land reform via expropriation without compensation. This was actually an EFF policy and the ANC had hitherto shrunk from it, for it quite obviously meant tearing up the compromise on which the Constitution had been based, whereby whites ceded political power but property rights were guaranteed. EWC – as it became known – was magic in the ears of poor Africans, for it meant free land, which in turn meant free money. True, very few wanted to be farmers, but the land issue was simply a metaphor for a wider African sense of dispossession. Equally obviously, such a policy, with its clear echoes of the Zimbabwean disaster, was nightmarish to anyone owning any assets, let alone would-be investors, domestic or foreign. Zuma was able to marshal behind the proposal only the KwaZulu-Natal ANC and the tame ANCYL.

The SACP vs Zuma: the culmination

The SACP's anger against Zuma had been building. Losing Durban had been a bitter pill. And by now the looting intentions of Zuma and his Gupta cronies were plain for all to see. Although Blade Nzimande had been left undisturbed in his cabinet post, for many in the SACP Zuma was now just an irreparable crook. Worse, the party was desperate to distance itself from Zuma because the EFF's propaganda against Zuma and his 'SACP enablers' was doing the party much damage among its clientele. Solly Mapaila, the party's second deputy general secretary, was bitterly outspoken in his criticism of Zuma, whom he referred to as an 'elite predator'[28] – making Nzimande's continuing silence even more of an embarrassment.

Indeed, Julius Malema warned that the SACP needed to increase the number of bodyguards around Mapaila for 'he is the only man that Zuma is worried about' and 'anything is possible'. The rest of the SACP didn't worry Zuma, said Malema, because they 'are scared like little kids'.[29] This followed an incident in which Mapaila had been due to give a speech on the anniversary of Chris Hani's assassination and had suddenly found himself faced, on the one hand, by an organised mob booing him and, on the other hand, by a gunman. The gunman bolted when he realised he was caught by surveillance cameras, but it was enough to abort Mapaila's speech. The fact that many SACP activists were among those who had been gunned down in KwaZulu-Natal had shown that the Zuma faction was in earnest.[30]

Nzimande faced an agonising choice: the SACP had grown so close to Zuma that any separation might well mean the party losing its representation in government. And Nzimande was only too keen to keep his ministerial salary, car and other perks. But the pressure within the party for a split from Zuma was now overwhelming, particularly since a strong lobby within the SACP wanted to replace Nzimande with Mapaila. So, the party made it clear that at its national conference in July 2017 it wished to purge all its pro-Zuma elements.

The party chairman, Senzeni Zokwana, straightforwardly denounced the Guptas, while Cyril Ramaphosa, who addressed the conference, openly inveighed against state capture.[31]

The problem was that these pro-Zuma elements included Willies Mchunu (premier of KwaZulu-Natal), Phumulo Masualle (premier of the Eastern Cape), S'dumo Dlamini (president of Cosatu), Senzeni Zokwana (SACP national chairman), and Buti Manamela (head of the Young Communist League, now a minister in the presidency). These were all leading figures who would doubtless fight their corner. The party was tearing itself apart. Nzimande was booed and barracked from the floor and the Mapaila faction was clearly very strong. When Jeremy Cronin, Nzimande's long-time number two, stood down there was some suspicion that he too had been disheartened by the party's failure to come out more clearly against Zuma. Mapaila was easily elected to replace Cronin after Nzimande had told delegates that he must persevere as leader: 'The debate is do you change or not change leadership when the truck is going down at fast speed on a slippery slope?'[32]

Zuma had thus greatly weakened and divided both the ANC and the SACP. He had also had the same effect on Cosatu. Its secretary-general, Zwelinzima Vavi, had also become bitterly critical of Zuma. (This was in marked contrast to his enthusiasm back in 2007, when he hailed Zuma as like 'the big wave of the tsunami'.[33]) As a result, the Zuma forces (led by the Cosatu president, S'dumo Dlamini) had railroaded him out of the federation. Vavi had taken a considerable body of support with him, and the biggest union, the National Union of Metalworkers of South Africa (Numsa), also walked out. The result left Cosatu a shadow of its former self. It was now composed mainly of white-collar public-sector workers, especially teachers and civil servants. In effect, the bureaucratic bourgeoisie had now taken over Cosatu.

A contest like no other

In the previous era, open contests for the ANC leadership had been rare; even in 2012 Motlanthe had come under strong pressure to withdraw, the Zuma faction insisting that it was wrong that Zuma should be challenged at all. Similarly, the ANC had banned all members, on threat of expulsion, from taking the ANC to court. In 2017 all this came apart. No fewer than seven candidates ran for the party presidency, openly campaigning for months on end and all making their own programmatic promises as to what they would do when elected. Nkosazana Dlamini-Zuma faithfully echoed Zuma's refrain about 'radical economic transformation' and 'white monopoly capital' and she also campaigned steadily for expropriation without compensation as the 'answer' to the land issue.[34] The other six candidates made little or no mention of these themes.

Dlamini-Zuma's campaign was formulaic and pretty much lifeless. It was not even clear whether the candidate was writing her own lines. To some extent this may have reflected the fact that she was cast in an old-style Soviet mould, highly ideological and little given to the requirements of modern political campaigning. But it may also just be that she had little control over her own campaign, which was mounted for her by the Zuma faction. Remarkably, her main spokesman and aide was Carl Niehaus, a man with a long record as a con man and liar.[35] Niehaus's serial criminality had forced him to drop from view but before the campaign he re-emerged as part of the Zuma faction, becoming spokesman for the MKMVA. It was difficult to believe that Dlamini-Zuma would have chosen such a front man herself.

Of the other candidates the two women, Lindiwe Sisulu and Baleka Mbete, made a fairly vigorous showing, as did Cyril Ramaphosa. The remainder – Jeff Radebe, Zweli Mkhize and Mathews Phosa – did little. To all intents and purposes, it was a two-horse race, though Lindiwe Sisulu gained ground during the campaign and was a clear third by the end.

During the campaign, at the behest of eNCA, I carried out a large-scale opinion survey and a number of focus groups with the help of market research firm MarkData.[36] Almost 5 000 people were surveyed, but we focused particularly on the 2 717 ANC voters among them. When we first interviewed voters in September 2017 we found that Ramaphosa was far ahead: among ANC voters he was preferred by 48.4 per cent against 21 per cent for Dlamini-Zuma. Indeed, he led in eight out of nine provinces, and even in KwaZulu-Natal he was close behind, with 32.8 per cent against 37.5 per cent for Dlamini-Zuma. Our focus groups showed why: everywhere there was a furious rejection of Jacob Zuma, who was blamed for corruption and bringing down the country and the economy. But ANC voters also exhibited a blithe confidence that once Zuma was gone the ANC could revert to its former self as the Mandela ANC. In any case, they asked, how could they vote for the DA, which would bring back apartheid and abolish all the social grants? This showed how effective ANC propaganda had been, for both suggestions were vigorously denied by the DA.

Ethnically, Ramaphosa's lead was built on a 2:1 majority among Xhosa-speakers, a 3:1 advantage among Sotho-speakers, 5:1 among Tswana-speakers, 8:1 among minority tribal groups, and 9:1 among the Pedi (Northern Sotho). This was interesting in two respects. First, ANC dominance since 1994 has been built on a solid bloc of Nguni (Xhosa, Zulu, Swazi) support, producing one Nguni leader after another. Indeed, this Nguni dominance goes back to the 1950s, that is, ever since the ANC became a mass party. Throughout that period non-Ngunis were always somewhat left out and, in opinion surveys, were more likely than other African groups to support non-ANC parties. With the coming of Ramaphosa – a member of the minority Venda group himself – this situation was reversed.

This sudden reversal of the old ethnic balance posed many questions: could the ANC really hang together in this changed form?

Normally, reversing the sociology of any party so completely comes at some cost. Secondly, the Venda are a small minority even within Limpopo province, and it was by no means clear that Ramaphosa would gain the support of the Pedi, who constitute the majority in that province. In the event, he was overwhelmingly adopted by the latter, with the 'favourite son' effect clearly trumping other factors. In Limpopo, Ramaphosa led Dlamini-Zuma among ANC voters by 77 per cent to 3.3 per cent.

It was striking that while popular opinion lay behind Ramaphosa, the power of Zuma's patronage meant that most ANC premiers adopted a firmly pro-Zuma position. There were two exceptions. First, Stanley Mathabatha (Limpopo) was a strong opponent of corruption and a firm supporter of Ramaphosa. He was, though, fiercely opposed by the provincial ANC secretary, Knocks Seabi, a Zuma ally.[37] Second, there was David Makhura (Gauteng), who calmly announced that the Gauteng ANC had examined Zuma's bugbear of 'white monopoly capital' and concluded that it did not actually exist.[38] But the key figure in Gauteng was the ANC chairman, Paul Mashatile. He had endorsed Ramaphosa early on.

However, Mashatile was greatly struck by the fact that David Mabuza (Mpumalanga), a pillar of the Premier League, had belatedly declared that he didn't wish to choose between Ramaphosa and Dlamini-Zuma. Instead he favoured a unity ticket. This positioned Mabuza firmly on the fence as a possible kingmaker. Mashatile was much attracted by such a notion and consorted with Mabuza a good deal, meanwhile rowing back from his initial endorsement of Ramaphosa.[39] This greatly annoyed the Gauteng ANC, a bastion of anti-Zuma sentiment.

The other ANC premiers – Sihle Zikalala (KwaZulu-Natal), Ace Magashule (Free State), Supra Mahumapelo (North West), Phumulo Masualle (Eastern Cape) and Sylvia Lucas (Northern Cape) – all took a staunchly pro-Zuma position. Masualle had earlier been very critical of Zuma, but a visit from the Zuma faction to let him know how much worse things could be for him if he failed to support Dlamini-Zuma had the desired effect.[40]

In all cases these premiers faced stiff opposition from a rival in their organisation who backed Ramaphosa and tried to use that to topple them. Zikalala had the easiest ride, for his rival, Senzo Mchunu, had already been dispossessed of the premiership and in any case Zikakala was supporting a Zulu (Dlamini-Zuma) against a non-Zulu (Ramaphosa).

Everywhere else, our survey showed that large majorities of ANC voters backed Ramaphosa. In the Eastern Cape, Ramaphosa led Dlamini-Zuma by 52.3 per cent to 24 per cent; in the Northern Cape by 50 per cent to 12.5 per cent; in the Free State by 48.9 per cent to 19.9 per cent; in the North West by 39.4 per cent to 11.8 per cent (with 41.9 per cent saying they supported no candidate, a clear sign of intimidation); and in Mpumalanga by 47.2 per cent to 15.9 per cent. That is to say, Ramaphosa was far ahead in all the Premier League provinces despite the strong commitment of their premiers to the Dlamini-Zuma ticket. ANC voters in the Western Cape also favoured Ramaphosa heavily but that province was dominated by the DA and the ANC section there was small and chronically disunited.

In the Northern Cape, the Ramaphosa camp had a virtual pushover. The premier, Sylvia Lucas, had joined the ANC straight from her previous job as a secretary for the National Party and had minimal popular support. A large lady, she had earned headlines (as well as a cartoon by Zapiro) as 'the Fast Food Premier', spending R53 000 on fast food in her first ten weeks in office. As her provincial ANC conference neared, she simply stood down as chairperson, allowing the Ramaphosa faction to sweep the board.[41] Naturally, she tried to have the conference nullified – but failed. She clung on as premier but was quite impotent.

In the Eastern Cape, the Ramaphosa forces were led by the provincial

ANC secretary, Oscar Mabuyane, who managed to displace Masualle as party chairman at a violent conference characterised by much chair-throwing.[42] Again thanks to presidential patronage Masualle managed to cling on as premier but with little power. He too tried and failed to have the conference annulled.

In the other provinces, the Ramaphosa forces faced far stronger opposition and, despite their clear advantage among ANC voters, they failed entirely to prevail. Not to put too fine a point on it, the Free State, North West and Mpumalanga were all de facto fiefdoms where the premier's will was enforced by every kind of administrative stratagem, rigging or by main force if necessary.

Why Ramaphosa?

Given that the whole weight of state and ANC patronage was exercised behind the candidacy of Dlamini-Zuma it was striking that rank-and-file ANC opinion lay better than 2:1 in the opposite direction. Why was this? The answer popularly given was that Ramaphosa appealed particularly to the better-educated and more middle-class voters. This argument was parroted even by TV commentators whereas a moment's thought would have revealed that such voters were a distinct minority within ANC ranks. In fact, when we broke down choices by employment, income and education we found the exact opposite to be true: there was a systematic bias towards Ramaphosa among the poorest, the less educated and the unemployed. Those with higher educational qualifications and better-paid jobs in the formal sector were distinctly biased towards Dlamini-Zuma.

Another striking finding emerged when we asked ANC voters whether they would prefer the ANC to move towards radical economic transformation aimed at complete redistribution of capital and income; whether they would prefer the existing policy mix; or whether they would like to see ANC policy move in a more pro-business direction in the hope that this would produce more jobs. Only one tenth of the electorate preferred the existing policy mix – a sign of how fed-up voters were with the status quo – but there was a 5:2 majority for more pro-business policies over 'radical economic trans-formation'. Yet the Zuma camp had been campaigning for radical economic transformation in the belief that such 'revolutionary' poli-cies would win the hearts of ANC voters and activists. To be fair, it is possible that such policies would have more appeal among ANC activists and conference delegates than among ordinary ANC voters. And it has usually been fatal in ANC politics to be termed a 'sell-out' for favouring an insufficiently revolutionary position. Even so, it is remarkable to see a party in which such a huge divide separates the leadership from its rank and file.

As one puts these factors together one should add that, in all polls and for many years now, the key issue in South African politics has been unemployment. Given the mountainous figures of the jobless it can hardly be otherwise. And therein, pretty clearly, lay the reason for Ramaphosa's large lead: there was an underlying assumption that he would be able to do more to create jobs than any of his rivals. At the level of the conference delegates, the power of patronage was clearly the dominant factor. At grassroots, the key was jobs.

Almost certainly, the jobs issue was also the reason why the battle continued to move Ramaphosa's way as the campaign lengthened. For we returned to our sample in late November to question those who had professed themselves willing to undergo a second round of interviews. Some caution is necessary here, for this final sample was self-selected, not random. Nonetheless, it was striking that this second set of interviews showed Ramaphosa leading Dlamini-Zuma by 64 per cent to 14 per cent, suggesting a further large slippage of support to him.

No one, however, could believe that popular support would be enough on its own. ANC conferences are prey to every kind of corruption, chicanery and manipulation. A great deal of money changes hands. And Zuma still had all the advantages of incumbency. The Zuma faction in the country at large clearly expected that Dlamini-Zuma would win and that there would be business as usual. The only cloud in the sky was that the Guptas had clearly decided that they had far too much to lose to make any bets on an ANC conference (and they may well have been conducting their own polls). In the run-up to the conference they sold off their media interests to their loyal client, Mzwanele (Jimmy) Manyi, transferred as much of their ill-gotten gains as possible abroad and quietly removed themselves to Dubai.

Chapter Four

The conference

Jacob Zuma still had some tricks up his sleeve. Just as the long-awaited conference got under way in December 2017 at Nasrec, he announced a new policy of free higher education for 90 per cent of students. This had been a student demand for some time, but the Heher Commission, set up by Zuma in January 2016 to examine the issue, had concluded that it was not an affordable option. The real situation was worse in two respects. First, students in higher education represented the most fortunate 20 per cent of their age group. Often, they were the sons and daughters of the new African middle class and all of them entered higher education in the hope of joining that class. That is to say, free higher education was a further diversion of scarce resources to an already privileged group. Second, Pravin Gordhan, as finance minister, had earlier made it crystal clear that the state simply had no spare resources for such an extravagance.[1] After all, far richer countries like Britain and America did not manage to afford free higher education.

But Zuma's calculation was that this populist defiance of economic logic would be a crowd-pleasing demonstration of what radical economic transformation might look like. It was also a major challenge to Ramaphosa: he knew the state was effectively bankrupt and that if he won the presidency this would be another albatross round his neck.

He could have made the case for economic rationality and resisted the idea. But, like most politicians in his position, he decided this was no time for heroic gestures and publicly signed on to the new policy. So that was the first round to Zuma: Ramaphosa had been publicly forced into a 90-degree turn against his will.

The result

The polling figures we examined in Chapter Three suggest that Ramaphosa should have won by a landslide. In fact, as we have seen (see Chapter One), he won by a wafer-thin majority of 179 votes. In large part this was because ANC conferences are far more a measure of patronage politics than political popularity. The fact that Dlamini-Zuma's advantage in KwaZulu-Natal was relatively slight in popular terms counted as nothing, for example, when compared to the fact that the power of patronage in that province was concentrated in the hands of the premier and the president, who could then use this to achieve an overwhelming majority for their candidate. Undeniably many votes were bought and many more were rigged.[2] This had been the way that ANC conferences were settled for some years past. What was remarkable was that the Free State and North West both cast overwhelming votes for Dlamini-Zuma, flatly against the wishes of ANC voters in those provinces.

President Zuma was clearly thunderstruck when the result was announced. It was obvious to all that David Mabuza had settled the contest by swinging the whole of his Mpumalanga delegation into the Ramaphosa column – in return for the deputy presidency. What made this all the more important was that Mabuza had hugely inflated Mpumalanga's delegate count to 736, giving it more delegates than any other province save KwaZulu-Natal. Some of these may have been bogus – after all, most provinces had 'ghost branches'.[3] In North West, Supra Mahumapelo, when faced with branches that did not follow his writ, simply dissolved them and recreated dozens of new branches to replace them. There was no little irony in the fact that Zuma was sunk in the end by this huge and artificial inflation of Mpumalanga's delegate count, for this was a trick Zuma had pioneered in KwaZulu-Natal, passing it on to Mabuza.

A rigged deck?

One of the reasons that Zuma had been so sure of victory was that he had ensured that Nomvula Mokonyane, one of his strongest supporters, was made head of elections for the conference. Mokonyane was widely held to have reduced her department of water affairs and sanitation to a bankrupt shell due to huge amounts of 'irregular expenditure'.[4] She was a quite open Zuma partisan, and even at the conference itself she made no secret of the fact that she was campaigning for the Zuma faction. Moreover, she accused David Mabuza of having 'sold out' by failing to support the Zuma bloc.[5] With such a Zuma partisan in charge of the election it was hardly surprising that she was accused of fiddling the registration process by granting accreditation to non-delegates. But, of course, when Mabuza swung his huge bloc of delegates towards Ramaphosa this had overwhelmed any such biases in the process.

The Zuma faction drew some comfort from the fact that at least it had managed to push two of its own faction into the top six – Jessie Duarte as deputy secretary-general and Ace Magashule as secretary-general, with Mabuza still an unknown quantity. Magashule's victory was a devastating blow to the Ramaphosa faction, whose candidate, Senzo Mchunu, had been the leader of the Ramaphosa forces in KwaZulu-Natal. Before the conference Mchunu had not minced his words, telling his supporters that the choice was between allowing the rot to continue and electing a leadership that would really confront the issues facing the country. Mchunu explained that 'pigs just eat, that's all they do all day', and that if things carried on as under Zuma then 'we shall become a nation of pigs'.[6] Mchunu's supporters were so confident that he had been elected secretary-general that they carried him shoulder high to the podium before the result. When the result was announced, Mchunu was clearly completely shocked and went up to ask to see the figures.

And well might he have asked. Magashule had won with 2360 votes to Mchunu's 2336, a margin of 24. There had been four spoilt ballots and eight abstentions. But that added up to only 4696 and 4764 delegates had voted – so there were 68 missing votes. These were declared to be 'quarantined' as unsafe in some way or another. Yet Stanley Mathabatha, the premier of Limpopo, confirmed that these were votes from his province's Vhembe district.[7] Given that Limpopo, Ramaphosa's own province, had voted monolithically for its favourite son, it seemed a racing certainty that, if counted, these would have pushed Mchunu over the top. This certainly seemed to be the view of the Zuma faction, which was emphatic that the 68 votes must not be counted. Naturally, fingers were pointed at Mokonyane. So, everything depended on what the Ramaphosa faction would do. The Zuma faction made it clear that if a recount was ordered for this post, it would demand a recount for all of the top six. This made the Ramaphosa faction nervous, for they felt unsure that Ramaphosa's own majority would survive another Mokonyane-organised poll. Others felt that conceding the secretary-general's post to the tainted Magashule might ruin Ramaphosa's presidency. It was too important just to give way.

Indeed, the stakes were even higher. Zweli Mkhize had not been returned to the top six and nor had Baleka Mbete – both of them Zulus. With Dlamini-Zuma also losing, this meant that the top six would go from having three Zulus in it, including the president, to having none at all. Ramaphosa had depended heavily on having Mchunu, a former premier of KwaZulu-Natal, to represent his cause in that most vital and explosive of provinces. As a Venda himself, he had no standing there. There might well be a powerful Zulu reaction against this loss of power. In the end Ramaphosa decided to concede. News24 showed a sneak video of him addressing his own supporters in closed session and telling them to accept the result: '... it may not be what we all wanted but the conference must not be allowed to degenerate into controversy.'[8]

This was almost certainly a blunder. Any attempt to unseat Ramaphosa after he had been elected would never have been accepted. Accepting Magashule was far too high a price; it could well mean that Ramaphosa would never be able to achieve control of the ANC. And it meant that Ramaphosa would be deadlocked in the top six. The only votes he could more or less rely on there were those of Gwede Mantashe (chairperson) and Paul Mashatile (treasurer-general). Both Magashule and his deputy, Jessie Duarte, were firmly in the Zuma camp – and they would have exclusive control over the party. This left any hope of a majority dependent on what David Mabuza, the deputy president, might do. Once again, the canny Mabuza had made himself the indispensable man.

One thing is certain: if the roles had been reversed, Zuma would have fought to the last round and beyond to keep the secretary-generalship, for he knew that in ANC politics control of the party apparatus was almost everything. He would certainly not have been afraid of things 'degenerating into controversy'. To the Zuma forces this was further proof that Ramaphosa lacked the steel to be president. The fact that he had been willing to give way on this cardinal point – and thus allow his ally Mchunu to fall under the bus – merely emboldened further opposition.

There was a final twist of the knife. Zuma knew that at an emotional level the land issue summed up all the African feelings of dispossession, of grievance against colonial conquest and anger against poverty and inequality. He had unleashed this ultimate weapon by getting Dlamini-Zuma to campaign for expropriation without compensation (EWC). But at the ANC's July 2017 policy conference he had found himself in the minority on this issue and had craftily shelved it, saying it should be dealt with instead by the December conference.[9] By that time the Zuma faction had spent most of the year campaigning for EWC and feelings were running high. So, on the last day of the conference the Zuma faction made an extremely determined push for EWC. This sensitive topic, emblematic for many black South Africans of their whole sense of loss and disadvantage, produced a rowdy debate with a great deal of shouting and screaming. Ramaphosa's faction feared that EWC might torpedo all hopes of economic recovery and more than suspected that the Zuma side was deliberately trying to set up the new ANC president to fail. After all, Zuma had had two terms as president – why was it only in his last days in office that he was bringing this issue up? If he felt so strongly, why had he not acted before?

The answer was, of course, that Zuma's use of the land issue had been entirely opportunistic and cynical. Throughout his presidency he had talked of the plight of poor rural people and there had been much rhetoric about land. Moreover, he had opened up so many new opportunities for land claims that it was estimated that it would take 700 years for the state to process all the claims.[10] But at the same time, year after year, next to nothing had been voted in the budget for land reform, thus making it impossible for the state to buy out even the many willing sellers.[11] In a very strict sense, Zuma's actual policy had been wholly irresponsible. In 2016 Parliament had passed an Expropriation Bill allowing the state to acquire land without the owner's consent at a price to be set by the Valuer-General. Yet Zuma had refused to sign the Bill and passed it back to Parliament, saying that MPs had not consulted widely enough.[12] The fact was that it suited him to allow the issue to peak at the December conference, but not before.

However, he had used its mobilising capacity to great effect, and at one stage actual scuffles broke out and conference marshals had to eject some delegates from the conference.[13] The Ramaphosa forces argued passionately against the EWC resolution. They attempted to pass a motion allowing EWC only if the 'willing buyer, willing seller' model failed, but this did not pass. They pointed to the disastrous effect of land seizures in Zimbabwe and how this had harmed the poor and delivered land only to the elite. It was no good: the Zuma faction was adamant, and on this issue it could rely on the raw emotions that it tapped into among delegates at large.[14]

The debate dragged on, but in the end the Ramaphosa faction decided to give way, contenting itself merely with adding a number of conditions – that EWC should only be carried out if it did not endanger food production or food security or the rest of the economy (and it would be bound to do all those things).[15] Their concern was that if they failed to concede it might even lead to an attempt to overthrow Ramaphosa's presidential win.

So, in the early hours of the morning, many hours late, Ramaphosa at last gave his maiden speech as ANC president in which he declared his own acceptance of EWC, thus making support for it unanimous. Diplomatically, he even praised Zuma's legacy, though there is little doubt that in the eyes of Zuma, who was stonily looking on, this would have appeared as merely a further sign of weakness.[16]

Ramaphoria

It was immediately obvious that most of the ANC, let alone public opinion at large, wanted Ramaphosa to take over the presidency of the country right away. Zuma resisted, claiming that at least he should be afforded a further three months in which he would be able to introduce Ramaphosa to international leaders and audiences. This was farcical. Zuma had not bothered himself much with foreign affairs, while Ramaphosa was already well known on the international circuit. But Ramaphosa was insistent: Zuma must go. He knew perfectly well that once the moment was allowed to slip it would become progressively harder to get Zuma out. Zuma would use all his networks to mobilise support and Ramaphosa, with his narrow victory and no tribal or regional base to speak of, would see his position erode. Indeed, Zuma's behaviour made it clear that had Dlamini-Zuma won, Zuma would have remained in office almost indefinitely.

So Ramaphosa kept up the pressure. But Zuma stood his ground for nearly six weeks, making Ramaphosa look weak. In the end, it became clear that Ramaphosa alone could not move Zuma and the decision would have to depend on the ANC's NEC. The NEC wanted a clean break too, and in the end it was made plain that if Zuma continued to resist he would be voted out by the NEC – in which case he would lose his various benefits. So on 14 February 2018 Zuma finally resigned, and Ramaphosa was duly sworn in as president of the republic the following day. The departure of Zuma and the advent of Ramaphosa set off a huge wave of enthusiasm, generally referred to as 'Ramaphoria'. In part, this was simply a matter of Ramaphosa's vast public majority finally giving voice to its relief at seeing the back of Zuma and its hope for a new and better era. But Ramaphosa was also mightily cheered by white business, which had contributed heavily to his campaign. What was not revealed was the price Ramaphosa had had to pay for Zuma's exit. Later it became clear that the state would continue to pay Zuma's legal costs in the various cases against him[17] – a major concession not just financially but politically, for it meant that Ramaphosa was helping to defend the corrupt old order.

These changes meant a sudden and large loss of power and patronage for KwaZulu-Natal, the province with the biggest ANC delegation – an intrinsically dangerous situation for the stability of the ANC. Ramaphosa showed that he understood the sensitivity of this issue by making a visit to KwaZulu-Natal in July. There he paid court to the Zulu king, Goodwill Zwelithini, clearly hoping to assuage Zulu resentment at this sudden loss of power.[18] It was, though, unlikely to be enough, particularly since an angry and embittered Jacob Zuma was bound to return to swim in those troubled waters. For Zuma had taken Ramaphosa's measure: he had given way on issue after issue, pursuing a mythical consensus. Zuma had lost the presidency, but in the wider game of poker he had outplayed Ramaphosa in almost every hand.

Chapter Five

The new struggle begins

Ramaphoria did not last long. Zuma had allowed his powerful barons to loot – unless they went too far and caused a peasant revolt. This is pretty much what happened in North West province, where the premier, Supra Mahumapelo, was alleged to have looted and tyrannised the population.[1] However, he had placed all his bets on Dlamini-Zuma, and when Ramaphosa won at Nasrec, the province's enraged citizenry rose up, demanding change. So serious was the civil disorder thus caused that Ramaphosa had to break off in the midst of a Commonwealth Heads of Government Meeting in London and fly home to deal with it.[2] But Mahumapelo's summary removal clearly threatened other party barons, particularly Ace Magashule, who was already under suspicion for his involvement with various Gupta pieces of criminality.[3] So Magashule did all he could to hinder the investigation into Mahumapelo. ANC meetings in the North West called to inquire into the complaints against Mahumapelo were arranged at awkward times in remote places, and sometimes in areas where there had been recent lion attacks, thus making it difficult to achieve quorums.[4] But Mahumapelo had provoked such popular hatred that the opposition to him was not to be discouraged, and after several weeks the errant premier was forced to step down – though even then he remained chairman of the provincial ANC, a post from which he was only dislodged later and with difficulty.[5] Mahumapelo was reinstated as chair of the North West ANC by court order in February 2019.

This was an early indication that Ramaphosa's position was not strong, an impression confirmed by his difficulty in forming a new cabinet. Under pressure from powerful factions in the ANC, he ended up with a cabinet that still included a number of ministers widely regarded as compromised. He managed to have more honest and competent boards installed at Eskom and Transnet (though even so the Eskom board included anomalies such as Professor Malegapuru Makgoba, who had all but destroyed the University of KwaZulu-Natal[6] and had neither business nor engineering experience). Ramaphosa struggled to impose himself, however, when it came to dismissing Tom Moyane, a crony of Zuma's who had misdirected the tax collection system while commissioner of the South African Revenue Service (SARS). When the judge presiding over Moyane's disciplinary inquiry recommended his dismissal, which recommendation Ramaphosa immediately acted upon, Moyane resisted fiercely and challenged the decision in court. Given that Moyane was believed to have cost SARS anywhere between R50 billion and R200 billion in lost revenue,[7] this was an extraordinary display of chutzpah.

Clearly, there were all manner of Zuma appointees and clients in powerful and lucrative positions throughout the public sector who were determined to fight their corner. Many, after all, had virtually no skills, and if they lost their government positions might end up unemployed. Under Zuma's patronage they had been able to steal, achieve rent-seeking goals and set up gatekeeping positions. They would fight under Zuma's banner or anyone else's, but they would fight. And the really disturbing thing for them about Ramaphosa was that, even in the case of Zuma, he had taken the position that the rule of law must prevail and that he would not interfere with it. The days of pliant police and prosecutors could well be over.

The problem was that Zuma had been in power so long and the odds on Dlamini-Zuma being elected had seemed so good – in which case the whole Zuma system would have continued undisturbed – that not a few of those in power had continued on their merry way. Thus, the managers and directors who were robbing the VBS Mutual Bank of its depositors' funds had felt secure because they had taken out insurance by extending a large 'loan' to Zuma himself and making a R2-million donation to ANC funds.[8] Had the Zuma faction stayed in office they would have got away with this, but once Ramaphosa won the bank failed amid huge scandal.[9] In Mahumapelo's case, the state arms firm, Denel – which had been suborned by the Guptas – gave Mahumapelo's son a R1.1-million bursary to help him become a pilot, although Denel had no history of making such grants.[10] This relatively small detail was one of the straws breaking the camel's back. A furious Pravin Gordhan, by now returned to the cabinet as the minister of public enterprises, ordered an investigation. After all, Denel had had to borrow money simply to pay salaries a few months before.[11]

Gordhan, the SOEs and the 'Indian cabal'

The key mover in this new dispensation was Pravin Gordhan, who began to comb through the SOEs, evicting at least the more notably corrupt individuals. He was not to be brooked, and when, for example, the board of Transnet, the mammoth state transport corporation, failed to take action against miscreants he simply replaced the whole board.[12] Moreover, miscreants might find themselves not only sacked but also reported to the Special Investigating Unit (SIU), and also relieved of substantial sums; the Transnet CEO, Siyabonga Gama, was sacked and ordered to pay back R151 million.[13] Gordhan was regarded with horror – as a veritable Robespierre – by the Zuma-ites, for they were long used to a culture of impunity.

Gordhan was fearsomely unpopular. He was a true believer in

the old ANC vision, and smart enough to know that whether or not that dream could be saved would depend not only on uprooting corruption but also on re-establishing a culture of accountability. But corruption had long been systemic and utterly pervasive, operating through the patronage networks that had put down roots in every corner of the country. The result was that when one centre of corruption was eliminated it was like pulling up a convolvulus weed in the garden – one would find that its tendrils reached everywhere, into the most surprising places.

A good example was the VBS Mutual Bank, a black-owned bank with Venda roots (it was formerly the Venda Building Society). Having a black bank had long been a BEE dream, and there was always much support for the idea of a state (ie black-run) bank,[14] though how yet another SOE was supposed to compete with the well-run commercial banks was not explained. VBS had solved this problem by corruptly inducing municipal treasurers and other notables to place deposits with the bank at attractive rates. However, the bank's managers and directors were just as busily stealing the money. When the bank began to founder in 2018, its CEO tried to claim ignorance,[15] but as the appalling scale of the thievery became apparent, his voice died away. It turned out that the bank's shorn depositors were widely spread throughout South Africa and even into Namibia and Botswana.

The scandal widened when it was revealed that money had been funnelled from VBS to the EFF via a network of front companies, and that a considerable sum had been paid to the brother of Floyd Shivambu, the EFF number two.[16] Certainly, it was the party's national chairman, Advocate Dali Mpofu, who had defended Tom Moyane, and it was at this point that the EFF began to make bitter and racist attacks against Gordhan and other Indian South Africans at SARS and the South African Reserve Bank. The EFF went so far as to accuse all Indians of racism against blacks and cleverly suggested that an Indian cabal was at work in Ramaphosa's engine room.[17] This was a quite conscious echo of complaints in the 1980s about an Indian cabal at the heart of the UDF[18] and showed that Malema had sensed that the Ramaphosa team was in part the old UDF reconstituted. It was a strange piece of targeting, though: the Guptas had been far more prominent, after all, and they weren't even South Africans. They had been a far greater affront to African nationalist sensibilities.

By April 2018 the Zuma faction was openly complaining of a purge against them, citing not only the removal of Mahumapelo and the changes to the Eskom and Transnet boards but also attempts to displace the Eastern Cape premier, Phumulo Masualle, and replace him with the pro-Ramaphosa Oscar Mabuyane. A purge, they warned, would cause the ANC to implode.[19] This was a sensitive issue. The fall of Mbeki, followed by a sweeping purge of his supporters, had seen a significant breakaway from the ANC in the shape of Cope. Zuma himself had repeatedly warned of the repercussions should the party axe him.[20] And, of course, in a patronage-based system like the ANC's, it was inevitable that there would now be pressure for jobs from a hungry throng of Ramaphosa supporters.

Zuma in court – again

Central to this unease was the fact that Zuma himself had already had to appear in court in Durban to face the reinstated charges of fraud and corruption: already his appearances were supported by a motley band of rent-seekers – Carl Niehaus (Dlamini-Zuma's ex-spokes-man), Mahumapelo, the extreme Black First Land First (BLF) group (an EFF breakaway), Kebby Maphatsoe's MKMVA and several leaders of black independent churches, such as Bishop Vusi Dube. Zuma's conduct – making speeches to the crowd, again depicting himself as a victim – showed that he was playing the situation for all it was worth.[21]

In effect, he was re-enacting his role of 2005, when Mbeki had sacked him from the deputy presidency. Zuma had then gone to ground in KwaZulu-Natal, seeking out allies and funders wherever he could find them and activating his extensive Zulu network, using his court appearances to rally sympathy and support by casting himself as the victim of unnamed political forces.[22] This had proven an effective way of campaigning without ever putting himself beyond the pale by mentioning either Mbeki or the ANC. Then, as now, Zuma was willing to enlist aid from anyone willing to help, including taxi bosses, crooked businessmen or religious charlatans. In effect Zuma was acting out Marx's maxim that history repeats itself, first as tragedy and second as farce, for it was difficult to take seriously the veritable circus that now followed Zuma around.

There were also reverberations from the fact that Ace Magashule's office in Bloemfontein had been raided by police in connection with the Estina dairy project, in which money voted for poor black farmers had allegedly been diverted into the pockets of the Guptas.[23] If it were truly needed, this was a sharp warning to Magashule that he might well end up in jail. Hence his bitter, back-to-the-wall resistance. Another Zuma die-hard, Kebby Maphatsoe, had been stripped of his responsibilities for military veterans by the new defence minister, Nosiviwe Mapisa-Nqakula – probably on Ramaphosa's instructions.[24] Under Zuma, Maphatsoe had used the MKMVA effectively as a gang of bully-boys for Zuma. Now all of that was in doubt and it was a matter of time before Maphatsoe was sacked. Which he duly was.[25]

David Mabuza was altogether different. He too had allegedly been involved in endless shady business but he had been careful to avoid entanglement with the Guptas, and there seemed to be no smoking-gun pieces of corruption in Mpumalanga to hold him accountable for. He had clearly decided to take a leaf from Ramaphosa's book and be a loyal deputy president beyond reproach. After all, if he had hopes of one day succeeding to the presidency he had much to live down.[26]

The ANC's sociological revolution

The key point was ethnic. Ever since Chief Albert Luthuli had become ANC president in 1952 the ANC leadership had been dominated by Ngunis – comprising the Zulus, Xhosas and Swazis – from the heavily populated eastern seaboard. This 65-year run had at last been broken by Ramaphosa's election in 2017, but beneath him, in the cabinet and the civil service, the Nguni predominance continued. There was no question of Ramaphosa's sweeping in with him other people from the minority tribes. This meant that Ramaphosa's position was precarious in a way that none of his predecessors' had been. Almost immediately there were reports of plots against him, of schemes to topple him from power.

However, the ANC had changed. In exile, the SACP and ANC leadership had had a monopoly of power and patronage, thus allowing for a tight party discipline reaching into every corner of a member's life; even the choice of spouse would be monitored by the movement, and individuals could only take up jobs or scholarships with the agreement of the movement. Once the ANC returned home and put down roots, that sort of discipline collapsed and patronage within the ANC became decentralised among many centres. So an ANC president no longer dominated the movement in the way that Oliver Tambo or Nelson Mandela had. Instead, he floated on a sea of quarrelling factions.

Ramaphosa had run behind Dlamini-Zuma only in KwaZulu-Natal, though not by much. And in the other provinces his slimmest majority had been in the (Xhosa) Eastern Cape. So he had had to overcome the Nguni bloc, and in the end he had done so only through the assistance of another Nguni – David Mabuza, a Swazi. Now he had to govern, and almost his first move had been to rush down to KwaZulu-Natal to pay his respects to the Zulu king.[27]

KwaZulu-Natal, the nub of the problem

The heart of the ANC's factional struggle lay in KwaZulu-Natal. The ANC there was used to being at the centre of national decisions and of receiving a large amount of patronage. Moreover, the rest of the Premier League had always been grouped around the central pillar of the KwaZulu-Natal ANC. But the ANC in the province was now a mess. Its provincial executive had been invalidated by the courts on evidence of blatant rigging of its elective conference.[28] Now the Zuma forces pressed hard for a new conference to be held in May in the expectation that they could again elect Sihle Zikalala, thus giving them a secure base from which to lead a Zuma fight-back. The pro-Ramaphosa faction resisted, believing their chances would be better later. Their candidate was James Nxumalo, the former mayor of eThekwini. They still felt somewhat bruised by the strong-arm tactics Zuma had used to translate a narrow plurality for Dlamini-Zuma in the province into an overwhelming delegate majority at Nasrec. And no one needed reminding that far more political assassinations happened in KwaZulu-Natal than anywhere else.[29] Politics there was an extremely dangerous game.

Even in April 2018 – four months after Ramaphosa's triumph – the ANC in KwaZulu-Natal remained recalcitrant. When Ramaphosa appeared in Durban the audience mocked him with songs in praise of Jacob Zuma.[30] The normal presidential portrait was not to be found in most official offices in Durban or Pietermaritzburg (even at ANC headquarters in Durban this was the case), and there was a similar shortage of Ramaphosa T-shirts in the province. They had arrived but were simply not being distributed. When Magashule came to address a party meeting in Pietermaritzburg, Ramaphosa supporters found themselves barred from the meeting.[31] And, they complained, similar gatekeeping techniques were being used to prevent them from participating in most other party meetings. In normal parlance, this was referred to as the work of 'the Dlamini-Zuma faction' but the fact was that Dlamini-Zuma was working away loyally enough in the presidential office in Pretoria. In reality, the faction was animated by Jacob Zuma.

Throughout his presidency Zuma had warned his critics that should they successfully bring him down they should remember what a strong reaction was provoked by Thabo Mbeki's defenestration.[32] This would be as nothing, he averred, compared to what would happen if he himself were brought down. It was a form of ethnic blackmail, threatening a Zulu revolt at one remove. This potentially included the foundation of a breakaway party, though since he retained decisive leverage within the KwaZulu-Natal ANC, he wanted to fight within the ANC too. This in turn meant that although he might give behind-the-scenes encouragement to a breakaway party, publicly he had to remain an ANC stalwart.

Zuma, the pied piper

In order to rally mass support for a new party, Zuma turned to a number of church leaders grouped in the South African Council of Messianic Churches in Christ – the Twelve Apostles Church in Christ, the Bantu Church of Christ, the Zion Christian Churches and the Ebuhleni sect of the Shembe Church.[33] Zuma himself had been an honorary pastor of the Full Gospel Community Church since 2007, but it may be more important that many of the independent black churches had long enjoyed the favour of the ANC government, which saw them as a handy counterweight to the mainline Christian churches, which tended to have a healthy critique of corruption and the abuse of power. Certainly, the South African Council of Churches had been strong critics of Zuma's state capture, so Zuma had found uses for the messianic churches long before his defeat at Nasrec. Specifically, these churches rallied support in the Free State, KwaZulu-Natal and the Eastern Cape for an alternative black party committed to radical economic transformation – free education, land expropriation without compensation, a state bank, and so on.[34] That is, these churches simply campaigned in clerical garb for the pro- gramme of the Zuma faction. Their new party was to be the African Transformation Congress (ATC).

To this Zuma added a second group – the political hangers-on seen outside during his court appearance, plus taxi bosses and black busi- nessmen grown rich on BEE procurement contracts from Zuma's government or the KwaZulu-Natal and eThekwini administrations. Such folk had known a wondrous prosperity under Zuma and nat- urally wanted him back in power so that it could continue. Their banner was 'Mazibuyele Emasisweni' (May the land come back) and their programme called for the restitution of all land to traditional leaders and 'the indigenous kings and queens of South Africa'.[35] A third group consisted of the BLF, the National Funeral Practitioners Association of South Africa (Nafupa), the Delangokubona Business Forum and various other groups who had come together to form the Radical Economic Transformation Champions.

It was a motley crew and, as ever, Zuma was happy to gather sup- port from any direction, including frankly criminal ones such as his nephew, the much-feared taxi boss Mandla Gcaba.[36] Similarly, the Delangokubona Business Forum was a mafia-style association that frequently invaded building sites in the Durban area and demanded, with armed force, that it be given at least a stake in the business. (The forum, which is supported by MK veterans, claims it is fighting against 'white monopoly capital'.[37]) For its part, Nafupa used strong- arm tactics to insist that 'Indian and white-owned funeral companies will not be allowed to enter our townships and villages'. Funerals are big business in African life, and Nafupa threatened serious repris- als against any business that attempted to undermine its monopoly.[38] Both Delangokubona and Nafupa are Durban-based, a testament to the violent and corrupt world that has prospered under the umbrella of the ANC administration in eThekwini. All these groups, like the ATC and Zuma's followers within the ANC, used as their anthem 'Wenzeni uZuma?' (What has Zuma done?), for Zuma presented himself, of course, as the victim of unfair treatment, claiming that 'the only crime I committed was to fight for freedom'.[39] Indeed, apparently forgetting that he had once apologised publicly for the obvious corruption involved in the extensions to his Nkandla homestead and paid back some of the money he had purloined for it, he now claimed that he had never done anything wrong and that 'I was raised in a way that taught me that it was wrong to steal'.[40] Be that as it may, Zuma's little private army was a perfect representation of the melding of the gangster and political worlds that had characterised life under the Zuma presidency.

At the same time, Zuma continued to wield considerable influence within the KwaZulu-Natal ANC. For while it suited him to have various other counters in the game – and there was talk of him deliberately sabotaging the ANC vote in KwaZulu-Natal in the 2019 election rather than let Ramaphosa win there – the main game still revolved around the province's ANC section. Since this was the biggest ANC section in the country, and since KwaZulu-Natal was second only to Gauteng in population, its affairs were of keen concern to Ramaphosa too. Zuma had rammed through a slate of his loyal followers to run the provincial ANC at a clearly rigged conference in 2015. This had been struck down by the courts later on, but it had nonetheless been sufficient to guarantee a solid body of support for Dlamini-Zuma at Nasrec in December 2017. Now the Zuma faction still in possession, led by Sihle Zikalala, faced off against the pro-Ramaphosa faction led by Senzo Mchunu.

Ramaphosa, realising that the factions would never make a deal on their own, intervened personally to hammer out a compromise – the so-called Zebra list – the idea being that a new party congress would be faced by a joint list, with Zikalala at the top, followed by Mike

Mabuyakhulu (a Ramaphosa supporter), and so on down. This was a perfect expression of the ANC unity for which Ramaphosa was campaigning as the necessary condition for a clear ANC majority in 2019. That unity was valuable enough for Ramaphosa to concede the provincial leadership to Zikalala. However, when Zikalala communicated this deal to Zuma, he vetoed it. He wanted nothing less than complete control and, in any case, had calculated that an ANC at under 50 per cent of the vote in 2019 would greatly weaken Ramaphosa and perhaps even create sufficient confusion for Zuma to be able to play a critical role.[41] Ideally, he hoped that Ramaphosa might then be thrown out by an ANC national policy conference or even by its NEC.

When it became clear that the carefully constructed compromise had fallen to pieces, Ramaphosa's supporters obtained a court interdict preventing the provincial conference from being held – though they did this in fear for their lives. As a result, the factions remained bitterly divided – though with Zikalala still in charge. In the end the conference was held a month later and both sides could take satisfaction from the final result: Zikalala kept his position, but two Zuma allies – Willies Mchunu and Super Zuma – were defeated, and Mike Mabuyakhulu was elected in the contest for posts on the new provincial executive.[42] Moreover, straight after his election Zikalala, who had previously been supporting Zuma in his court appearances, announced that he would no longer be doing that since it was wrong for the ANC to support the ex-president in that way. This suggested that Zikalala was succumbing to the gravitational pull of Ramaphosa's presidential patronage, or at least hedging his bets. There remained a complete absence of trust between the factions, hardly surprising given that political killings continued at a lively pace in the province.[43]

Zuma vs Ramaphosa

The struggle in KwaZulu-Natal was one Ramaphosa could not afford to lose, but even with the weight of presidential patronage on his side, the ultimate result was no better than a draw, if that. Zuma was an immensely shrewd party strategist with an encyclopaedic memory for names and the positions their bearers occupied, as well as how to exert leverage on them. He was also a keen chess player. While he would have preferred a provincial conference that confirmed his ticket in power he knew that rather than allow Ramaphosa to come into his home province and be responsible for brokering a constructive compromise in the local ANC organisation, it was better to go for the scorched-earth option. This would deny Ramaphosa any foothold, with the likelihood that in the resultant confusion Zuma would remain the dominant force. One ANC NEC member who knew Zuma well described him as being 'obsessed' with the notion of revenge against Ramaphosa and his faction.[44] Mahumapelo, who faithfully followed the Zuma circus around, frequently inveighed against 'the triumphalists', meaning the Ramaphosa faction, which was 'arrogantly' presuming to sweep the decks clean. Naturally, this sentiment was shared by the bevy of disgraced former Zuma ministers and placemen who queued outside the courthouse in Durban to greet 'our president'.[45]

What made Zuma such a dangerous opponent for Ramaphosa was that Zuma seemingly had a psychopathic inability to distinguish right from wrong and an apparently limitless ability to reshape the facts in order to portray himself – to himself and others – as an abused innocent. When Vusi, one of his many sons, died of lupus, Zuma claimed that it was the media's 'harsh reports' that had caused his son's death.[46] Similarly, Zuma told his followers that judges often made mistakes and wrongly convicted people (preparing them in advance to see any conviction against him as wrongful). He ridiculed the notion of state capture by the Guptas: 'I've heard that there was a certain family which spoke to a few people, including ministers.

You can't just say that by speaking to those people the state has been captured.'[47]

In his own eyes Zuma was being persecuted by a politically biased justice system. Thus he demanded to know whether the prosecuting authorities or anyone else had made payments to Fezekile Ntsukela Kuzwayo, known as 'Khwezi', with whose rape Zuma was charged in 2005.[48] (Ms Kuzwayo died in 2016.) No doubt Zuma's extensive intelligence system had unearthed the probability that some well-wishers may have made donations to Ms Kuzwayo when she was forced to flee into exile after the trial in which Zuma was acquitted. But the point was to suggest that the prosecution was and always had been biased against him. Naturally, he complained insistently that he lacked the funds to defend himself in court – though the state had paid his costs to date. In December, however, Zuma suffered a crushing blow when the North Gauteng High Court ruled that the state should not continue to fund his legal costs, and should take steps to recover monies spent so far.[49]

Zuma thus felt no compunction in using whatever methods he wished in order to fight his corner. Indeed, he constantly threatened to reveal what he knew about his enemies and warned menacingly that he was 'tired of behaving', how he had been a skilled stick-fighter as a young man, and that he 'had no fear' of any conflict, no matter how bruising.[50] At the same time Zuma insisted on attending every NEC meeting after he stepped down as president – although neither Mandela nor Mbeki ever attended an NEC once they had ceased to be president. Many NEC members complained that they found Zuma's silent presence inhibiting and even intimidating. Necessarily there had to be discussions as to how best to clear up the mess Zuma had left behind. Zuma carefully observed all these debates, noting who said what.

Against this, Ramaphosa was not well armed. He had a reputation as a great negotiator and a shrewd businessman, though it was not really clear whether either was truly merited. As a trade union leader he had led the miners' strike of 1987, perhaps the most disastrous strike in South African history, which cost tens of thousands of jobs and gained nothing at all for the strikers. It was the opposite of skilled negotiation and may well have been carried out in obedience to SACP dictates from Lusaka. Ramaphosa was then credited with the successful negotiation of the new Constitution. This was not, however, a difficult task. De Klerk had declared in advance that a new Constitution must be negotiated in time for an election to take place in 1994, thus giving himself an absolute deadline. The ANC had no such deadline and could afford to hang tough, with all the pressure building on De Klerk.

Ramaphosa was also lauded as having had a tremendously successful business career – he was halfway to being a dollar billionaire. But his business career had been essentially about his being placed on boards of businesses built and run by others. He never launched a product of his own and never served as a CEO. He was the perfect exemplar of the BEE success story, attaining board positions and share deals essentially because of his political contacts and credentials. In a word, his reputation, indeed his success in every sphere, was overblown.

Politically, Ramaphosa had played a straightish bat for a few years in the early 1990s but he was not a very shrewd player of the political game. Moreover, he had been absent from active politics from 1996 to 2012. It had been naive of him to imagine he could solve the problem of the KwaZulu-Natal ANC merely by getting all the factions round the table. This presupposed that everyone wanted a deal of some sort, while the truth was that the most important negotiator – Zuma – was not in the room and was certainly not going to let Ramaphosa invade his turf and dictate terms.

The next crisis blew up suddenly in May when, at an ANC land summit, ex-president Kgalema Motlanthe attacked the way in which the Zulu king's Ingonyama Trust had begun to levy rents on land traditionally parcelled out free – a practice now emulated by chiefs in other parts of the country too. Motlanthe, conscious that this had always been regarded as community land and that the ANC was much to blame in tilting the balance more and more towards the chiefs in return for their electoral support, now declared that this was really state land and ripe for expropriation and redistribution, with power removed from the chiefs who were mere 'tinpot dictators'.[51]

Ramaphosa gives way

This produced a predictable explosion from King Goodwill Zwelithini and the Zulu chiefs, the *amakhosi*. Speaking at an *imbizo* (assembly) called to commemorate the battle of Ulundi in 1879, the king told thousands of his followers, 'The issue we are faced with now is very similar to the one our forefathers were faced with' – then the white man had come to take away the Zulus' land, now it was a black government. 'The war our fathers faced before is the same war we are faced with today' – and he ominously threatened 'a clash of nations'.[52] Observers said that they had never witnessed the *amakhosi* in such a state of angry excitement, and that the *impis* (the king's regiments) were being mobilised. Plans had been made to cut KwaZulu-Natal off from the rest of South Africa by blocking all major roads leading in and out of the province – a threat of secession at one remove.[53]

The terrible danger now existed of a link-up between the recalcitrant Zuma faction and Zulu traditionalist elements furious at the threat to the Ingonyama Trust. This was a fire that had to be put out, so Ramaphosa rushed down to Zululand to assure the king that he had no intention whatsoever of taking 'his' land. This cut short the immediate crisis, but it was recognised that Motlanthe had been quite right and that Ramaphosa now had merely confirmed the feudal 'rights' of the chiefs. Worse, pictures circulated on social media of Ramaphosa kneeling before the king. Ramaphosa angrily insisted that he had merely been showing the king his book on cattle,[54] but the damage was done. In the popular view Ramaphosa had been humiliated.

At much the same time, the government again gave way to the public sector unions and conceded a three-year pay deal of a six to seven per cent compound increase, despite the fact that the public service was already swollen in size and massively overpaid. The increase again burst budget limits, leaving the Treasury looking around for ways to fund it. Then the Eskom workers won a 7.5 per cent increase despite the fact that Eskom was 66 per cent overstaffed and even more overpaid.[55] This too drove a coach and horses through any semblance of a sensible economic policy, and Ramaphosa found himself having to give newspaper interviews to insist that he wasn't weak – a sure sign that he was perceived to be just that.[56]

Plots, factions and polls

In early September 2018, the *Sunday Times* ran a front-page story about Zuma meeting secretly at a Durban hotel with Magashule, Mahumapelo and other presumed members of the Zuma faction in order to plot Ramaphosa's overthrow. Naturally, the participants angrily denied that that had been their purpose, and Pule Mabe, the pro-Zuma ANC spokesman, attempted to insist that no meeting at all had taken place – despite the fact that the *Sunday Times* had published a photo to prove that it had.[57] Magashule angrily declared that 'there is no ANC leadership which I am part of that is going to stop me and many others from meeting President Jacob Zuma'. He also added, clearly referring to Ramaphosa, that 'I am not a product of white people ... there are people who are products of the white man in the ANC'.[58] A few days later at the Cosatu congress, with Magashule sitting in the front row, Ramaphosa referred to the alleged plotters: 'So if you are working to divide the ANC tell us what your agenda is.'[59]

In effect, it was a standoff. Along with Zuma devotees such as Dudu Myeni (the former chairperson of SAA and the chairperson of the Jacob Zuma Foundation), the Durban meeting had included Thanduxolo Sabelo, the secretary of the ANCYL in KwaZulu-Natal and Meokgo Matuba, the secretary-general of the ANCWL, who then tried to claim she hadn't been there.[60] It was of no small significance that Zuma could assemble such a cast, particularly since there were clearly many others in the party and government who still owed their loyalties to Zuma. Despite that faction's allegations, Ramaphosa had not carried out any purge and was not paying the price for it. His only strategy was the passive one of allowing the law to operate. To the Zuma faction that was threatening enough, but the law was both slow and uncertain in its progress, while Ramaphosa clearly needed to stamp his authority on the ANC right away.

This was, equally clearly, not going to happen. In truth, the ANC was in a mess. Quite apart from the two main factions, there were many minor factions in the provinces, and no fewer than four of the provinces (KwaZulu-Natal, Eastern Cape, Limpopo and Gauteng) were fighting court cases against the party leadership. Magashule furiously tried to insist that such court actions were illegitimate and contrary to the principles of the movement ('Who are they? Are they still part of us? Which agenda are they serving? Do they want to reverse the gains of our revolution because of their selfish interests?'),[61] but this was quite in vain because party members had long since lost confidence in their leaders and the party's own processes to deal with their grievances fairly, and so they sought justice in the courts instead.

Meanwhile, unemployment reached 9.6 million, with over 800 more people losing their jobs every day. No issue mattered more and none better illustrated the failure of ANC governments. Even old ANC stalwarts spoke of the movement having 'just one last chance' – and that was optimistic.

The damage was increasingly clear in the polls. An SAIRR survey of 28 September 2018 found the EFF had doubled its support to 13 per cent, reducing the ANC to just 52 per cent. Worse still, the survey showed how land reform was mentioned by only four per cent of black voters as a significant issue.[62] In effect, the EFF had lured the ANC into making land the centrepiece of political debate – very much to the EFF's benefit. It was also notable that the EFF students' association had won the Student Representative Council elections at the universities of Cape Town and Zululand, as well as at the Mangosuthu and Durban universities of technology.

If these polls were correct, the EFF would more than double its parliamentary seats and Ramaphosa would get the blame for leading the ANC to its lowest level yet. Indeed, if the ANC got only 52 per cent its majority might depend in fact on a KwaZulu-Natal bloc of ANC deputies controlled by Zuma. Worse still was the notion that South African history was repeating itself, that just as JBM Hertzog's more moderate Nationalists had finally been pushed off the stage by DF Malan's more radical National Party, so the EFF's populism was beginning to do the same to the divided and tattered ANC.

Chapter Six

Why did South Africa copy Africa's mistakes?

Sometimes during the long sojourn in exile of the ANC anxious commentators, eyeing the generally calamitous state of independent Africa, would ask ANC leaders, 'But how do we know that you won't just repeat all the mistakes made elsewhere in Africa?' To which the reply was always given that precisely because the ANC had travelled so much in independent Africa and seen the many blunders made there, they knew what those mistakes were and were intent on avoiding them. They pointed out that South Africa was very different from other African countries, with a far more developed modern economy and, consequently, a far larger working class. Moreover, so the argument went, proletarianisation had led to detribalisation, so Africans in South Africa were far less divided by tribalism or national difference of any kind. What this meant was that the struggle against apartheid was a national and not a tribal one, and that the struggles against apartheid and against capitalism were much the same thing. Thus, when apartheid collapsed, so would capitalism, allowing an immediate transition to socialism – and the resultant socialist state would not tolerate racial or tribal divisions. In any case, the ANC was not an ordinary African nationalist movement. The Congress Alliance, of which it was part, included whites, coloureds and Indians, and its philosophy was firmly non-racial. The ANC was also careful never to formally adopt socialism as its programme – despite the fact that in exile it toed the Soviet line almost completely, even supporting the Soviet invasion of Czechoslovakia in 1968.

In retrospect, this glib response stemmed purely from the needs of the ANC's propaganda department to reassure outsiders, particularly liberal sympathisers around the world – though there is also no doubt that most ANC activists sincerely believed it. When some among the movement's Soviet supporters warned that they were severely underestimating the role of tribal and national differences, this was confidently brushed aside by Pallo Jordan and other ANC leaders: 'our Soviet comrades have not really understood our struggle'.[1] This dismissal was absurdly arrogant, for many of these 'Soviet comrades' had spent a lifetime studying the dynamics of national struggles. But, of course, the assumption was that, even after decades in exile, the ANC knew their own best.

In fact, the ANC's activists had absorbed little or nothing of the huge and expanding literature on post-independence Africa and, as a result, they had no real understanding of the dynamics of African national-ism or, indeed, of the nature of their own struggle. Unsurprisingly, in power the ANC has indeed replicated the mistakes of their brother regimes to the north.

The dynamics of African nationalism

Most African nationalist movements were led by small educated elites – mainly civil servants, schoolteachers and a few lawyers and minis-ters of religion. These elites used a populist nationalism to mobilise the peasant masses (and the few workers) below them against the ruling colonial regimes. They raged against these white occupiers whom they wished to displace, using the language of democracy and human rights to denounce them, thus exciting the dissatisfied masses to action and gaining international sympathy. In fact, their key aim was to replace their colonial masters by becoming masters themselves and then rewarding themselves with all the privileges (and more) that those colonial administrators, planters and businessmen had enjoyed. This was painfully visible even before independence when, for example, African civil servants' unions in French West Africa made one of their key demands that their members should, like their French administrators, enjoy paid leave in France.[2] But this was nothing compared to the way the leaders rewarded themselves. A Houphouët-Boigny or a Mobutu accumulated many times what any of the colonial governors had owned or earned: the governors were, after all, mere colonial civil servants, while their successors were lords of all they surveyed.

Once this educated elite took power it immediately lost interest in democracy and human rights. Typically, it set up one-party regimes, would not allow opposition parties to exist and threw opponents into jail with or without trial. During the independence struggle they had relied quite heavily on unionised black workers, on black military veterans of the Second World War and on the support of one or more small newspapers run by their supporters, which bitterly criticised the colonial regime. Once in power they lost all interest in the military veterans, and even the most radical regimes – those of Kwame Nkrumah in Ghana, Sékou Touré in Guinea and Julius Nyerere in Tanzania – cracked down on the unions and made them mere creatures of the ruling party. They also did away with the free press, allowing only those newspapers that slavishly followed the party line. This loss of interest in democracy and human rights did not prevent them, of course, from adopting a radical anti-Western policy at the United Nations (UN), denouncing colonialism and apartheid as crimes against humanity. At the same time, they affected a complete indifference to similar abuses in communist or Third World countries. They were completely unembarrassed by these obvious hypocrisies.

The logic was simply that Western countries were the colonialists; the others were not.

This new elite spent an astonishing proportion of the national budget on the salaries of the civil service, which was generally corrupt and non-productive but which included many of their brothers and cousins. Many of the political elite became extremely rich. Jomo Kenyatta, in Kenya, owned many farms and the country's biggest dairy industry. Léopold Senghor of Senegal owned a chateau in Normandy, Félix Houphouët-Boigny of the Ivory Coast owned a whole portfolio of foreign property, including luxury homes in Paris and the South of France, while Mobutu Sese Seko of the Congo (Zaïre) became one of the world's richest men.

As political scientist Jean-François Bayart argues,[3] the most striking thing about the new regimes was the creation of these new and extraordinary inequalities. Pre-colonial Africa had seen nothing like it: the gap between the greatest chief and his subjects was not that great. But now the top levels of the political elite were as rich as even rich men in developed countries, while their countrymen often continued to slave away for a dollar a day: the gap was enormous. And yet the political elite continued to speak the language of socialism even as it energetically created these inequalities, again quite unabashedly.

The bureaucratic bourgeoisie

The French agronomist René Dumont was the first to point out[4] what soon came to seem a truism, that all these countries were now ruled by a 'bureaucratic bourgeoisie' consisting mainly of civil servants, teachers and other public employees. This term has become so widely used that it would be rather wilful to avoid it, but it refers more to an elite status group than a real bourgeoisie. What was important was that the bureaucratic bourgeoisie had middle-class levels of consumption and was only ambitious to consume more and to amass capital by hook or by crook. This had dire implications for their countries' development. Given the inordinate share of resources that was now diverted to the political elite and the bureaucratic class on whom they depended, this inevitably implied a redistribution process from poor to rich, with the mass of the peasantry and the growing class of poor urban dwellers paying the price. Most African countries were predominantly agricultural, and resources were siphoned off from the peasants and farmers by means of state-operated marketing boards (an inheritance of colonialism) as well as taxes. This stunted the growth of agriculture, and so very quickly all these countries ceased to be agricultural-surplus states – from time immemorial they had fed themselves or starved – and began to rely on imported food.

This was obviously bad for the economy. The new elite typically had large ambitions to diversify their economies and industrialise, for they associated that with developed-country wealth, so their vision of modernisation envisaged the creation of large numbers of jobs in manufacturing. Invariably this did not succeed. For a start, their economies were too small to justify the steel plants, car factories and other large industries they wanted to build. Then again, the bureaucratic elite wanted to skim off whatever they could by acting as gatekeepers to the development process, while the political elite often wanted to take decisions that defied economic rationality, in order to placate some tribal or party faction. On top of this, the new rulers were somewhat wary of foreign investors, whom they were not confident of controlling. They felt much more comfortable with SOEs, whose management they could hand-pick, often placing their family members or loyal cadres of their ruling party at the top.

Almost invariably, though, these SOEs ran at a loss. They were incompetently managed – their managers had not, after all, been chosen for their competence – and corruption was endemic. With neither customers nor shareholders being a consideration, it was easy for the enterprise managers to loot them. Naturally, the political elite, knowing that these enterprises would be robbed blind, decided to get their own take. Not infrequently this meant that the president himself or his family members were the biggest thieves. In Angola, President José Eduardo dos Santos's daughter, Isabel, used her position as chairperson of the state oil company, Sonangol, to become Africa's richest woman. Daniel arap Moi, when president of Kenya, derived income from more than a score of enterprises. Robert Mugabe, as president of Zimbabwe, owned multiple farms and took a large cut from diamond mines in both the Democratic Republic of Congo and his own country. Indeed, it is almost misleading to give examples, so normal was this practice of self-enrichment.

The ruinous consequences of a bureaucratic bourgeoisie

Again, ideology was a misleading guide. Regimes that professed socialist principles – and most did – were just as likely to steal as the minority of pro-capitalist regimes. In 1968, Guinea was Africa's most left-wing state. Its leader, Sekou Touré, was an avowed Marxist-Leninist (producing his own Little Red Book in imitation of Mao) but his half-brother, Ismael, who was minister of industry, was regarded as even more to the left. The Guinean franc was so weak that when my wife and I set off for a two-week trip upcountry we had to take one suitcase entirely full of paper money. One of the state enterprises under Ismael Touré's control was the cigarette factory making Sily cigarettes – Sily the elephant being the ruling party's symbol. I spent some time in Guinea then – and I was then a smoker – but could never find even a single Sily cigarette. Only after persistent inquiry did I discover that Ismael smuggled the factory's entire production across the border into Côte d'Ivoire and Sierra Leone where it could be sold for hard currency, all of which he pocketed. (I was naive enough to be incredulous that Ismael could square this with his radical views.)

The result of all these developments was that many African

countries were run for the benefit of a small elite that gobbled resources but was itself unproductive. A key point was that money that should have gone on capital expenditure and maintaining the infrastructure was appropriated by this elite through higher salaries, bonuses or simple stealing. Over time this diversion towards consumption of what should have been capital expenditure had a dire effect on the infrastructure and, indeed, on the whole economy. Fifty years after independence few African countries had reliable electricity supplies or decent roads. Economic growth was, accordingly, slow and investors generally wary. The masses below had soon lost the euphoria of independence and fell back into apathy and, often, sullen resentment. Occasionally coups or violent seizures of power would take place. Mass discontent meant that these were always greeted with initial euphoria, though this seldom lasted. Even when there were elections, turnout was generally very low. Governments thus rested on minimal or no consent and were weak. Many could not – and many more certainly did not – maintain law and order. Corruption was structural and went unpunished. Many states verged on complete failure. It was a truism that in many African countries the government only really maintained and controlled the road from the presidential palace to the main airport.

A curious feature of most African states was their foreign policy. On the one hand their biggest investors, aid donors and trading partners were Western countries, yet this was not reflected in their foreign policies, which were at least neutralist and sometimes more pro-Soviet than that. The Cold War was, however, a very helpful climate for African governments: by balancing between the blocs they could hope for aid from both sides, and East-West competition prevented either side from making any difficulties about African deficiencies in democracy or human rights. The end of the Cold War made things more difficult: there was less aid, more pressure for good behaviour and, worst of all, a loss of relevance. There was less interest in whatever

Africa said or did and growing impatience with its endless disasters – wars, famines, unhappy socialist experiments and state failure. All of these, even the famines, usually came down to poor governance. Most of the UN's time and peacekeeping deployments were spent on Africa.[5] Asia and much of Latin America moved powerfully ahead but Africa remained stuck.

Sticking to the script

This was, so to speak, the script and the ANC followed it almost word for word. Very quickly it became clear that South Africa too was ruled by a small political elite and a bureaucratic bourgeoisie, namely, its 2.2 million civil servants.[6] True, the trade unions continued to have a significant role, but by 2018 Cosatu, the main union federation, consisted largely of white-collar and public-sector workers. The Umkhonto we Sizwe (MK) guerrilla fighters, peasants and unorganised workers – who had played a vital role in bringing the ANC to power – were quickly discarded. Corrupt cliques took over many of the unions and the MKMVA.[7] Indeed, many MK veterans lived in abject poverty, while the unorganised workers were simply thrown under the bus: the number of unemployed rose from 3.7 million in 1994 to 9.6 million by 2018. The ANC leadership made only empty promises of more jobs and it was quite clear that the political elite did not really care.

There were and are differences, of course. Even in its reduced state as a 'formerly developed country' South Africa boasts a better infrastructure, a larger industrial base and a bigger private sector than other African countries, and although much of the media is now under ANC control, a relatively free media exists alongside it. South Africa is, crucially, also far more integrated into the world economy and more open to it – and to the world's media.

Which is all well and good. But the obverse point is that precisely because South Africa is more developed, so its bureaucratic elite has had opportunities that its peers in the rest of Africa could only dream of. There are simply much richer pickings to be had in South Africa. So that new class – which everywhere acts like a swarm of locusts, devouring whatever it can – has had richer looting opportunities than anywhere else in Africa. Not only has there been more extensive looting in South Africa – as much as R100 billion may have been stolen through state capture by the Guptas and others[8] – but the looting class is correspondingly bigger and the structural corruption penetrates deeper. Many ANC ministers have become multi-millionaires, as have a number of fly-by-night BEE 'entrepreneurs' and SOE managers, while corruption has also become endemic all the way down the system: municipal politicians and managers get rich through corrupt tenders, policemen take bribes and collude with gang bosses, hospital staff sell off drugs, blankets and other materials, and so on.

In other words, what is happening in South Africa is essentially a repetition of what happened a generation and more ago in the rest of Africa. The difference is just one of scale – South Africa has become a real looter's paradise – and also one of effect. For it is one thing to steal in a cash-crop economy: the peasants are immiserated but they have no option but to continue to grow their crops. But in a more developed economy the damage is far greater, for there the economy depends on a continuing inflow of investment. As investors get burnt by South African realities or see how corruption has become institutionalised through BEE, they retreat. Mines and factories shut, capital flight becomes generalised and a full-scale investment strike sets in.

The sociology of ANC rule

How did redistribution work in South Africa? Apart from the straightforward corruption outlined above, the new bureaucratic and political elite sucked up money from the haves by redistributive taxation of every kind. These haves were not only whites – the coloured and

Indian minorities also suffered (they were now regarded as not properly 'black', as they had been during the struggle). Naturally, the ANC (and even naive opposition politicians such as Mmusi Maimane, the DA leader) tried to present these inequalities as a confrontation between 'white privilege' and 'black poverty'. This was quite misleading. To be sure, many whites remained well-off, and certainly whites had benefited from their privileges during the apartheid years, but they were now much more heavily taxed than before.

Whites found themselves virtually barred from public-sector employment, and even private firms often didn't want them because they were struggling to meet their BEE and affirmative action targets. Aspiring academics or researchers would find that many universities had a 'blacks only' appointment policy. And so on. What whites had going for them was mainly social capital – the product of more secure family lives, more affluent parents and better education. While whites generally continued to do well, sometimes spectacularly well, there were plenty of white beggars in the new South Africa and whole squatter camps of whites outside Pretoria. There were also many poor whites now barely scraping a living.

In any case, white privilege was nothing new. It explained only the old inequalities. The dynamic factor that explained the new – and much increased – inequality was the now-dominant bureaucratic bourgeoisie, which added a whole new privileged layer without providing much in return. Neither the government nor the opposition really wanted to confront this situation, for that class was too important to them politically, and it was also the articulate class that claimed to represent (and helped to shape) African opinion. The trade unions were increasingly turned into a mere wing of the ruling party. They now represented only a small labour aristocracy consisting largely of the bureaucratic bourgeoisie and their juniors. All labour legislation reflected their interests, which were often directly opposed to those of the unemployed.

The rise of the labour aristocracy

The origins of this labour aristocracy lay back in the apartheid years when the Nationalist government had exercised strict influx control through the pass laws, allowing only those Africans with jobs to stay in the cities. Whole townships were built to house these workers, and urban Africans were treated as a separate class, more sophisticated, modern and better educated than their rural cousins. Naturally, this artificial situation pushed up the wage levels of the urban Africans: had rural Africans been allowed to flood into the cities, wages would have dropped. Thus, the black, coloured and Indian urban workers all had a vested interest in the continuation of influx control, though this could never be publicly admitted. Everyone knew that influx control was basic to the apartheid system and the leaders of all three of those communities were dedicated to ending apartheid. To admit that non-white urban workers had an interest in the continuation of influx control meant admitting that, in a sense, they had a vested interest in the perpetuation of apartheid. This was unthinkable.

The answer to this conundrum was provided by the rise of black trade unions from 1973 on. By this time the influx-control system was beginning to collapse, but as trade unions developed among these non-white urban workers, they used the whole panoply of Marxist terminology and protective labour legislation to advance their cause – and, of course, to maintain and increase their wages. Finally, when the ANC came to power, the unions quickly championed highly restrictive labour laws such as the Basic Conditions of Employment Act. These reduced labour mobility and set up such strong protectionist barriers around those in work that even though huge numbers of new migrants had flowed into the cities with the end of influx control, they were effectively locked out from competing for the jobs of the unionised. This strange triangular interplay between black trade unions, influx control and urbanisation, although the key to much recent South African history, remains almost completely unacknowledged and unexplored.

Ultimately this eventuated in the present situation in which a tiny labour aristocracy, organised mainly within the Cosatu unions, fights under the Marxist banner to maintain artificially high wages and salaries. Bureaucratic 'workers' are absurdly privileged, often earning 30 to 40 per cent more than their private-sector counterparts. Civil-service salaries take up no less than 35 per cent of the national budget, and year after year such workers enjoy inflation-plus increases, even when the economy is not growing.[9] In May 2015, the public-service unions won a pay increase of seven per cent at a time when the economy was actually contracting.[10] Again in 2018, both the public service and Eskom workers won large inflation-plus increases at a time when the economy was in recession. The predictable result has been to squeeze spending on infrastructure and capital projects, that is to say, the requirement of the bureaucratic bourgeoisie for a high and rising income effectively becomes the supreme national objective ahead of all other needs and requirements. This expresses exactly the dominance this bourgeoisie has in the new South Africa. The extraordinary result is that effectively South Africa is now run for the benefit of a smaller minority than it was under white rule.

The Bantustan dividend

Under apartheid the Bantustans were also a potent source of inequality. The Bantustan policy involved the elevation of a chiefly elite to rule these new 'states'. Moreover, considerable sums flowed every year into propping up a number of Bantustan institutions – separate black universities, police forces, armies and, above all, civil services. At the same time, preferential advantages were conferred on the border industries – white-owned industries lured to set up just inside the Bantustans, thus providing much-needed jobs. Thanks to tax breaks and generous subsidies, these industries were highly competitive with their counterparts in white South Africa.[11] All of this was denounced bell, book and candle by the ANC.

When the ANC took power, however, they completely reversed themselves. The Bantustans were welcomed back into South Africa and their debts paid off. Their 'bush colleges' were suddenly rechristened as 'historically disadvantaged institutions'. Their civil servants, soldiers and policemen were incorporated into the corresponding national institutions – often with a pay increase. All of this could be well justified under the rubric of 'national reconciliation' but it was to have dire consequences. Moreover, the Bantustan border industries were simply deprived of their preferential tax rates and made to pay the same wage rates as in the big cities. Cosatu, representing the urban workers of the big cities, was loath to allow such factories to continue to undercut the high wage levels achieved in the metropoles. This quickly closed them down, resulting in thousands of lost jobs. The result was to drain the life out of many smaller and more remote towns. It was, in other words, the sort of deal that soon became characteristic of the new South Africa, with priority given to public-sector professionals, with private-sector workers being sacrificed. More than 20 years later, during the eNCA survey of 2017, our focus groups recurrently found a degree of nostalgia for the Bantustans because of the job opportunities they had afforded.

Most surprising of all, after 1990 the chiefs who had collaborated with apartheid were welcomed back into the fold. The ANC set up a new affiliate, the Congress of Traditional Leaders of South Africa, and in every province and nationally Houses of Traditional Leaders were set up as part of the legislative process. The chiefs now received handsome emoluments from the state, in return for which they were expected to shepherd their people towards an ANC vote at election time. The authority of the chiefs was given legal recognition and strengthened, although there were increasing complaints that many of them had become, in Kgalema Motlanthe's words, 'tinpot dictators',[12] usually with gangs of muscular bullies as their enforcers. Naturally, the chiefs

91

wanted to emulate the privileges of the Zulu king, so by 2010 there were no fewer than 13 kings or queens in South Africa's strange republic. In that year, it was decided to reduce the number to seven,[13] but the pressure to increase that number again would be insistent.

The extent to which the ANC had effectively handed back power in the countryside to traditional chiefs was emphasised by Cyril Ramaphosa's backing down to King Goodwill Zwelithini in 2018 over the issue of traditional communal land.[14] Chiefs everywhere had begun to charge rent on land that had historically always been bestowed free, thus using their power to transform themselves into a wealthy landlord class. With the state caving in to that, a fateful step had been taken. This had in a sense been foreshadowed in 2003 with the death of Kaiser Matanzima, one of the most notorious of the Bantustan rulers. Astonishingly, he was given an official funeral with President Mbeki delivering the eulogy and Nelson Mandela sending a message of acclamation. Nothing could have better symbolised the ANC's embrace of the old Bantustan elite, including the chieftaincy. This too meant further encouraging redistribution from the poor to the rich, this time in rural areas.

To this long and dismal list of wealth transfers in the wrong direction – from the poor to the rich – one must add the BEE policies introduced under President Mbeki, obliging companies to give away large chunks of their equity to black partners and to source a high and rising share of all their procurement from black-owned companies. The whole emphasis of the policy was bent towards the creation of black fat cats, a preoccupation shared by the government department that monitored affirmative action: it was far more interested in how many directors of large companies were black than with black advancement at lower levels. The only real attempt at redistribution towards the poor lay in the system of social grants, which at least kept many of the most poverty-stricken from starving. This was largely paid for by the minority of taxpayers.

As may be imagined, the ANC's boast that it was a non-racial alliance disappeared fairly rapidly. It was soon evident that the only members of the minorities allowed to play any significant role in the movement were those who had been in the struggle: there was zero opportunity for young Asians, coloureds or whites to climb up the rungs of the movement. As soon as serious spoils and patronage were at stake, such upward mobility quickly became an all-African affair. Support for the ANC from the minorities waned electorally. Ever since Mbeki, the ANC's tone had been fiercely nativist, even racist, and by 2018 there were very few members of the minorities still active within the ANC. This was mirrored electorally as minority support for the ANC dwindled.

In foreign policy too, the script established by radical states to the north was religiously followed. Having campaigned for democracy and human rights for its entire existence, the ANC promptly shelved such concerns on coming to power. When the brutal and dictatorial regime of Robert Mugabe was threatened, the ANC propped it up. It expressed great friendship for Cuba, Libya, North Korea, Iran, China and a whole host of undemocratic African regimes while adopting a suspicious, often paranoid attitude towards the Western democracies – despite the critical role that the sanctions deployed by these countries had had in ending apartheid. In March 2018, the US State Department's annual analysis of voting practices at the UN listed South Africa as one of the ten countries least likely to vote with the US.[15] Strikingly, when there was a call for international sanctions against such human-rights offenders as Syria, Iran, Sudan or North Korea, Pretoria's stance was that it did not believe that sanctions were a desirable or effective mechanism – this despite the ANC's having campaigned for decades for sanctions against apartheid and the fundamental role that these sanctions had in ending that regime.

We have seen that most African nationalist regimes lost their interest in human rights as soon as they gained power. It was the same with the ANC, not just in foreign relations but also at home. A voluminous literature now exists on torture and ill treatment in South African jails and police cells. It is clear that the incidence of such maltreatment has become much worse since the end of apartheid, so much so that maltreatment is the new normal. One study showed how in a three-year period (2011–2014) 3 440 assaults in police custody had been documented, with doctors attesting to the large number of burns, swellings, bruising, lacerations and contusions. Despite that, this evidence secured only 40 convictions.[16]

In large part this brutality resulted from the fact that the SAPS was a complete mess, corrupt and out of control. This was made shockingly clear at the time of the Marikana massacre in August 2012 when the police shot dead 34 black strikers and wounded 78 more. Not only did the police appear not to be taking orders from any higher authority, but in the days that followed, the police detained many hundreds of strikers. When lawyers representing the strikers made urgent applications stating that their clients were being tortured in the police cells,[17] the minister of police made no attempt to deny this and could only suggest that the prisoners be transferred to the custody of the army instead, thus tacitly admitting that he had lost control over the police.[18]

Having to live with democracy

In one direction, ANC rule diverged sharply from its brother African nationalist regimes to the north. Most of them had attempted to insulate the ruling elite from all political competition by setting up de jure or de facto one-party states. There was no doubt that the ANC in exile had leaned in the same direction, but the compromise deal that brought the ANC to power meant that the party had to get used to living with democracy. At first the ANC found this difficult. It was a naturally authoritarian movement. Within its own ranks there was little or no democracy; during the struggle, party conferences were not held regularly, and when they were, the norm was a single candidate nominated for each position. Similarly, its idea of a newspaper – *Sechaba* – was one that slavishly followed the party line, allowing no debate or discussion and providing little information at all of the movement's inner (factional) life. It was also completely humourless and ignored all sides of human life other than the political. Above all, the private sector and other political parties were regarded simply as 'enemies' to be destroyed, not just opponents or simple facts of life.

Yet when the ANC was allowed to return home it found itself agreeing to a Constitution guaranteeing free elections, multi-party democracy and a free press. In good part this was because the ANC was still in so oppositional a frame of mind that it imagined it would need all these devices in order to keep on fighting the National Party government. When the Nats were as good as their word and handed over power in 1994, the ANC found itself, somewhat grudgingly, having to accept the implications of this bargain. There even began to be (a few) contested elections within the ANC itself, though well into the democratic era the movement remained under the control of a Soviet-style democratic centralism. The party continued to view its electoral rivals not as opponents but as 'enemies' and it exercised tight party control over the national broadcaster, the SABC. It was extremely angry if criticised in the press, and for many years the press was intimidated so that little real criticism was published.

This only changed with Jacob Zuma's fight-back after he was sacked as deputy president by Thabo Mbeki in June 2005. The ANC divided into two factions and suddenly its hegemonic unity was no more – and so the press felt free to comment and debate. The ANC's response to this more critical press was to mount its own paper, *The New Age* (owned by the Guptas), and then to use the resources of the civil-service pension fund to help Iqbal Survé, an ANC trusty, to buy Independent Newspapers. This allowed Survé to turn the titles in the Independent stable into slavishly pro-ANC publications. Even this still left a number of truly independent media, such as the *Mail & Guardian* and the upstart *Daily Maverick*. Moreover, all the ANC-line publications suffered disastrous falls in their circulation and began to lose money hand over fist. Once *The New Age* was deprived of Gupta subventions, in the form of lavish government advertising, it quickly collapsed. The South African audience was simply acculturated to a free press. Similarly, it responded to the party-line SABC by turning instead to independent radio and TV stations.

The land question

As we have seen, a key characteristic of independent Africa was that it very rapidly ceased to be able to feed itself and became heavily dependent on food imports, usually from the USA. In numerous cases there were actual famines, alleviated only by emergency food aid – again, usually from the West. The oddity was, of course, that African political leaders simultaneously made strong speeches about their determination to do away with any remaining vestiges of colonialism, even as in fact their dependence on Western food supplies was increasing.[19]

South Africa and Zimbabwe were initially strong exceptions to this pattern, remaining large food exporters until 2000 when Robert Mugabe's land invasions had the effect of returning large acreages of productive Zimbabwean land back to subsistence farming. Food production collapsed and thereafter Zimbabwe depended heavily on food imports, often emergency famine relief. In South Africa the land-claims process involved numbers of productive farms owned by white farmers that were either the objects of restitution to African communities or were transferred. Many of these farms were soon returned to subsistence agriculture or lay fallow altogether.[20] As in Zimbabwe, the greatest casualty of these changes was the farmworkers, most of whom lost their jobs.

Commercial farmers in South Africa were treated to a far tougher regime than they had enjoyed under the Nationalists. Specifically, a series of new laws made the employment of farm labour far more onerous. The farmers naturally reacted by radically trimming their workforce, thus again increasing the number of unemployed and redistributing away from the poor. Large numbers of commercial farmers also deserted the land, so that by 2018 there were about 40 000 of them left on the land, many of them aged over 50, so that one could already glimpse a future in which food production in South Africa might collapse as badly as it did in Zimbabwe. For the moment, however, thanks largely to the productivity of a small number of mega-farms, agricultural production held up remarkably well.[21] Nonetheless, the usual food surplus (excess of food exports over imports) gradually declined and by 2014 had fallen into deficit, which had widened sharply by 2017.[22] These mega-farms are what stands between South Africa and starvation. Right on cue, however, Gwede Mantashe, the former ANC secretary-general, has proposed to limit the size of farms in future,[23] a measure clearly aimed at exactly those farms.

In Zimbabwe, the farmers had lost their farms without receiving any compensation. This naturally created a wave of anxiety about the security of property rights, which crippled the Zimbabwean economy for years thereafter. South Africa avoided this disastrous example until 2018 when it too accepted the principle of EWC. Thus, both countries seemed intent on following the general African trend into food dependency. The extraordinary thing was that this was a policy with no winners. The Zimbabwean farmers lost their farms, their farmworkers lost their jobs, the national economy saw its balance of payments deteriorate. There was a loss of economic sovereignty and a loss of trust and confidence, which crippled the country far into the future, the state lost tax revenue from the now idle farmers and farmworkers, and, of course, consumers suffered badly as their dependence grew on (more expensive) imported food. South Africa now stands poised on the edge of repeating this bizarre lose-lose strategy.

The strange economics of African nationalism

The African states to the north of South Africa had gained independence while declaring that they intended to industrialise their countries. There was much talk of massive hydroelectric schemes, steel plants and the like. Little of this ever actually transpired. Only a few capitalist states such as Côte d'Ivoire and Kenya built on their natural advantages by increased cash-crop production, which gradually bred a considerable merchant class. The ANC clearly belonged in the former group, declaring that it intended much greater industrial development. Initially, according to Frene Ginwala,[24] the party had decided that mining – the heart of the South African economy for over a hundred years – should be relegated to a lesser position and instead a more futuristic economy would be built around high tech of one sort or another. This was absurd: South Africa's comparative advantage lies largely in its mineral wealth, easily the greatest in the world, and South Africa also lacks the large nexus of computer and engineering skills required to sustain a Silicon Valley. There was also insistent talk – Ramaphosa repeated it once again in 2018 – that development had to be 'manufacturing led' and that the jobs produced must be 'decent jobs'.[25]

In fact, ANC policies have had the effect of deindustrialising the economy. On its watch, manufacturing as a share of GDP has almost halved, to 11 per cent. In May 2018 South Africa's manufacturing output was still 7.4 per cent below its mid-2008 level, compared with a 51.4 per cent increase for all other emerging markets in the same period – and these are South Africa's peers and competitors. Even developed economies saw a 1.2 per cent increase in manufacturing in the same period.[26]

Mining has been crippled by a highly interventionist regulatory policy, so that most of the big mining houses have decamped and many thousands of jobs have been lost. This effect has been exaggerated by the fact that excessive wage increases both at Eskom and for the mineworkers themselves have created a situation where it has become harder and harder for mines to make a profit: their two biggest costs, after all, are electricity and wages. The result can be seen in the country's once-dominant gold mines. By 2018, employment in these mines had fallen by 30 per cent (48 000 jobs) since 2009,[27] and, even so, less than 20 per cent of the remaining mines were profitable, making further large job cuts inevitable.

This decline has had a large knock-on effect on the many supplier industries. Legislation enforcing affirmative action and BEE has had negative effects on investment, as has the cancellation of all the outstanding investment protection treaties.[28] In general, the government has also damaged industry by subjecting it to the demands of the new black bourgeoisie – for more directorships, more managerial and professional jobs, for rules forcing companies to procure goods from black-owned companies, and so forth. This drives up costs, creates inefficiencies and drives away investment. By the mid-Zuma period these policies had led to a generalised investment strike, low to zero growth and steadily falling per capita incomes.

The other features we have noted in independent Africa were also duly to be seen in South Africa, including the strange combination of highly acquisitive behaviour and socialist ideology. Thus, the ANC government continued to profess its commitment to the National Democratic Revolution (NDR), an old-style Soviet notion of how developing countries might move to socialism. Yet none of the government's ministers are poor men and many are extremely rich. Take Jeff Radebe, who has served continuously in all ANC cabinets since 1994. His wife, Bridgette, owns considerable mineral wealth and is one of the richest women in Africa, and Radebe himself, a one-time communist trained in East Germany, is a multi-millionaire – yet Radebe still preaches the NDR. Gwede Mantashe, another communist, and ANC secretary-general under Zuma, is a prosperous farmer. As the Zondo Commission into state capture revealed, Mantashe – like many other ANC ministers – was quite happy to try to bully the South African banks into keeping open the Guptas' accounts despite clear evidence of malfeasance, money laundering, and so forth.[29] Other examples are legion.

President Zuma was the most prominent example of this strange combination of radical sloganeering and unalloyed acquisitiveness. In a sense, he summed up a regime whose primary feature was public-sector theft. He preached 'radical economic transformation' and crusaded against 'white monopoly capital' – even while he was stealing public money and earning continuous subsidies from wealthy backers to whom he granted favours.[30] With some of this misbegotten money he built an imitation royal kraal at Nkandla, and in a gesture beyond satire the SACP, its leader, Blade Nzimande at the forefront, demonstrated *in favour* of this construction project, which it termed 'rural development'.[31] Similarly, the government continually stresses its concern at rising levels of poverty and inequality while devoting billions to a fund to create '100 black industrialists', ie more business moguls and thus more inequality.[32]

One could go on, but that has to be sufficient. Whatever the ANC may have said about avoiding the mistakes and excesses of African nationalism elsewhere on the continent, in practice it has followed the script almost to the letter. This is to say that the evidence suggests that there is a single sociological phenomenon, African nationalism, of which the ANC is merely a local exemplar, its claims to be distinct and different notwithstanding. And the uncomfortable truth has to be faced that the Afrikaner Nationalists were quite correct in their designation of their opponent: they pointed to the disasters wrought by African nationalists elsewhere and argued that if the ANC was allowed to come to power in South Africa, the results would be the same. For obvious reasons a large section of international opinion found it convenient to accept the ANC claims of exceptionalism. Nobody today would argue that apartheid was ever justifiable, but it is a bitter truth for liberals in South Africa today (myself included) that in this respect, at least, their National Party opponents have been vindicated.

Why did it happen?

The question remains as to why this has happened. We can dismiss out of hand the claims by white racists that this disastrous result is due to defects in character or personality. Africans in next-door Botswana are governing a whole lot better, after all, with much better results. And there is no doubt that most black South Africans are appalled by South Africa's decline since 1994: this is certainly not a result that anyone wanted. Even the ANC elite are uncomfortable about many results of its own rule, for they had set out with high ambitions for national growth and prosperity and made many large promises to the electorate predicated upon that – promises that they cannot now fulfil. They are distressed at the fall in the ANC vote and (by 2018) the crescendo of civil unrest these failures have produced, though they look in all other directions except at themselves for an explanation as to why this has occurred.

As we can see, the puzzle doesn't cease there. Why were the ANC so wrong in their confident predictions that they would avoid the failures of independent Africa? There is no doubt that they didn't *want* to fail as others did, didn't *want* these results. And how does it come about that there is such a contrast between the ideology of African nationalism in its campaign phase and the behaviour of African nationalists when in power? How do we explain, for example, that African nationalists invariably campaigned for greater equality but have also always presided over dramatically greater inequality when in power? Again, it is no good simply to impute Machiavellian insincerity to every African nationalist. There is no doubt that many of them actually believed what they said, at least when in opposition. Indeed, some still believe those now-exploded ideas despite all factual evidence to the contrary. One can see here both the appeal and the genesis of magical thinking.

An important part of the answer is that both the ANC and African nationalists seldom, if ever, understood the nature of the populist revolution they were seeking to achieve. What they knew with great certainty was that they wanted to displace the ruling white supremacy, or the white colonial/settler elite. To this end they appropriated whatever radical ideologies served their purpose. These ideologies – various mixtures of Marxism and African nativism – were then used to mobilise the black electorate behind them. But what they were actually carrying out was a particular sort of capitalist revolution – a bureaucratic capitalism. A few African leaders understood all along that their revolution would necessarily be a capitalist one – Félix Houphouët-Boigny, Hastings Banda and Jomo Kenyatta certainly did – but even they could not grasp in advance the central role that a new black bureaucracy would play, for the simple reason that that class would not come fully into existence until independence/liberation.

The seeds of this new revolution had been sown in the colonial period, when, throughout Africa, a small black middle class began to emerge – small businessmen, planters and small farmers, lawyers, journalists, teachers and ministers of religion, though the most numerous group were the clerks, civil servants and office workers. They were often the sons and daughters of chiefs, whether colonial or pre-colonial. This latter group were among the better educated and they also worked most closely with white administrators, managers or businessmen. They thus formed a clear picture of how much more privileged such folk were. Moreover, the members of this educated black group had frequently been students abroad where they had seen at first hand how the metropolitan middle class lived. Inevitably, this sharpened their own appetite for the good life. All these forces were at work in South Africa too, with the added fact that the ten Bantustans all spawned large black bureaucracies.

Under colonial rule or apartheid, the development of this black middle class – and would-be middle class – was artificially and deliberately restricted. Thus, the end of colonial rule or of apartheid saw a veritable explosion of opportunity for this group. Even in those countries where the most radical ideologues held sway – Ghana, Guinea, Mali and Tanzania (and later Mozambique and Angola) – such groups could be seen pushing for 'a better life'.

In South Africa, this new middle class grew very quickly from 1994 on, and the ANC government quickly became its vehicle, not only pressing for every development that would assist the development of such a class, particularly affirmative action and BEE, but also from the top down the government's administration was soon riddled with corrupt schemes to enrich politicians or civil servants. In South Africa, the greatest such scheme was the massive arms deal of 1999, which saw the great enrichment of a number of politicians and their associates.

But if African nationalism was everywhere the vehicle for a new middle class to come to power, it was a very peculiar form of capitalist revolution. The new bourgeoisie was not, after all, really a bourgeoisie. It seldom owned factories or farms, and its relationship to the means of production was essentially parasitic. The new middle class was mainly a salaried class of bureaucrats. It was intent on achieving a higher income and a better lifestyle and was adept at corruptly turning its position to advantage through contracts, tenders, licences and permits, and by running businesses on the side towards which it pushed business opportunities of one kind or another. Its principal objective often seemed to lie in gatekeeping, constructing rent-seeking opportunities for itself and securing employment for relatives, romantic partners and clients.

The ANC liked to believe that it represented the African masses, but in reality its large majority gave unfettered power to this new bureaucratic bourgeoisie. This group tended to see everything through its own lenses. Thus great attention was paid to how many black directors the top companies had because these positions were of interest to the new elite. The far more numerous positions lower down the scale never attracted the same interest. As we shall see, it is more correct to term this group the 'politically predominant class', not the ruling class. But what was not to be doubted was its zeal for primary accumulation. Its appetite was voracious.

The blind leading the blind

In exile, the ANC did not foresee or understand this sociology – and it had not really understood the social dynamics of the African regimes that hosted the movement. For in South Africa this class was only constituted after 1994 (when the civil service was sweepingly Africanised) and only then discovered its interests. A partial – though large – exception to this were the numerous bureaucrats of the ten Bantustans. However, throughout the struggle period they had been vilified as apartheid collaborators and tended, accordingly, to keep their heads down. After 1994, with the reincorporation of the Bantustans into South Africa, this numerous class gravitated naturally into the new state structures where, given the skills shortage among black applicants, they were welcomed with open arms as historically disadvantaged individuals requiring special and sympathetic treatment. Moreover, in the wake of the bureaucrats proper there followed a small army of interpreters, clerks, supervisors, and so on. This ex-Bantustan group had already learnt all the tricks of how a corrupt bureaucracy works and they became a key part of this new politically dominant class. The last thing that the exiled ANC had expected was that liberation would bring Bantustan bureaucrats into their own.

The notion that the ANC did not understand African nationalism, did not understand even their own movement, may seem a surprising conclusion – though in fact many people ride on tigers without knowing much about tigers. It was perfectly clear that Mandela was one of these, that for him the movement really was all about democracy and human rights. When he discovered corruption within his first ANC government, he was shocked and said so. His generation, the struggle generation that had suffered in prison, had not been like that. In a sense prison had anaesthetised the prisoners, for had they but known it, there was considerable corruption in the exiled ANC.[33] Similarly, Jacob Zuma spent ten years on Robben Island and gave no indication of how he might behave later on. But before long corruption was virtually the new normal within the administration and no one turned a hair about it.

Like all the other African nationalist movements, the ANC steadily lost favour with urban dwellers and became increasingly dependent on its support in the countryside, where it was seldom challenged. But by 2017 we found in the eNCA poll and focus groups that there was a countrywide revulsion against the corruption of the Zuma regime.

Perhaps the most pathetic group were the ANC's white supporters, who had joined the movement believing strongly in its professed ideals. In truth, they had failed entirely to understand what sort of party they were choosing and were horrified as they discovered corruption, factionalism and thuggery. There is a real pathos to books such as Andrew Feinstein's *After the Party: A Personal and Political Journey Inside the ANC* (2007) or Crispian Olver's *How to Steal a City: The Battle for Nelson Mandela Bay* (2017). At the outset both these authors see themselves as fighting the righteous fight against a particular set of corrupt arrangements that they take to be exceptional. Only towards the end of their books does one sense that they glimpse that actually the problem is general, that patronage networks and corrupt deals are everywhere, that they are interlocking and inescapable, and that this is simply the world their party has created and inhabits.

To sum up, then, the real reason why, despite all the ANC's averrals, African nationalism in South Africa has taken an almost exactly similar course as it did in the rest of the continent is that once in power it is driven by the same politically dominant class, the bureaucratic bourgeoisie. Moreover, the explosive factor that drives them far off course is also the same, the almost irresistible (and apparently bottomless) appetite of that class for primary accumulation. The fundamental problem, of course, is that a bureaucratic bourgeoisie is not productive in the way that a commercial and industrial (or even agricultural) middle class is. Because it does not itself generate wealth, it is inevitably parasitic and can achieve its goals only through patronage and corruption.

In the years since the independence era of the 1960s, fewer and fewer African states espouse socialist policies. Even in Ghana and Tanzania, where the names of Nkrumah and Nyerere still resound, no one today would dream of returning to their economic policies. Doubtless in time this will happen in South Africa too. But here the question is different. It is whether Mandela's vision of racial reconciliation and a united nation can be preserved or whether the country will fall apart amid racial division and civil strife.

Chapter Seven

The leaderless world of the bureaucratic bourgeoisie

Ever since it took power the ANC has, in its own eyes, been working to bring about the NDR, which is to say a Soviet model for the advance of a developing country towards socialism through incremental reforms and without a bloody revolution. The fact that this model died with the USSR and is ridiculed by today's Russians has had no impact on the ANC which, ideologically speaking, is happily stuck in the 1950s and 1960s.[1] According to this theory there is a longish preliminary phase in which the productive forces of society are strengthened not only through the push of the working class but also by the efforts of the 'patriotic bourgeoisie'. This last term refers to a bourgeoisie that is willing to throw in its interests in helping develop the budding socialist state, a group counterposed by the 'comprador bourgeoisie', which exercises a mediating and parasitic role vis-à-vis the forces of imperialism. Since its interests are ultimately aligned with the imperialists, this group can never work wholeheartedly for the assertion of the national economy, which must, necessarily, diminish the power of the imperialists.

The 'patriotic bourgeoisie' and the compradors

When the ANC took power in 1994 a black middle class hardly existed in South Africa, and the party worked energetically to build it. The idea that the principal purpose of the state was to build this new class was summed up by Jacob Zuma's plan to create '100 black industrialists', a quite extraordinary objective both in its belief that the state could create such a group and with the priority given to producing a few score very rich people rather than helping nearly ten million unemployed. Even more extraordinary was the fact that, upon taking office, Cyril Ramaphosa adopted this programme and even spent good money on it.[2]

In the ANC's racialised consciousness it was a simple matter to designate this new black middle class as the patriotic bourgeoisie and the old white middle class as the comprador bourgeoisie. This notion fitted easily with the assumption that the whites, Indians and even coloureds were mere settlers, not fully rooted in South African society.

In the quarter-century that followed the ANC's accession to power, the black middle class grew at great speed. Primarily it was composed of the overpaid workers of the massively overstaffed public sector, particularly its affluent upper ranks, but increasingly a black business class came into existence, usually feeding off state and other public-sector contracts and the preferential procurement laws applied to both public and private entities.

Despite the theory that this patriotic bourgeoisie was merely afforcing the principal driver, the working class, it was apparent from the first that the former group was granted an absolute supremacy over the latter. Thus, for example, the forced sale of white farms to black interests invariably led to the loss of large numbers of farmworker jobs as production collapsed on the farms taken over, but usually the bankable asset of the land ended up in the hands of the black elite. An even more clear-cut case was the mines, in which successive editions of a Mining Charter compelled higher and higher equity shares

(30 per cent by 2018) for black investors. The result was to stifle the mining industry almost completely, and many thousands of mining jobs were lost.[3] Clearly, these lost jobs mattered much less to the ANC than the help they were trying to give to would-be black capitalists.

South Africa possesses greater mineral wealth than any other country on the planet. Yet by 2017 these policies had created a situation in which no new money had been invested in a new mine for over ten years and in which mining companies had stampeded towards opportunities in other countries with less onerous regulatory regimes.[4] The mining industry was dying on its feet, with more workers laid off every year. This was a perfect expression of how the ANC had created an investment strike by its attempt to insert a new and parasitic upper social layer – the owners of that 30 per cent equity share – into the existing social structure. In effect, the insertion of this new layer would destroy the profitability of the capital already invested in the mines.

This in turn would both guarantee that no new capital was committed – the investment strike – and that more and more labour would be shed in order to try to preserve profitability. At the same time, Eskom took the decision to recruit 66 per cent more 'workers' than it needed, pay them an average of over R700 000 a year, and divert all its coal procurement to BEE companies (at considerably greater cost).[5] It was a textbook example of how the determination to create a new black bourgeoisie was pursued at the expense of both the economy as a whole and the African working class in particular. This is the fundamental reason why unemployment has tripled under ANC rule to 9.6 million by late 2018. It is bizarre that this policy has been pursued by a party that declares itself to be committed to the interests of the working class and even more bizarre to see such policies fêted and supported by 'revolutionary' activists dressed in red.

It is worth pausing to consider how fundamental are the implications of this policy. By insisting on the primacy of the interests of this would-be black bourgeoisie, the ANC guarantees that South Africa will be unable to compete internationally – after all, where else in the world do governments insist that investors simply give away 30 per cent of their equity? Even without mentioning the dire effects of EWC this is quite sufficient to prevent investment. That is to say, the policy of 'transformation' is a fraud, for the key change wrought by this policy is not anybody's empowerment but ever-higher unemployment and immiseration.

We should note that the big multinationals that have invested in South Africa in recent years ('the imperialists') have usually ignored these laws. Thus, none of the large motor manufacturers present in South Africa – Ford, Volkswagen, Honda, Toyota, Mercedes, etc – have any BEE partners. Their attitude, in effect, is that South Africa is fortunate that they have invested so heavily, and if they are subjected to unreasonable demands they will simply close down their local plants (as General Motors has done). Similarly, Amazon, who have set up in Cape Town, have not bothered much with the affirmative action laws. If their life were to be made difficult by the application of unreasonable rules they would simply move – there would be no shortage of takers for their jobs and investment, after all. Similarly, the big mining companies have easily found new mines in other parts of the world.

At local level, the imposition of BEE procurement practices inevitably pushed up the price of services to the poor. Similarly, affirmative action privileged a small elite of white-collar and professional workers at the cost of worsening service delivery for the poor. And so on it went. In effect, the anti-working-class bias of the new regime was both severe and consistent. Soon the rot spread to the unions, where union leaders revelled in high salaries, pillaged pension and union investment funds, and where corruption became endemic. Across society as a whole one could measure this bias by reference to the increasing Gini coefficient, as this new black bourgeoisie made South

Africa more and more unequal. The new bourgeoisies of developing countries are notoriously ruthless in their treatment of the workers and the poor, and South Africa's black middle class was no different. The idea that this could ever help to build any real kind of socialism was laughable.

However, a perverse quasi-socialism was not only possible but also distinctly desired by this new black bourgeoisie. Early on it had noted that when any enterprise was brought into the public sector this allowed it to be staffed by highly paid black executives and looted by its managers and then bailed out when required from the public purse. Fat pickings, in other words, though only for a few and only until the enterprise in question had been so undermined by corruption that its collapse became inevitable. A prime example is the Passenger Rail Agency of South Africa (Prasa), where a combination of massive corruption and inefficiency has pushed this vital public service to the brink of collapse.[6]

This merely served to underline another problem. Crudely put, the 'patriotic bourgeoisie' was anything but patriotic. It looted and undermined national institutions and showed no sign of any collective commitment to building a new society. No large sum of money – whether in a pension fund, a government department, a municipality or a public utility – was safe from peculation. When the Guptas arrived on the scene they found no shortage whatsoever of figures in the local black elite happy to cooperate with them in their destructive work. Indeed, government departments, the police and judicial institutions bent over backwards to smooth their path.

What is one to make of this alacrity with which the large majority of the governing elite succumbed to the blandishments of this foreign family, which was, transparently, set on robbing South Africa of enormous sums? These collaborators were, in effect, the modern analogues of the West African chiefs who chased down and corralled their subjects so that they could sell them to the next slave ship. In both cases what was missing was any conception of a national or common good. And without that such a group was incapable of patriotism.

The absence of a new nation-building ruling class

The group that the ANC and SACP misnamed as the 'comprador bourgeoisie', ie, the white business classes, really constituted far more of a 'patriotic bourgeoisie'. Over many generations the white and Indian business class had built thousands of productive and lasting businesses, a powerful and independent financial sector, highly successful retail chains that fed and clothed the population and a successful commercial agriculture sector that grew the country's food. These were deeply rooted institutions that had invested massively in South Africa over the years and had also contributed philanthropically to many schemes and NGOs with the aim of furthering the national future. They had of course done this for profit and their ranks included the normal number of scoundrels, but their overall achievement was not to be denied.

This comparison serves to make the point that the black middle class is clearly still, in Marx's terms, only a class for itself – a multitude of individual interests all pushing and manoeuvring for personal advantage. Marx believed that only later might a class become 'a class for itself', that is to say, a social group that develops a strong sense of solidary consciousness and seeks to advance the interests of its class as a whole rather than just the individual interests within its ranks. Crucially, the group has to develop a strong attachment to the notion of a common good, even though that is perceived in class terms.

Marx greatly admired the way in which the British cabinet – 'the executive committee of the ruling class' – governed in this spirit. Naturally, its conception of the national interest was defined entirely within the perspective of the ruling class itself, but the result was a strong national infrastructure, great economic development, a powerful army and navy, and well-established institutions of governance that functioned smoothly and worked determinedly for the national interest thus conceived. But one only needs to adumbrate this model to see how very far South Africa's black middle class still is from being a class for itself.

This situation has numerous consequences. The prescriptions of the NDR are, of course, more than dubious to start with; one reason the Soviets themselves started to doubt the theory was that nowhere in the Third World had it actually worked. But even in terms of that theory the ANC's course is chaotic. In the first instance the new black middle class is allowed complete dominance over the interests of the poor and unemployed – clean contrary to the theory. Second, the ANC still views the white business and professional class – the true 'patriotic bourgeoisie' – as its enemy, while claiming to rely on a patriotic bourgeoisie that is incapable of any solidary commitment, patriotic or otherwise.

Finally, while the old white ruling class has either stepped aside or been pushed aside, there is no replacement ruling class at all, and nor can there be. Despite all the communist rhetoric about the leading role of the working class and the masses, there is only a small labour aristocracy amid a huge mass of the unorganised poor – who are more impoverished than ever. And the bureaucratic bourgeoisie that rules the country (with a smattering of a BEE business class) is incapable of becoming a class for itself. This is, in fact, entirely typical of bureaucratic elites throughout Africa. Inevitably, this produces and reproduces the African phenomenon of the broken-backed state.

Thus, the South African ruling group is a quasi-ruling class that is disunited, chaotic, torn by individual, regional and sometimes tribal interests, a melange of patronage, bossism, gatekeeping and rent-seeking. It is simply idle to imagine such a group generating and then carrying through a coherent programme of reform. This is the sociological reality that underlies the irreducible factionalism of the ANC.

113

The party likes to issue calls for unity, but any real basis for unity was lost long ago. The chaotic state of the ruling group is reflected in a high turnover of cabinet ministers, with endless reshuffles. In a paper published by the SAIRR, Gareth van Onselen counted 215 changes in ministers, deputy ministers and directors-general of departments in the period 2009–2017, with an average 'life' in office of 14 months. He correctly termed the result 'chaos'.[7] He noted a similarly high turnover among ANC MPs.[8]

What is the meaning of such frantic turmoil? Clearly, it has nothing to do with good or even 'normal' governance. Instead, what it bears witness to is the constantly changing needs of special interests and factional struggle, as reflected through a patronage-based system. (It must be remembered that in South Africa MPs can be swapped in and out of Parliament by leadership fiat.) This is, in other words, the perfect institutional expression of the fact that there is no proper ruling class. One is not far from the model perfected by Mobutu in the Congo, where there was a frantic turnover of ministers so that no one could acquire a base from which to challenge the president. Accordingly, every minister stole all they could as quickly as they could, knowing that their opportunity would not last.

Naturally, the ANC is aware that all is not well. It looks back to and hankers for the euphoria of the Mandela period, but this cannot be truly recreated now. That unity was born through a party in exile, trained in Leninist discipline, united by charismatic leadership and, on its return, presiding over a black electorate that had not yet begun its headlong process of social differentiation. There existed then a real possibility for a united multi-racial advance towards a high-growth market economy. Such a perspective was dismissed out of hand by the ANC for ideological reasons. The party's failure to take that path is the single greatest tragedy of post-liberation South Africa.

There is a final point that must be made in considering the sociology of the ANC ruling elite. In the black townships of the apartheid era, the natural elite were the gangsters – smooth, savvy, well-heeled, often controlling the shebeens and often, too, with their own arrangements with the local police. The anecdotal reflection of this is found in the popular folk opera of the era, *King Kong*. King Kong is a champion black boxer with the world at his feet, but he is forced by local gangsters to throw a boxing match. This destroys his career, his woman deserts him (for the gangster boss), and ultimately the hero kills himself. We meet a range of local characters – including the local policeman – but there is no doubt that the gangsters are in charge.

This gangster elite was part of the ANC from the start, for during the struggle the party recruited not a few men from this violent underworld. In the Mandela government, the most commanding cabinet minister was Joe Modise, a former criminal boss.[9] He was able, against strong opposition, to push through the multi-billion-rand arms deal. Modise and his friends are alleged to have profited massively from this. As I have argued elsewhere,[10] Modise was also very likely involved in the assassination of the Communist leader, Chris Hani, another hugely influential event.

As patronage bosses came to dominate the ANC, a tough-guy style – natural anyway in a movement that had attempted guerrilla warfare for 30 years – came to the fore. By the time of the Zuma era gangster enforcement (including death threats and assassinations) was part and parcel of the system. This too was hardly conducive to good governance. But good governance was by then not the name of the game anyway. Government was a spoils system, pure and simple.

Chapter Eight

The rise of magical thinking

It has been observed elsewhere in Africa that as nationalist or soi-disant 'revolutionary' regimes begin to fail they indulge increasingly in magical thinking. Essentially this is a way of retaining key ideological beliefs in the face of realities that keep breaking in. Of course, the whole history of movements like the ANC has been replete with magical thinking from the start. Think how for decades ANC activists talked confidently of a coming 'seizure of state power' when it was always obvious that its guerrilla forces were quite unable to challenge the apartheid state's military forces. Similarly, questions of tribal, ethnic and linguistic difference were treated by the ANC as if they did not really exist apart from the apartheid state's divide-and-rule strategy. But during the struggle the 'magical' quality of such thinking did not really matter. Later it was even strengthened by the fact that apartheid did come to an end, allowing the ANC to attribute this, somewhat disingenuously, entirely to its struggle.

The situation now is very different. The ANC has been in power for a quarter of a century and its policies have resulted in failure on almost every front. Above all, it has comprehensively lost the confidence of investors, both foreign and domestic, producing an investment strike that has throttled both the economy and the government. When Cyril Ramaphosa first came to power there was great optimism that he would be able to break with that situation, restoring confidence and, with it, investment and growth.

Ramaphosa himself clearly hoped the same. He speedily announced a drive to attract $100 billion in new investment and predicted a leap in growth to three per cent in 2018. He was soon able to boast of promises of new investment by the Saudis, Chinese and the UAE. In all three cases this involved promises by friendly governments, but everyone knew that success depended not on state initiatives but on regaining the trust and confidence of the markets in general, that is, of a host of international institutions and private individuals. Of this there was no sign. In October 2018, the government held an investment summit at which the local business community duly announced investment decisions already taken (often purely for maintenance purposes), but it remained unproven that the government had really changed the investment climate.[1] Indeed, Trevor Manuel, the former finance minister appointed as one of Ramaphosa's investment emissaries, admitted that he had found his mission a tough sell.[2]

The best way of understanding this was to talk to the South African middle classes. During the Zuma years such people had taken very much to heart the notion that their savings were safest if they could push them abroad. And very much like so many South African companies, they exported their capital to such effect that for some years South Africa as a whole became a net exporter of capital, a remarkable statistic for a developing country.[3] Even at the height of Ramaphoria there was not the slightest sign that any such folk were considering bringing their capital back home.

This is a fact of large significance. As I have argued elsewhere, no South African government has ever survived a prolonged investment strike.[4] As it was, the unpopularity of the Zuma government derived in large part from the fact of falling real incomes and ever-mounting unemployment – both results of the investment strike. But despite the very different aura of the Ramaphosa administration, it is far from clear that the investment strike has ended. Everything suggests that the fix is still in. Moreover, the government has yet to grasp the full nature of the situation. This was evident from the way in which it introduced a new version of the Mining Charter, which still included sufficient BEE provisions to ensure there would be no new investment into South Africa's mines.[5]

Magic and the land

This is the context against which the rise of ANC magical thinking must be observed. This 'thinking' – in fact wildly irrational wish fantasies – is both a cause and result of the present crisis. The best-known example is the idea of EWC, proposed as an answer to the highly emotive land question. The argument has been that little land has been transferred to blacks since 1994 and that this is the fault of white landowners who resist land reform and demand exorbitant prices for their land. Accordingly, EWC will break the constraint of the 'willing buyer, willing seller' principle and at last see the transfer of valuable commercial farms into black hands, thus constituting considerable redress of existing social inequalities.

Every single part of this proposal is wrong. Land reform has been held up by administrative incompetence, corruption and inadequate government funding, and despite that large acreages have been transferred to black hands. Almost 90 per cent of the farms thus transferred have failed because farming is a highly specialised, competitive and tough business. In fact, relatively few Africans want to be farmers: far more want urban land or land that they can develop or sell for cash.[6] Land is simply a proxy issue for feelings of black dispossession and inequality, feelings that can never be assuaged by any mere legislative proposal.

EWC also threatens food security and has the capacity to undermine the entire agricultural economy, and with it the banking system.

One needs only look at the irreparable damage done by the farm invasions in Zimbabwe to see how hugely damaging a step this would be. EWC not only tears up the 1996 Constitution but also undermines the rule of law itself. Indeed, should this step be realised it would be so self-destructive that it could be compared only with what the older generation of historians used to term the 'national suicide' of the Xhosa in 1857. It was then that the messianic prophetess Nongqawuse persuaded her people to kill all their cattle and destroy their crops – which, she claimed, would cause the dead to arise and the British to be swept into the sea. The results were catastrophic and despite the intervention of the colonial administration, there was widespread starvation.[7]

Yet, despite all the evidence and arguments, the ANC leadership presses on headlong ...

Mineral magic, magic health

Almost equally fantastic are the various iterations of the Mining Charter that seek to impose wildly unrealistic BEE and affirmative action targets on the mining companies. There has been no new mining investment in South Africa for ten years and the industry is shrinking rapidly under the weight of poor commodity prices and the dead weight of existing BEE requirements.[8] Yet the minister of mineral resources, Gwede Mantashe, blithely upped the BEE requirements yet again – and yet at the same time he attacked as 'backward' those mining companies that responded to repeated and heavy losses by laying off workers.[9] There is clearly a complete disconnect here between economic realities and consequences with, one suspects, a simple-minded notion that mine owners are rich men who will always pay in the end. The fact that all the world's major mining companies have quit South Africa seems to have eluded the minister. Mantashe also wants to restrict farm size to 12 000 hectares – ignoring the fact that the vast bulk of South Africa's food is grown on a small number of mega-farms.[10] Rather like EWC, if realised, such a proposal would quickly lead to food riots.

The expectation that the mining industry will miraculously lay golden eggs despite the squeeze is matched in its irrationality by the sweeping proposal for National Health Insurance (NHI), essentially a scheme to introduce a national health service and forcibly integrate the private health sector into it.[11] Since the existing public health sector has been severely weakened under ANC rule, everything suggests that any new national health service would be just as pillaged and mismanaged as its predecessor. In addition, NHI would cost between three and six per cent extra of GDP, and no one has any idea where such colossal sums of money would come from, let alone how they could be afforded. In any case, for such a public health system to work it would need to rely on the taxes paid by a fully employed population, whereas 27 per cent of South Africans are unemployed. The NHI proposal is rooted in the fantastic assumption that, alone in Africa, South Africa can somehow afford a Scandinavian-style health system, though without Scandinavia's resources.

However, if that were not damaging enough, what really distinguishes NHI is the clear objective of nationalising the private health sector on which about 15 per cent of the population depends. That 15 per cent includes pretty much the whole of the South African middle classes of whatever colour. They are used to getting (and paying for) First World standards of healthcare, and if the private sector is nationalised or abolished not only will many more doctors, dentists and nurses leave the country but so too will enormous numbers of the professional and managerial middle classes. This would strip the economy of many of its most necessary skills and cause a major depression. It would also remove a large portion of the current tax base and cause the collapse of the present civil service and much else besides. NHI is a doomsday weapon.

Why is the ANC so destructive?

What is remarkable about these proposals is not just their magical quality. It is almost as if the ANC is intent on throttling the economy. Mining and agriculture are, after all, the historic mainstays of the economy and the Mining Charter and EWC seem almost designed to bring both to a halt. The most dynamic economic sector in recent times has been tourism, and here too the government brought in cumbersome visa requirements, which had the effect of repressing this vital sector (though some of these requirements were eased in September 2018). As I have argued earlier, the effect of ANC policy has been to repress the economy more or less across the board.[12] This is a circular process, for it produces ever higher unemployment and thus increasing desperation among the poor, which in turn leads ANC and EFF politicians to cater for that mood by proposing further populist 'solutions', which are really destructive non-solutions. The result is a downward spiral.

How is this possible? Magical thinking too is a reflection of the leaderless state of South African society. For there is no doubt that most ANC leaders are blithely ignorant or uncaring about the dangers posed by such populist proposals and magical thinking. Ramaphosa has chosen to go along with EWC and to champion NHI although he must surely know that both policies would lead to complete disaster. So what are we to make of 'leaders' who cheerfully advocate policies that would clearly destroy the national economy? More broadly, how do we account for a leadership that seems bent on repeating policies that have already failed elsewhere? As Einstein said, it is madness to repeat the same actions time and again, expecting a different outcome.

The answer is, as we have seen, that the ANC has failed to provide South Africa with a new ruling class capable of developing the country. At most it seems capable of managing just its patronage networks. We are back to the problem of 'the vacuum at the centre', instead of a replacement for the Afrikaner ruling class that so ruthlessly governed the country in its own interest. That old ruling class had many sins to its name but over the 84 years since Union in 1910 it built a formidable infrastructure, a developed economy and a series of powerful and efficient institutions – the armed forces, Eskom, Transnet (including a large railway and port system), the civil service, a strong police force, a highly developed water distribution system – and much else besides. It was able to do all this because it was *a class for itself* with a strong solidaristic consciousness of itself. This was crucial, for it ensured that individual or sectional interests within that ruling group were held in check and subordinated to a strong sense of a national interest – conceived, of course, within an Afrikaner, indeed a Broederbond, perspective.

Because the ANC has been unable to constitute a ruling class in that sense we have a political elite that is a mass of conflicting interests, with no solidaristic sense of itself and, as night follows day, little or no sense of the national interest. Instead it adopts magical thinking simply as a way of placating various factions, of not disturbing various vested interests by telling them uncomfortable truths, and because the leaders themselves wish to continue to dream rather than face up to the consequences of their own actions. Magical thinking is thus the negation of proper leadership. Real leadership is Churchill telling his listeners that all he has to offer them is 'blood, toil, tears and sweat', De Gaulle spelling out the grim alternatives France faced in Algeria, or even PW Botha telling his followers that it was a case of 'adapt or die'. In all these cases leaders faced their audiences with the blunt truth, risking their own popularity but knowing that only if they levelled with the electorate could they at least direct their efforts to a realistic end.

Mbeki, we have seen, was frightened of spelling out the economic imperatives that necessitated Gear. Zuma, throughout his term, made impossible promises and played to the populist gallery. Ramaphosa has begun in the same vein. This failure of leadership is not accidental

122

but derives directly from the fact that the new ruling elite is a merely a bureaucratic bourgeoisie. Again, Marxist terms are useful. This group has no settled relationship with the forces of production in the way that a class of farmers or industrialists might have. Instead, it is an artificial creation, existing only on the taxes paid by old productive businesses and the white middle classes, which it resents and despises (though also seeks to emulate). It is pumped up in size and income purely as a matter of political fiat and without any regard to function or utility. Inevitably it is opportunistic, with its members continually seeking to build business careers by means of illicit family companies to which they attempt to divert state procurement. All attempts to prevent such practices have failed and, indeed, they are endemic.

The point is that as public servants they are mere employees, supplicants for patronage, while if they can build business careers they can become self-employed – with an independent relationship to the forces of production. This would – such is the dream – turn them into patrons themselves, instead of just clients. As a whole, this public servant class is characterised by its dysfunctionality. It is quite normal for failures of the state's administration to be put down to 'a lack of capacity'. This is quite literally true.

As the situation tightens ...

As the economic situation has inexorably tightened, so the various sections of the bureaucratic elite, which all feed off the state in one way or another, found themselves facing the reality that things would have to change. As a whole, this group had gorged itself and also greatly increased in size since 1994. As we have seen, in 1998/99 there were 1.17 million civil servants. By 2014 there were 2.161 million – 455 701 at national level, another 1 118 748 in the nine provincial administrations, 311 361 in local government and 275 851 in other government organisations (though not including SOEs). This was ludicrous overstaffing and featherbedding. In the Zuma period, more such jobs were added all the time, so that by 2018 there were well over 2.2 million civil servants, earning average salaries of R338 000 per annum. It was what Stephen Mulholland quite rightly called 'the largest gravy train ever seen in Africa'. The salaries of this group absorbed over 14 per cent of South Africa's GDP, compared to 6 per cent in Thailand and Chile and 10 per cent in the rich OECD countries.[13]

But the collective appetite of this dysfunctional and largely incapable group had now far outrun what the state could provide. The result was, immediately, to open up fissures in the ruling group, rather than cause it to stand together in face of the crisis. Thus, the new finance minister, Tito Mboweni, who replaced Nhlanhla Nene in October 2018, immediately made it clear that the state had no funds to keep bankrupt SOEs like SAA afloat and that it also could not pay for the huge new salary increases just awarded to the public service.[14]

The result was interesting. Tahir Maepa, the spokesperson for the Public Service Association, responded furiously: 'There is no way that we are going to sit back and allow a situation where dysfunctional SOEs keep on taking from the fiscus and we take the brunt for it. We are going to take [Mboweni] on … We are being put to failure and when we fail we are being blamed on both sides.' Maepa said that civil servants were 'easy prey' because of the government's failure to provide services, and called on Mboweni to tackle corruption and maladministration in government before blaming civil servants.[15]

Thus, under the first onset of pressure the various sections of the bureaucratic bourgeoisie turn on each other, the civil servants against the political elite and the staffs of the SOEs: a perfect example of this group's fissiparous nature. In truth, all these groups have been stealing as hard as they can, but, until now, all were shielded by a general rule of impunity. Their non-solidary behaviour derives directly from the fact that all these groups depend directly on the state. As the piglets get larger and lustier, and the mother pig becomes less keen to suckle them all, so they begin to fight harder and harder over the same teat.

Mboweni had pointed to the harsh fact that jobs would have to be lost in the civil service and that SAA could not be bailed out forever. Yet Ramaphosa rushed forward to say that SAA would be saved and that there would be no public-sector redundancies.[16] This was pure magical thinking. Even as he spoke the SABC, the state broadcaster, was announcing a thousand redundancies. The government quickly stepped in to prevent this, despite the fact that the SABC did not have sufficient money to pay its employees.

Vulnerability to populism leads to external intervention

Thus, South Africa's polity and society are leaderless. This weakness has been exhibited in many ways. Under Mandela the ANC's leadership elite bowed entirely to his leadership and his vision of a harmonious rainbow nation. But as soon as this was replaced by Mbeki's naked appeals to race, equal fealty was given to that. Even when Mbeki's Aids denialism cost hundreds of thousands of African lives, no voices were raised against this policy. Similarly, even as Zuma allowed the state to be captured by a family of foreign origin, there was no open dissent from within the ANC. In effect, the ruling group was a completely malleable supplicant for patronage. A more self-confident and cohesive ruling group with a clearer sense of the national interest would have held these leaders to act within its own terms.

Because the ruling group is so weak it is extremely vulnerable to populist appeals of any kind, so that the tiny EFF has had no difficulty in continually destabilising government and driving it along whichever paths it chooses. A stronger and more self-confident leadership would dismiss such marginal actors with contempt. It is this vulnerability to populism that explains why the ANC leadership has ended up espousing a set of policies that it knows would ruin the country.

This leaderless nature of the South African polity is thus the reason why the ANC government is blundering along so blindly, apparently incapable of carrying out the structural reforms that the world has been trying to press on South Africa for a decade or more.[17] Indeed, the government has even proved incapable of achieving the far lesser goal of fiscal consolidation. Year after year it has promised lower budget deficits – and then failed to produce them. Inevitably, this weakness means that, once again, South Africa finds itself trapped within a political prison of its own making.

This has happened repeatedly before. In the 1890s, the Cape and Natal were unable to surmount the growing economic power of the Transvaal, but the Transvaal was also blocked from finding its own route to the coast. This log jam was only 'solved' by massive British military intervention during the Anglo-Boer War.

In the 1930s, South African politics was trapped within the uncomfortable world of 'Fusion', a solution forced upon the country by the economic crisis of the early 1930s. There were always strong tensions within the Fusion government, with its more liberal elements horrified by the reactionary policies of the Hertzog leadership. It was only a huge external crisis – the outbreak of a world war – that enabled Smuts to overturn Fusion to his own advantage.

Finally, of course, after two decades of fruitless attempts to reform apartheid, it was only when external pressures became overwhelming that FW de Klerk was able at last to abolish apartheid and launch South Africa on a new post-racial trajectory.

And now again South Africa seems unable to escape from the prison it has made for itself. Accordingly, the country seems destined to drift until its economy hits the rocks, when, at last, there will be no option but to seek another external intervention, in the shape of the help of the IMF.

Chapter Nine

The DA alternative

We have seen that the ANC has been unable to constitute a ruling class capable of steering the national state. But one of the options for the future is coalition government, so what of the DA, the main opposition? The DA, a classically liberal party, has been tremendously successful, rising from 1.7 per cent of the vote in 1994 to 22.2 per cent in 2014. What of the future?

The problem of racial dynamics

As the DA grew from its all-white core to be a fully multi-racial party it was faced with a difficult choice. Almost no organisations in South Africa have managed to surmount the strong centrifugal forces generated by racial difference and the race-based policies of the past. One may see this process at work in all manner of organisations. As soon as the organisation grows to encompass all races, one begins to find separate racial caucuses forming, often running their own electoral lists and each lobbying for its own advantage. This soon leads to allegations of racism and threats of withdrawal. Similarly, one may find successful multi-racial schools with a careful balance between the racial groups but once one group attains a majority of pupils the school will quickly slide further towards that group. It is as if it has been captured by one of the racial communities. Dynamics of this kind tend to paralyse organisations and to pull them apart.

The only exceptions to this rule have been the major Christian churches. They have succeeded due to several factors, including a strong hierarchical organisation and a body of beliefs that all communicants adhere to. Often, this is reinforced by an international authority (the Papacy, the Anglican Bishops' Conference, etc) that monitors developments and may intervene if necessary.

If the DA was to follow this example it had to insist on a strong, clear and consistent liberal ideology, in terms of which differences of race would not be allowed to sway the principle of meritocratic selection for all posts. This was how the DA's predecessor, the Progressive Party, had started out. As the DA grew larger, chiefly by repeated amalgamations with other breakaways from the two major parties, so the usual pressures of political opportunism were felt. Under the leadership of Tony Leon these pressures were contained, though with increasing difficulty as the party grew to incorporate all three of the minority groups.

But there was the rub. The minorities all shared many of the same fears and grievances and they identified socially with each other. Spreading the party further – into the African electorate – was an entirely different matter. For a start, there was a basic presumption that South Africa was now and forever an African-majority country and that therefore to be competitive a party had to have African leaders. This was problematic not only in that it meant that one group had a presumptively prior claim to leadership, but the African world had its own set of political traditions and liberalism was not one of them. In addition, of course, it meant that the African group had a presumptive right to leadership of the DA despite the fact that African voters were only a small minority of the DA electorate – an inherently fragile position. All these problems surfaced powerfully during Helen Zille's leadership of the DA in 2007–2015.

The dam walls go down

More or less by definition, Africans recruited by the DA would come from an ANC/SACP tradition, a chiefly tradition, the Black Consciousness tradition or the world of the Pan Africanist Congress or the Azanian People's Organisation – or often one of these traditions overlaid by another. Inevitably, this affected the assumptions, beliefs and behaviour of these recruits. Few, if any, had emerged from within the liberal tradition. Moreover, the ANC was promising special privileges for Africans via BEE or affirmative action. Could the DA afford to offer less? The party's electoral strategists urged that if the party was to appeal beyond the confines of the three minority groups it had to make exceptions to its principles and encourage the accelerated and affirmative promotion of Africans within its ranks and also modify its opposition to both affirmative action and BEE.[1] Once these dam walls went down, others quickly followed, so it was easy to find young DA MPs who no longer knew what the party's principles were.

With this coherence lost, the party soon fell into all the predictable tramlines of racial differentiation. The party grew a separate black caucus, something that should have been anathema in a liberal party. Race became a leading basis not only for policy but also for appointment and election within the party, with any group that didn't get its way crying racism. Policy formulation, candidate selection and everything else became a wrestling match between the various racial groups. This suited the ANC well, and it did all it could to stir the pot, repeatedly calling the DA racist and insisting that it was still a white party, which, accordingly, could never attract much African support.

This was clearly incorrect, but the DA leadership was never self-confident enough to simply shrug this off and constantly sought to 'prove' that they were anything but racist. This was foolish, for nothing they might do would stop the ANC repeating the charge of racism like a stuck record. Nonetheless, this led to the insistent suggestion that what the DA needed was a black leader. Yet the problem was that none of the party's African recruits had yet worked their way up through the usual *cursus honorum* of municipal, provincial and shadow cabinet experience at the political coalface. So, fatally, it was decided to simply omit this process and opt for a black leader anyway. This led to a series of initiatives that were disastrous for the party.

An experience-free leadership

First came Lindiwe Mazibuko, an able young woman recruited straight into the DA staff from university. By 2009 she was an MP and was immediately jumped to being a shadow deputy minister and the party's national spokesperson. By 2011, at the age of only 31, Mazibuko became the DA's parliamentary leader – an astonishing rise for someone who had spent no time as a local councillor or provincial legislator, had not shadowed a major ministry and had spent only two years as an MP. She immediately set her sights on the party leadership and even gave interviews in which she spoke of becoming the country's president one day.[2] Party colleagues criticised her for being 'arrogant and autocratic',[3] she quarrelled with Helen Zille, the party leader, and in 2014 she resigned, having blown a spectacular opportunity.

It was a textbook case of how accelerated promotion through affirmative action can lead to overconfidence and an overdeveloped ego. For the curious nature of affirmative action is that even those who are most in favour of such a policy are wholly unwilling to believe that they themselves are affirmative action appointees. The seductive alternative is to believe that one's own talents are so extraordinary that one earned such accelerated promotion on merit. This leads, all too often, to a dangerously enlarged ego, a peremptory style of leadership – and disaster.

Meanwhile, in 2014 Helen Zille had come up with the idea of giving her party another black presidential candidate, Mamphela Ramphele, with a further plan to then relaunch the DA as simply the

Democrats, with Ramphele as leader. This was always a dubious idea. Ramphele had had a decidedly mixed record as vice chancellor of the University of Cape Town and, when recruited to the World Bank, had been unable to deal with its sharply meritocratic atmosphere (which she found 'toxic'[4]) and had fled back to Cape Town, where she then stayed. In addition she had no background in the DA, was indeed a Black Consciousness stalwart, and had never held political office at any level. In fact, the whole arrangement fell apart in three days, creating a major public-relations disaster for the DA.

Unabashed, in 2015 the party elected Mmusi Maimane as leader – aged 35. Again, it was a story of astonishingly accelerated promotion. Maimane had only entered the party in 2010 when he became a city councillor for Johannesburg, immediately becoming its mayoral candidate despite having no council experience. Indeed, he had previously only worked as a pastor for his (fundamentalist) church and in an NGO. Nonetheless, by 2011 he had become the DA's national spokesperson and the year after that he was elected as the party's deputy chairman – despite having no provincial or parliamentary experience. The next year he became the party's candidate for the premiership of Gauteng, although he had never served in the provincial legislature. He then became an MP and, instantly, the party's parliamentary leader despite a complete lack of parliamentary experience. The next year he became the party leader, although he had had no shadow cabinet experience.

The result of this giddying climb is a leader with almost no experience at any level, someone who has never had to labour at the coalface and who has had no time or opportunity to win the respect of his colleagues. Not surprisingly he proved to be a weak leader, heavily influenced by his handlers and unable to manage the shadow cabinet. Instead, he wandered around the country giving speeches, which was clearly what he imagined his job to be. He remained a pastor, preaching to his flock, but the tough organisational world of leading a political party was foreign to him. He came from an ANC tradition and had, apparently, been quite happy with Thabo Mbeki as president, despite Mbeki's Aids denialism. This, together with his furious rejection of evolutionary theory,[5] led to raised eyebrows among the party's traditional supporters.

To complete this picture one should mention Solly Msimanga, who is the same age as Maimane and is already seen as his probable replacement should Maimane falter. Msimanga worked for the DA from when he was 26. He became a councillor for Tshwane (Pretoria) in 2011, a member of the Gauteng provincial legislature in 2014, chairman of the Gauteng DA in 2015 and in 2016 he became mayor of Tshwane. As he was the first to observe, the city was in a considerable mess after years of ANC administration and required a major turnaround operation. Hardly had he begun this huge project than he put himself forward for the post of national chairman of the DA (effectively the party's deputy leader), and when that failed he put himself forward as the DA's candidate for the premiership of Gauteng.[6] By January 2019 he had been forced to resign as mayor after an undistinguished term in office.

Again, Msimanga had had a remarkable history of accelerated promotion. Traditionally, one might have expected him to build a solid five-year record of turning around the country's capital city, acquiring experience and being able to point to a solid achievement. But Msimanga, like Maimane, was on a far faster track than that and wished to waste no time at all in getting to the very top.

Invidious comparisons

The DA's decision to skip all the normal stages of leadership development in order to fast-track a black leader for the party has proved to be a huge and perhaps irreversible mistake. There is little doubt that the party would have fared far better if it had remained colour-blind and insisted that its African recruits should move through the same sort of career development as their white, Indian and coloured peers. This is a mistake that a properly liberal party could never have made.

The result so far is that the DA now has a weak and inexperienced leadership, which to date has shown no sign of attracting large numbers of black votes. This matters particularly in the DA for, ever since its birth as the Progressive Party in 1959, the party has counted among its leaders a number of extremely able men and women – Helen Suzman, Colin Eglin and Zach de Beer, Frederik van Zyl Slabbert, Tony Leon and Helen Zille. The party leader has traditionally provided strong leadership in Parliament and has generally been more popular than his/her party in the country. Now the party is led by someone who cannot provide leadership in Parliament, who is easily outsmarted by Julius Malema, the EFF leader, and whose popularity may well lag behind the party in the country. The contrasts are painful.

In addition, the sight of African candidates being given such accelerated promotion was bound to create resentment and demoralisation among more earthbound politicians from the minority groups. Instead of being a party offering a real alternative, a party open to all the talents, as it had traditionally been, the DA now seemed to be just another public-sector institution in which members of the racial minorities could expect to be also-rans. And, importantly in a (supposedly) liberal party, it was profoundly illiberal to treat individuals so differently on the basis of their inherited characteristics and not on their individual merits. Maimane made it clear that he wanted far more Africans on the party's electoral lists[7] and this led to resentment and resistance from other quarters in the party.

The question of centralism

When the new Constitution was being hammered out at Codesa (the Convention for a Democratic South Africa) the DA's predecessor, the Democratic Party, fought tooth and nail for federalism, with local determination of local problems. Under the leadership of Maimane, who had grown up in the centralist tradition of the ANC, this principle simply vanished. Thus in 2017–2018, when the DA-led Cape Town city council faced problems both with its controversial mayor, Patricia de Lille, and a severe drought, Maimane simply announced that he was both taking control of the water crisis and dealing with De Lille and even forbade councillors to interfere.[8]

The result was beyond farcical. Maimane reached a deal with De Lille whereby she agreed to stand down – but it then emerged that the deal was not watertight and she might elect to stay after all. Maimane then wrongly asserted that five councillors were implicated in criminal allegations – and had to apologise and retreat in disorder.[9] Had he wished to provide an example of why party leaders should leave local politics to the locals, he could not have done better.

Meanwhile, the DA nominated Dan Plato as the next mayor, although Helen Zille would undoubtedly have been the popular choice. Plato had already served a very undistinguished term as mayor and was chosen again, presumably, because he would do as he was told by the DA leadership. This was not only a complete denial of the principles the DA had historically stood for, but the DA's hold on Cape Town itself, the jewel in its crown, could also be at stake. Nothing could have made it clearer that the party had lost its way.

In late 2018 it became known that Maimane was considering a carpetbagging expedition to become premier of the Western Cape. The resultant publicity forced him to jettison the idea.[10] This served to emphasise the fact that the only consistent strand in his experience-free career was a propensity for continual job-hopping within the DA. As may be seen, this was not atypical of the party's new black leadership.

No new ruling class

The avoidable disaster that has overtaken the DA's leadership is of large potential significance. Just as the party's enlarged multi-racial electorate has made the leadership a more difficult and demanding task, so the party has responded by choosing weaker, inexperienced and less capable leaders. It has done so out of a simple-minded belief that an African leadership will bring more black votes. This has been a major failure of the party's strategic imagination. It ignores the fact that the party's dramatic multi-racial expansion occurred under two white leaders, Leon and Zille, and that all the evidence suggests that their abilities were more important than their race. Everything suggests that the DA would have done far better to stick to its principles and simply elect the most able person as its leader, regardless of race.

It is not impossible that this is merely a stage in the DA's disintegration. The DA's best hope, we have seen, was to be a strictly principled liberal party in both its policies and its internal practice. Now that it has departed from those principles it is difficult to see why it should not become the same sort of vehicle for patronage, racial and ethnic politicking, and the same Big Man behaviour one sees in the ANC. Already there is racial tension over the question of candidate selection and muttered threats of a 'true liberal' breakaway.[11] All these trends have emerged while the party is still some way from sharing governmental power. If and when that happens, powerful new tensions are bound to open up as opportunities for patronage, perks and, yes, graft, increase.

But the DA's weakness has a broader significance. We live, I have suggested, in 'the leaderless world of the bureaucratic bourgeoisie' – and, indeed, the ANC's leadership has never been weaker or more divided than it is today. But given the trends at work inside the DA it is not likely that the country can look to the party for an alternative leadership that is any better or even very different. The best that can be said in its favour is that historically it has been less corrupt. These weaknesses of the DA could have practical consequences in the near future. At local level coalition politics has already become quite normal and the possibility clearly exists of the DA entering coalitions at national level too. But if one is looking to the DA to remedy the lack of a new, post-apartheid ruling class, one will look in vain.

Chapter Ten

Ramaphosa begins: optimism deferred

When Cyril Ramaphosa was campaigning for the ANC presidency in November 2017 he launched his own plan for the economy, the New Deal for Jobs, Growth and Transformation. This, he insisted, would be the product of a shared commitment by all stakeholders. Drawing heavily on the government's National Development Plan (NDP), Ramaphosa set a target of three per cent growth in 2018, rising to five per cent by 2023. The aim would be to create at least one million new jobs in five years, a development that would be 'largely manufacturing led', though he also spoke of how the agricultural sector should create a further one million new jobs by 2030, with many more small farmers.[1]

In a speech in September 2017, Ramaphosa asserted that there had to be 'far more effective exploitation of our natural resources', that is, a revitalised mining industry. Investment would increase from 20 per cent to 30 per cent of GDP. Manufacturing costs would be cut through a reformed Eskom (ie, cheaper electricity) and there had to be far greater use of renewable energy. There had to be R1.5 trillion spending on infrastructure over five years and a multi-billion-rand fund to assist start-ups. Education would be improved by 'working together with education department officials and teacher unions'. The economy 'must reflect in every respect the demography of the country'. The overriding aim of policy would be that it 'promotes growth and secures our economic sovereignty',[2] which he later explained meant avoiding any recourse to the Bretton Woods institutions – the IMF and the World Bank.[3]

This was, of course, all pie in the sky. Long before the end of Ramaphosa's first year as president, it was clear that growth would be under one per cent – with hardly better outcomes expected over the medium term. Indeed, the first quarter of 2018 saw negative growth of -2.6 per cent, followed by -0.7 per cent the next quarter, thus signalling a full-blown recession. This in turn was likely to mean that South African bonds would soon be consigned to junk status by all three of the ratings agencies, which in turn would cause financial institutions to dump some R100 billion of the country's bonds. The currency, already down 20 per cent in the year, would be bound to feel the impact of that. Moreover, far from providing cheaper electricity, Eskom had agreed to inflation-plus wage increases for its hugely bloated workforce, guaranteeing higher costs – and renewable electricity was not always cheaper than the alternatives. There was no sign of increased investment by either the public or private sector and unemployment was continuing to mount.

But it was also obvious that Ramaphosa's whole approach was mistaken. He had begun with a flurry of commissions, joint working parties, a job summit and all the other paraphernalia of the corporatist approach. This is very much his traditional modus operandi and also the language preferred by the ANC's wide and fractious coalition, for it meant that all their interests would be consulted. Yet the sort of structural reforms the economy needed could not possibly be delivered in that manner.

It is worth reiterating what the IMF and other international bodies have been saying for over a decade now, that South Africa must:

(i) liberalise its labour laws, making it easier to hire and fire workers, and also adopt a far more liberal attitude to the immigration of skilled labour;

(ii) radically overhaul its education system, weeding out incompetent teachers and raising standards throughout the system;

(iii) make large cuts in the number of public servants and also cut their remuneration so as to bring South Africa more into line with its peers;

(iv) clean up the SOEs so that they cease to require government bail-outs. This would involve reduced workforces, wage restraint, a crackdown on corruption and at least partial privatisation.[4]

Even to list these necessary reforms is to show how inadequate the corporatist approach is. How to improve education if such plans had to be approved by the corrupt and Luddite South African Democratic Teachers' Union (Sadtu)? How to slim down the bloated civil service or SOEs through consultation with unions intent on preserving all those jobs? How to increase the number of small farmers while conciliating the traditional chiefs, who are opposed to granting secure rights of property ownership anywhere in the old Bantustans? How to liberalise the labour laws in consultation with the unions, who are committed to defending the existing laws at all costs?

It was perfectly clear that all of these reforms could only be achieved by cutting Gordian knots – in the teeth of strong resistance from vested interests at every point. But that in turn would require a strong and determined government, while the Ramaphosa administration was weak and uncertain.

The view from the IMF

A very different perspective was provided by the IMF team that visited South Africa in mid-2018 as part of its regular Article IV consultations. Such teams work closely with the officials of the National Treasury and Reserve Bank and their work is presented to the cabinet as well. This guarantees that such reports are couched in diplomatic language – sometimes rather pulling their punches. However, the June 2018 report[5] was quite outspoken: 'Bold structural reforms are urgently needed … these include tackling corruption and strengthening governance, promoting competition in the product markets and by restructuring weak SOEs, advancing labour market reforms and enhancing the quality of education, and leveraging digitalisation and stabilising debt and reducing inflation.'[6]

The report then appended a 27-item list of 'must do' structural reforms, including such firm injunctions as to train and retrain teachers and strengthen their accountability – enough on its own to send Sadtu into paroxysms. The last item on the list dealt with the notion of EWC: 'This debate is undermining the credibility of the government's stated priorities to attract investment. In line with best international experience land reform should focus on enhancing agricultural productivity, improving land administration and reducing poverty.'[7]

The IMF forecast economic growth of 0.8 per cent in 2018 and 1.8 per cent per annum over the medium term, which is to say it forecast that the fall in real incomes that had already been going on for the previous five years would continue into the future. This absolutely dire result was in part a consequence of the inflexible labour laws. Again, the IMF was emphatic: 'The rigid labour market practice that hinders job creation by inflating labour costs needs to be revisited. Wage agreements between large unions and businesses through a centralised wage settlement process are imposed on SMEs [small to medium enterpises] and other firms that often cannot afford them. Wage levels thus become too high to absorb the unemployed. Further, wage increases exceed the pace of productivity improvements ... presenting a barrier to entry.'[8]

Moreover, the report continued, the increase in the minimum wage, proudly announced by Ramaphosa, was probably a false step: '... the envisaged wage level is relatively high by international standards and may have adverse employment effects on SMEs and the youth, with the possibility of renewed informalisation'.[9]

This last point is not made often enough. Cosatu and the government are keen to better the lot of those in work by allowing complete job security, a higher minimum wage, and so on. But it seldom gets noted that such measures will inevitably price some workers out of work by making their services too expensive for others to afford. The result is that these workers are forced down into the informal sector, where they make private bargains with possible employers to perform these services at a cheaper rate. Usually such transactions are for temporary work only; there is no observation of a minimum wage or of any health and safety standards. Such work is normally performed strictly for cash, thus falling outside the tax net. Other workers, finding themselves unemployed, sink into the informal sector in other ways – selling fruit or vegetables by the roadside or marketing various goods to passing cars at the traffic lights. Large numbers of young women are driven, ineluctably, into prostitution. It goes without saying that all careers in the informal sector are lower paid, uncertain and sometimes quite dangerous.

The IMF also warned that South Africa's public-sector employment and wage levels are both way out of line with those of other emerging markets. This all amounted to a strong warning that the economy had become completely unbalanced, that as things stood the population would continue to get poorer and poorer, and that without urgent and sweeping change there could be a complete collapse. Again, the IMF tone was urgent: 'Ambitious reforms in labour and product markets need to be launched now ... private sector participation in all areas of the economy would help drive growth by increasing efficiency and promoting competition ... a bigger role of the private sector in the provision of basic services is warranted. Meanwhile SOEs should operate on a commercial basis.'[10]

This was as near as the IMF would allow itself to go in recommending sweeping privatisation. This was a far stronger and more urgent set of recommendations than was at all usual. Reading between the lines, the IMF team was clearly quite alarmed at the way the South African economy was beginning to founder.

The IMF: the big bad wolf

Contrary to popular impression, the IMF is by no means keen to intervene in Africa's economies, for it knows that it will be vilified for requiring austerity measures as a condition for its aid. In addition, it is aware that a bail-out for South Africa would be particularly problematic given the extravagant hopes aroused by the Mandela period and the likelihood that the sort of measures required to rebalance the economy would elicit accusations that the IMF was seeking to reinstate white supremacy. Accordingly, the Fund would greatly prefer it if South Africa could set its own house in order and avoid a bail-out.

When I first wrote (in May 2015)[11] that South Africa was headed for an IMF bail-out, this was treated as a shocking suggestion. Since then, references – by politicians and journalists – to such a possibility have multiplied, usually accompanied by dire warnings about the loss of sovereignty that this might entail. In effect, the IMF is the big bad wolf.[12] Thus its very strong warning in June 2018 was met merely with the usual response – that South Africa would concentrate on fiscal consolidation only (ie, keep the budget deficit down), thus ignoring the long list of 'must do' reforms.

Down the years – and South Africa has been receiving such advice for 20 years now from a range of international institutions – this has been the country's standard response. In effect, the IMF has been warning in sharper and sharper tones that the ship is headed for the rocks, but those on the deck respond only by trimming their sails, never by altering course. The result is that an IMF bail-out looks increasingly likely.

Generally, the best way for a country to avoid recourse to the IMF is to carry out pre-emptively the sort of reforms upon which the IMF would make any loan conditional. This is very much what happened in 1996 when Mbeki launched his Gear policy. Indeed, Mbeki argued that, with the budget deficit then reaching almost eight per cent of GDP, recourse to the IMF would soon have been inevitable had he not introduced Gear.[13]

Advice ignored

Under Ramaphosa such pre-emptive action was nowhere to be seen. Indeed, Ramaphosa backed down before one pressure group after another, allowing through a ruinous settlement with public-service workers in June 2018, which added an unbudgeted R30 billion to expenditure, and an unaffordably generous settlement in August 2018 with striking Eskom workers as well. With Eskom needing a government bail-out and the public-service workers' settlement merely increasing the budget deficit, both these pay settlements could only be financed by increased borrowing.[14] The folly of going further into debt merely to pay salaries needs no emphasis.

And Ramaphosa had adopted as his own Zuma's unilateral announcement of free higher education, albeit with some modifications. This was yet another catastrophic error, not only because it meant slashing provincial budgets for health and social assistance – thus directly redistributing from the poor to the better off – but also because such a move was bound to produce chaos in the higher education system itself.

Ramaphosa doubtless took the path he did in part because he was in such a weak position in the ANC that he felt he could not afford to offend anyone else, and in part because this was a pre-election period. What was more worrying was the possibility that Ramaphosa had failed to understand just how serious the situation was, that he simply feared being outflanked on the left or that he lacked the character to face up and dare to be different.

It was difficult to find another interpretation for Ramaphosa's decision to take over responsibility for the NHI programme from the health minister, Aaron Motsoaledi, apparently with the idea of making it central to his election campaign ('We are going to lead it and we are going to be talking about it all the time … in my view it is achievable'[15]).

For years, Motsoaledi had made rather messianic speeches about NHI while the Treasury had carefully refrained from costing the programme or giving any indication as to how it could be paid for. Other ministers were generally loath to talk about it for it was obvious that, if it were ever introduced, it was bound to be a huge disaster – and no one wanted paternity for that. Yet here was the president cheerfully taking responsibility for it and making its implementation a matter of confidence in himself. It was pure folly.

Ramaphosa's response to the economic crisis was threefold. First, he appointed a four-person team – former finance minister Trevor Manuel, economist Trudi Makhaya, former deputy finance minister Mcebisi Jonas, and former Standard Bank CEO Jacko Maree – whose task it was to scour the world for investors and persuade them to invest in South Africa. What was needed, according to this view, was some arm-twisting and some charm and, thus convinced, those with capital would decide to disburse it in South Africa's direction. Ramaphosa's business career should have taught him that investment doesn't work like this: investors need to be wooed with tax breaks, enterprise zones, cheap labour and the cast-iron security of their investment. None of these things are on offer in South Africa, and meanwhile the media is full of countries advertising themselves as investment destinations, many of them with much more competitive offerings.

Second, Ramaphosa launched, with much fanfare, a stimulus plan 'to kick-start growth'. Fitch, the ratings agency, was typically underwhelmed, saying that the plan was unlikely to deliver 'a significant boost to growth'.[16] The reprioritisation of R50 billion in spending was fine, but no new money was involved, and while Ramaphosa had also announced a new R400-billion infrastructure fund, it was unclear where the money for that was supposed to come from. If it was not new money, there would be no fresh stimulus. If it was new money, it could only come from borrowing, of which the markets would take a dim view. Many of the other measures announced were either things announced a while back, or were still not certain to be implemented, or were of dubious value. For example, Ramaphosa hailed the 'policy certainty' introduced by the new Mining Charter, but since that Charter was still extremely unattractive to investors, it was doubtful that this certainty could help.[17]

Finally, Ramaphosa held a jobs summit with business, unions and government. Some 70 growth-friendly administrative 'interventions' were identified and the three 'partners' in Ramaphosa's initiative were asked each to put something in the pot. The government gave a guarantee that there would be no retrenchments anywhere in the public service or in any SOE[18] – an amazing commitment given the unsustainable state of the SOEs and their known overstaffing and overpayment. The unions wanted business to give a similar commitment about private-sector jobs, but business contented itself with a statement that it would seek to avoid any retrenchments if at all possible. This meant little. The unions gave nothing.[19]

Astonishingly, the government claimed that the summit would lead to the creation of 275 000 jobs annually henceforth. It seemed inherently implausible that merely administrative interventions could do anything of the sort. But Rob Davies, the minister of trade and industry, praising the 'vigour' of these calculations (presumably he meant 'rigour'), suggested that actually 825 000 new jobs would be created annually as a result of the summit.[20] This was, again, nothing less than magical thinking, as was the idea that the way to solve the unemployment crisis was to get people together so they could all make good resolutions about it.

It was of a piece, really, with the proposal to commence NHI by pouring hundreds of billions of rands of taxpayers' money into an NHI Fund and place it under state administration.[21] This was simply asking for more looting. Just as pools of stagnant water inevitably attract mosquitoes, so in modern South Africa any large pool of capital – amassed for whatever purpose, in a bank, trust, pension fund or state account – will attract looters. The sky is full of vultures. Anyone who doesn't know that simply hasn't been paying attention.

Down on the farm

In August 2018, I attended an AgriSA/Landbou conference on land reform at Bela Bela in Limpopo. Because AgriSA is the main farmers' union, taken very seriously by government, Deputy President Mabuza helicoptered in to address the conference. Both he and the president of AgriSA, Dan Kriek, spoke earnestly about their keenness for 'partnership',[22] but everybody also acknowledged that there was a complete lack of trust.

I was left reflecting that it had taken fully a quarter of a century for things to get down to brass tacks. During the struggle, the ANC always referred to its enemy as 'die Boere' – and here indeed were *die boere*, for most of the conference speakers gave their profession as 'boer' (farmer). The ANC had seen such people as the true heart of Afrikanerdom and racism, and also as a semi-militarised group, for farmers had guns and organised their own self-defence in the shape of commandos. Hence the ANC song 'Kill the boer, kill the farmer'. And here were the two sides facing one another, with the ANC wanting to take the farmers' land without payment and the farmers determined to resist. Many of the farmers had heart-warming stories to tell of how they had helped some of their farmworkers to become smallholders, but it was always clear that these do-it-yourself land reforms would not be enough to stem the tide of land populism.

Both sides had changed a lot. The number of farmers had more than halved since 1994 under the weight of murderous farm attacks, the abolition of all the farmers' old exemptions and privileges, and the process of farm concentration common to all developed countries. And yet the reduced number of farmers fed the whole country and produced a large volume of exports too. But the ANC had changed more. Here it was represented by a man whom *The New York Times* had openly accused of presiding over large-scale corruption and even political killings[23] – accusations to which neither Deputy President David Mabuza nor the ANC made any reply. And Mabuza was extremely rich. No one in 1994 would have guessed that the ANC would be represented by a man like that.

What was completely gone, disappeared down the memory hole of history, was the notion of either side as a fighting unit. The commandos had long since been abolished, while the ANC as a disciplined Leninist phalanx, ready to do battle with *die boere*, had equally disappeared. It took a moment to comprehend that. All that ideology, that passionate commitment, that courage – gone. Who wanted a fight now? Neither side had soldiers.

What often seemed to unite the two sides was God. There was a very great deal of God at the conference – grace was said, as were lots of prayers (and EWC got mentioned even in the prayers), and there were all manner of born-again speeches. I noted that some of the farmers were outspoken admirers of liberal figures of one sort or another – again, an amazing transformation.

As I listened to the psalms I realised how the struggle in front of me was almost biblical. The psalms spoke of sheep being reared, protected, stolen and sacrificed, of people being killed, or people being subjugated and then being freed from that subjugation, of land under threat from others, sometimes of the need to flee – and the myth of return. All these themes run through contemporary South Africa like a river. I was hardly the first to notice these things. When Henry Kissinger first met with John Vorster in 1976 he told his aides, 'I have just met a character from the Old Testament.'

The farmers were all yearning for a final settlement, for a deal where the goalposts stopped moving, where there was certainty. And the problem was that the African cry for land echoes endlessly, and is not even that much about land. It is a cry of dispossession and alienation, a feeling of being unequal, of 'wanting our country back'. This guarantees that politicians will continue to use it, and the more they fail, the more they'll use it.

The whole debate is, of course, an anachronism. The United States has the world's most productive farm sector, but less than 0.3 per cent of its population produces almost all its food. This number is constantly shrinking, as it is bound to do, for the average American farmer is aged just over 57.[24] The number of South Africa's commercial farmers is also constantly shrinking. This is a worldwide trend. Agriculture stands to become the world's first wholly automated industry, particularly when the robotics revolution gets into its stride. Within a generation in the developed world, agriculture may employ just a handful of people. Such realities never impinge on the South African land debate, based as it is on emotion rather than rationality.

Mere fingers in the dyke

Several things seemed obvious. Ramaphosa's investment drive, stimulus plan and jobs summit were going to be insufficient to turn things around. Indeed, they seemed mainly to do with pre-election public relations. The ANC was ageing but its decaying hulk could probably hang on a while longer. At the same time, it seemed certain that the continuation of ANC government would, as Carol Paton put it in *Business Day*, lead to 'a long and painful downward trajectory of the economy, living standards and social cohesion'.[25]

Ultimately, such a course is suicidal for any political party, so it still seemed likely that the ANC would have to go, cap in hand, to the IMF, because, in effect, it was incapable of carrying out the necessary structural reforms itself. But, as we have seen, Ramaphosa and the ANC are both determined to avoid the IMF. This suggests that there could be a protracted period of low growth and social misery – a sort of dragging along the bottom – before the government is forced to go to the IMF after all. In the end, such recourse seems inevitable. Ramaphosa's expressed horror at the thought of resorting to the IMF was either parochial or simply political.[26] Other African countries go to the IMF all the time. At the time of writing, Pakistan was negotiating its 13th IMF bail-out in 40 years.[27]

Given that it was already obvious by early 2018 that recourse to the IMF was an immediate necessity, such a decision to delay the inevitable increased the risk that there could be a sudden collapse. Such a possibility already existed by mid-2018. The Land Bank warned that if the government proceeded with EWC the bank's loans would be at stake and the government would find itself having to bail out the Land Bank to the tune of R41 billion.[28] In addition, another R160 billion was at risk for the commercial banks in loans to farmers.[29] Already the debate over EWC had lowered the value of virtually all farms and rendered most of them unsellable.

Despite all the evidence, Ramaphosa continued to speak of EWC as if it would be a blessing to the economy, sparking growth and investment, but already it was having a catastrophic effect. All told, South Africa's banks have extended R1.6 trillion in property loans, and a great deal of that was now at risk, for investors are well aware that farmland is a fungible asset, and that EWC might well be applied to other types of property as well. By July 2018 agricultural land prices were down 32 per cent on December 2017 – and 43 per cent down on April 2016[30] – while listed (urban) property was down 20 per cent in 2018, which meant that it had 'performed worse than all other major listed property markets in the world'.[31] No wonder that Mike Brown, the CEO of Nedbank, one of the big four South African banks, warned that EWC could trigger 'a classical banking crisis'.[32] Given the already rocky state of the economy, that would capsize it altogether. Despite Ramaphosa's reassuring platitudes, it was clear that he was playing with fire.

The trouble with Eskom

The other pressure point was Eskom. By February 2019 it owed R420 billion and its credit rating was deep into junk status, meaning that commercial banks and other financial institutions would no longer buy its bonds. With the government and the unions both effectively forbidding any staff cuts except by natural wastage, it was hard for Eskom to reduce its costs – and already it had pushed electricity prices so high that demand had fallen significantly. Despite this, in 2018 it not only increased prices by another 4.2 per cent but then applied for three years of increases of 15 per cent per annum. This would mean that in three years' time electricity would cost an extra 58.5 per cent. Such an increase would be ruinous for many other parts of the economy, would undoubtedly cause many to go off-grid, and would undoubtedly see a large further fall.[33]

Moreover, Eskom had been disastrously mismanaged by its previous

CEO, Brian Molefe, who had closed down the tied coal mines in which Eskom had itself invested and which had provided it with its coal. Instead, the coal was to be provided by 'emerging suppliers' (in effect, through all manner of corrupt BEE deals), with the coal being trucked in at a higher price. By late 2018 there was insufficient coal at many power stations and Eskom's ability to produce electricity was down by around 30 per cent. As a result, Eskom was having to spend billions on diesel fuel to run (very expensive) gas turbines to supplement normal production.[34] If the economy were to recover, Eskom might well be unable to meet any increase in demand.

Eskom had approached the Public Investment Corporation (PIC), which manages the public-service pension funds, to turn its R84 billion holding of Eskom debt into equity. Given that Eskom's equity may currently have a minus value, this was a desperate throw, which Eskom then had to abandon when it realised that this might trigger covenants that it had with other lenders; in effect, such a move would be viewed by the market as a default.[35] But the very fact that Eskom had approached the PIC in the first place suggested that it was finding it difficult to meet its debt repayments. This was hardly surprising, given that its debt was expected to soar to R600 billion by 2022.[36] It was very hard to imagine how all that extra debt was to be funded unless the government returned to the apartheid-era policy of prescribed assets, forcing financial institutions to buy bonds. This in turn would be seen in such a negative light by the markets that the government might have to bring back tough exchange controls and other siege-economy measures. Again, the whole situation was pregnant with huge risk for the whole economy.

Nevertheless, the new three-year wage agreement signed by Eskom in mid-2018[37] committed the utility to above-inflation increases costing R2.21 billion per annum in the first year and R6.79 billion per annum by the third year. The remarkable thing about this was that Eskom was already running at a loss and was having to borrow simply to pay the interest on its outstanding debt. Ramaphosa had drawn plaudits when he appointed Eskom's new 'clean' management, but a glance at these figures showed that this management was unequal to its task. The utility literally had no idea how it was going to pay for those wage increases,[38] and its debt projections showed that in effect it was planning to go bankrupt. It was due to pay back R250 billion in loans over the next three years, and it was difficult to see how it could do this.[39] Such a bankruptcy would on its own compel an IMF bail-out.

The closest parallel would appear to be Argentina. When Mauricio Macri became president in 2015 he launched a programme of conventional market-led economics in an effort to clean up the mess left by 12 years of Peronist populism under Néstor and then Cristina Kirchner. It is sometimes said that the key characteristic of Third World governments is that they attempt to defy the laws of economics, and this certainly applied to the Kirchners. Macri's victory was accordingly greeted with much the same euphoria as attended Ramaphosa's victory two years later in South Africa. By 2018, however, Argentina was experiencing negative growth of 2.5 per cent, a steeply plunging currency and interest rates of 60 per cent when Macri was forced to go in great haste to the IMF for a $56-billion bail-out. The fact was that Macri's clean-up could not really compensate for the dreadful dead weight of all those years of populist defiance of economics under the Kirchners. In particular, over-generous salary and wage settlements had been locked in under their regime and Macri found himself powerless to stop them. Macri himself admitted that he had been guilty of 'excessive optimism'.[40]

The sudden collapse that forced President Macri to go running to the IMF (and then to plead for accelerated disbursement of the loan) was the fall of the peso, down over 50 per cent in the first eight months of 2018.[41] As one surveys the South African scene, one can see that it is in many ways far worse than Argentina. Macri, after all, carried out a large number of sensible reforms (removing taxes from exports, reducing the fuel subsidy, cutting the cabinet to just ten ministries, etc). But, in South Africa's case, to such woes as a recession, a falling currency and an investment strike, one has to add such enormous unforced policy blunders as EWC, NHI, the huge overpayment of the public service, promises to set up state banks, an (unaffordable) sovereign wealth fund, the costly (and pointless) nationalisation of the Reserve Bank – and so on.

The coup that never was

As one surveys the scene, one realises why many voters have concluded that the ANC (and EFF) are intent on destroying the economy and with it the country. Why should that be? After all, the ANC certainly didn't start out with such intent.

The answer is, as we have seen, that almost immediately after 1994 the ANC became the vehicle and instrument of essentially parasitic elements – not just the patronage bosses and their gangsters but the bureaucratic bourgeoisie, traditional leaders and a whole legion of rent-seeking wannabes. To a large extent these groups now *are* the ANC, though it still has hundreds of thousands of humble members. As we have seen, however, when it comes to an ANC conference these humble members are easily ignored. What the parasitic groups have in common is that they are hell-bent on primary accumulation but produce nothing in return. Collectively, this is a burden that the economy cannot bear.

The arrival in power of Ramaphosa has done nothing to change this situation. At a time when considerable horror was expressed at the shameless looting of VBS Mutual Bank, where nearly R2 billion had disappeared in a feeding frenzy,[42] the auditor-general, Kimi Makwetu, attracted less attention when he told Parliament that unauthorised, fruitless, wasteful and irregular spending in government departments and SOEs in the previous year had been more than R50 billion.[43] It can be assumed that most of this money was stolen. Moreover, despite supposed austerity drives and cutbacks on foreign travel and other privileges, this sum was still rising strongly – the year before that it had been 'only' R45 billion.[44] And while there was a general hue and cry, demanding that the several dozen thieves who had looted VBS should pay the price, Makwetu pointed out that there was an entire 'lack of consequence' for this far greater looting by ministers and public servants. Indeed, if the matter were taken seriously many thousands of them would have to go to jail every year.

In addition, it is these parasitic groups who produce (and endlessly reproduce) the phenomenon of ever-mounting inequality and who also hollow out the institutions of the democratic state. A widespread example is to be found in many municipalities, where the local municipal officials collect payments from local citizens for electricity and water, steal that money, and then default on the town's payments to Eskom and the water boards. This process ends up with a few rich individuals plus bankrupt municipalities and utilities, with many very poor people feeling the brunt of such service failures.

These parasitic elements have used the ANC to insert themselves at every level of the system. Their appetites, sharpened by all the years of enforced constraint under apartheid, are omnivorous and insatiable. All notions of the public or national interest are foreign to them. For them it is a simple matter of *enrichissez-vous* and devil take the hindmost. Any attempt to 'satisfy' them is merely feeding the crocodile. However, the mass unemployment and ever-greater inequality that results from feeding that beast is bound to be unpopular, so this elite seeks to stay in power by a desperate attempt to distract the poor with populist promises such as EWC and NHI.

Gradually, this parasitic greed and its accompanying populism are capsizing the state and the economy. There seems to be no force capable of reining them in or even of keeping order: the police are corrupt, incompetent and unmotivated to intervene, while the armed forces are in a desperate state of disrepair. This last is important. South Africa has already reached a point that would have triggered a military coup d'état in most African states, but this does not appear to be an option in Pretoria's case.

Chapter Eleven

What is to be done?

Sooner or later, structural reform is likely to come to South Africa. Much depends on how thorough-going that is. In an ideal world this opportunity would be grasped with both hands: never waste a good crisis. After all, nearly quarter of a century has passed since the ANC came to power and it is obvious that the current mix of policies has failed very badly. The country is stuck in very low growth, unemployment (and with it, inequality) is at record levels, investment is stuck in bottom gear, and over this period there has been a huge and continuous process of de-skilling. Not only has the country been exporting scarce skills hand over fist but it has simultaneously been lowering educational standards – which are at rock bottom – thus ensuring a further loss of skills. Probably only Venezuela and Zimbabwe have managed their affairs as badly as this. So why on earth would anyone want to keep the current policy mix?

Instead, let us imagine that the government – of whatever political complexion – decides to turn over a new leaf and to go all-out for economic growth. Perhaps spurred by the fact of an IMF bail-out (or the threat of it), this would mean that the government embarks on a sweeping liberalisation of the economy and society. What would this look like?

The problem of the labour aristocracy

One has to start with the fact that ever since apartheid made special provisions for the minority of Africans allowed to migrate to the towns, there has been a relatively privileged group of African urban dwellers. Whites, coloureds and Indians were free to live in towns if they wished, but Africans required an endorsement on their pass to do so. Most Africans lacked this. Parts – but only parts – of this African urban elite gradually morphed into a small labour aristocracy. Naturally, rural Africans wanted to migrate to the cities but were held back by the pass laws until the collapse of the pass system in 1986. The huge influx of migrants to the towns might have been expected to erode the position of the labour aristocracy, but the latter was able to protect its position with very rigid labour laws.

This is what has created South Africa's great economic conundrum. The country cannot compete with developed economies because it not only lacks the technical and industrial infrastructure with which to do so, but the productivity of its labour is also far lower. But it also cannot compete with many other developing countries because its labour is too expensive, that is, wages are higher.[1] The South African labour movement claims, that its members are desperately underpaid, but, in comparison to their emerging-market peers, this is emphatically untrue. So investment and jobs flow to far cheaper Asian or African rivals (Vietnam, Ethiopia) or to more productive developed countries (Germany, Australia, Canada).

Let my people go

At present there are nearly 10 million unemployed, living mainly in the countryside and shack settlements near the big cities and the larger towns. Many of these poor people have families, so in all there are some 20 or 30 million people in this situation. Usually they live off some pension or social grant, paid to one of their household, that gets spread around many people, together with whatever work they can do in the informal sector. These are South Africa's wretched of the earth. Under present labour laws they are unfairly locked out of competing for jobs in the formal sector. This is an intolerable situation. They have to be allowed in. They are in any case crowding more and more around the major cities and they have to be allowed to play a role in the life of those cities. In effect, the ANC has replaced the old job-reservation policy with a job-reservation policy of their own devising. This too has to go.

Thus liberalisation of the labour laws would be the key to many necessary changes in South Africa. If it were made easier to hire and fire workers one would expect the unemployed to pour into the labour market. Many of them would be willing to work for far lower wages than those currently paid, so one would thus expect a sharp reduction in wages for all unskilled and semi-skilled jobs, plus at least some reduction for the more skilled categories as well. At the same time, since employers would be more likely to hire under such a regime, employment would expand. Much the same effect could be achieved at the top of the scale by allowing the free inflow of skilled foreign labour. In a sense, the passing of the Minimum Wage Act, signed into law in November 2018, was a step in the wrong direction, since the imposition of a minimum wage could lead to further job losses.[2]

As will be seen, this would be South Africa's version of the 'shock therapy' applied to the Soviet bloc economies in the 1990s. There is no doubt that life will be hard for those whose wages fall. The trade unions will rage against this and will demand that we show sympathy for those in this plight. This indeed we should do, though it has to be tempered by sympathy for the far larger numbers hitherto locked out of the economy by restrictive labour laws.

The net effect of such a change would be that perhaps the same amount of money would be spread among more, lower-paid workers. Some of this adjustment would be made simply through inflation, with wages staying steady and thus falling in real terms. South Africa would thus gradually become a low-wage country and better able to compete internationally. Once it was clear that these changes were real and would last, investment would pour in and the economy would revive sharply. At the same time, many prices would fall as wages fell as a cost factor. This would ease the plight of the previously employed to some extent. Current workers would be angered by their reduction in wages, but they would be outnumbered by previously unemployed workers delighted by the change, particularly since revived growth would increase the total quantum of jobs. It would be an age of opportunity.

Such a change would also usefully underline the fact that the only justification for higher wages would be greater skills or higher productivity. It is even possible that under such a regime the motor plants of the Eastern Cape could be operated without government subsidy.

Trade unions would attack such a policy as a 'race to the bottom'. In part that is true, though once wage levels subside to a level that matches productivity, one would expect wages to rise along with economic growth, the rising tide lifting all boats. This has already happened in China. In 1952 the average wage there was under $100 a year. By 2017 the average wage was $10 680, or R152 824. Moreover, in a country of 1.39 billion the jobless rate in 2018 was just 3.82 per cent. And that average wage is now increasing very quickly; it rose over two and a half times between 2008 and 2017.[3] Living standards have risen manyfold since the 1990s. It is all very well for trade unions to thunder against 'a race to the bottom', but there is also a race up from the bottom. In any case, what is the alternative? At present, one can find many people in South Africa who are at best semi-literate but who hold middle-level or even highly paid positions. This is a pretend world. It does the country no good and cannot, in the long run, be sustained. Far better to adjust to the real world outside and grow our way upward.

For many years now we have seen ANC delegations returning from China, deeply impressed by what they have seen and saying insistently that 'we must learn from China'. And, indeed, that is exactly what needs to happen. The Chinese would not for one moment tolerate the inflexible labour laws that hold back the development of South Africa and immiserate its people.

The inevitability of globalisation

South Africa's integration into the international economy is far too deep and pervasive for the country to be able to escape the effects of globalisation. Indeed, most of its citizens hungrily devour the new technology that links them into that globalised world. They use their cellphones to transmit money to other countries, they watch American TV, they buy cheap Chinese clothes and shoes, they happily use social media. They are, in that sense, already global citizens. What is not imaginable is that South Africa can continue to exist behind the fence of its own peculiar job-reservation laws when everywhere else in that global market such restrictions do not exist. It's not just the billions of Indians, Chinese and Indonesians offering their labour in that global market – there will soon be another billion Africans doing the same. So no matter how hard it is to envisage this 'shock therapy', one has to realise that it is inevitable anyway in the long run. Indeed, even if the present labour laws are not scrapped, that long run may be quite short.

The culture of victimhood is so strong in South Africa that it is quite normal for African politicians to claim that they have suffered unique poverty and deprivation, even that they have endured 'slavery'. This is, of course, simply not true. South Africa is a middle-income developing country. Many hundreds of millions in Asia and elsewhere in Africa are far poorer than the average South African. Apartheid was a dreadful, inhumane and degrading system, but it was a long way short of slavery. West and East Africans, who really did endure slavery and the loss of family members to slavers, would be able to explain how much worse a plight that was than anything suffered under apartheid. Indeed, not a few East Africans were brought to South Africa as slaves and suffered under that system while the black South Africans around them did not. (Ironically, the West and East Africans who throng to South Africa today have little or no sense of victimhood and frequently comment on how curious it is that black South Africans exhibit this trait so strongly, together with an accompanying sense of entitlement.)

Nonetheless, that culture of victimhood is so strongly entrenched that it is politically impossible for any politician to advocate lower wages. In that sense, to write as I have above is to break a very large taboo, and I would not expect what I say to be popular, or even acceptable. Economists Nicoli Nattrass and Jeremy Seekings have made the argument for lower wages in the textile industry, where only plants that have disregarded the centrally bargained minimum wage have been able to survive, but they are quick to say that their arguments cannot be generalised.[4] But they can be, and should be. Indeed, globalisation will soon make such a development inevitable whether one likes it or not.

Two objections would be raised to this. First, it would be said that by lowering wages one was increasing the rate of exploitation. The answer to that is yes, indeed. But, as the Marxist economist Joan Robinson remarked long ago, 'the misery of being exploited by capitalists is nothing compared to the misery of not being exploited at all'.[5] If in doubt, ask South Africa's nearly 10 million unemployed. Second, local employers long ago realised that migrant workers from Zambia, Malawi, Zimbabwe, and so forth, work far harder and better than do many South Africans. There would be a danger that labour law liberalisation might merely result in greater inflows and employment of migrants, leaving a large, sullen and xenophobic local proletariat. That is not tenable, and stricter immigration controls would be required.

Market liberalisation

The liberalisation of the labour market would need to be accompanied by a general market liberalisation, including far more competition in product markets – breaking up the cartels that dominate South Africa. Probably all the SOEs should be privatised, and preferably split up so as to create competition. For example, there is little point in merely privatising the Airports Company of South Africa; one needs to allow all the airports to compete independently with each other. One would need to retain a national electricity grid and an integrated national system of water distribution, but the power producers and local water boards should be privatised. In a situation of 'natural' local monopolies (for example, Umgeni Water in KwaZulu-Natal), the operating contract could be re-awarded every so many years, subject to public review and competing bids. As we saw earlier, this is not a matter of free-market ideology but simply a recognition that state ownership is a very bad idea in independent Africa.

The same principles should be followed in general throughout society. What the last-quarter century should have taught one and all is that during the early stages of primary accumulation there is effectively no hope of avoiding massive corruption and mismanagement in any bureaucracy unless one can harness market disciplines on one's side. That is to say, the concerted effort currently undertaken by Cyril Ramaphosa and his minister of public enterprises, Pravin Gordhan, to clean up the SOEs, although extremely well intentioned, is probably doomed to fail. First, because it is highly unlikely that it will be effective – the opportunities for corruption are simply too great – and, second, because the minute Gordhan's 'great purge' of the corrupt and incompetent from the SOEs has been completed, all the same processes will begin again.

162

On top of this, the track record suggests that it will be impossible to stop continued government interference in the SOEs. This has already meant that Eskom has had ten different CEOs and six different boards in the last ten years.[6] No business can possibly work on that basis. The only way to make the SOEs work is if all the workers and managers know that if they fail to make a profit their jobs are at risk. Similarly, in a private company managers who engage in corruption will rapidly get fired – or their company will go bust. Either way, the risks of corruption are dramatically reduced.

I hasten to add that I am not a free-market ideologue; indeed, I have spent much of my life voting for social democratic parties. It is purely a question of what works or does not work under present conditions. And, of course, a free-market solution does not mean that one necessarily avoids all corruption and mismanagement: think of the (free market) minibus-taxi industry, plagued by incessant taxi wars, involvement with drug traffickers, its refusal to obey traffic rules or pay traffic fines, and the irresponsible and dangerous behaviour of the drivers, producing a hideous casualty rate. Quite clearly, under present conditions even free-market competition needs iron-fisted policing and regulation, including a tough inspectorate that punishes policemen who take bribes from taxi bosses. This regulation, policing and policing-the-policemen ought really to be almost the state's only job. It is quite enough. The same market principles need to be extended even into health and education, for everything suggests that under South Africa's present conditions these sectors cannot work well under state control.

It may be objected that this would make bankers and big businessmen too powerful – and that is probably true. But at least one could be sure that all enterprises had to serve their customers first or die. One could also be sure that the overpayment of managers and the featherbedding of industries with enormously inflated staff numbers, both a key feature of SOEs today, would cease automatically. And, in any case, look at the situation produced by a quarter-century of ANC rule. The SOEs plead, in vain, for loans from bankers. The president implores (his word) private businessmen to invest and not to make anyone redundant – in vain. The government pleads with the big car manufacturers to double their workforces (again in vain). The government goes in fear of the rating agencies and the bond markets. There is no doubt on which side of the equation power lies. For the sheer fecklessness of ANC rule – in a word, the lack of a proper ruling class – has hollowed out the state, which is less and less capable as time goes on. On the other hand, in a thriving and prosperous society one businessman or banker, more or less, doesn't make a lot of difference. It is the investment strike caused by the ANC that has made the investor king.

Having a national objective

At the moment, South Africans don't know where they are going. Notionally, the country is moving towards an NDR, but who can believe that? Are we really supposed to believe that the corrupt arms deal, the killing of over 300 000 African mothers and children in an Aids genocide, almost ten years of presidential looting under Jacob Zuma and nearly 10 million unemployed have all been purposeful steps towards that objective? It has been more like the career of a drunken sailor. But part of the large move towards liberalisation would be a redefinition of what the country is aiming at.

A key objective would be to make South Africa as internationally competitive as possible in order to maximise investment and job creation. For a start, all taxes on investment would have to go. This would mean the abolition of BEE, of all rules governing racially directed procurement, of the Mining Charter and the various other industry charters, and also of affirmative action. This would doubtless produce some resistance, but once it became clear that these changes would vastly increase the number of jobs, that would soon fade away. South Africa needs to study such African success stories as Rwanda, Mauritius and Ethiopia – none of which allow any of these taxes on investment – and copy them.

It would be important that the government was quite explicit about the reasons for these changes. In general, the philosophy would be meritocracy: the best person for the job. It would need to be emphasised that this applied quite equally to all races, tribes and religions, to men and women, and to those of all sexual orientations. None of the gains in social equality of recent times need be lost and, indeed, they would be greatly reinforced by having so many more people in jobs, with all that means in terms of social support and regained self-respect. It would be pointed out that BEE and affirmative action were merely more recent varieties of social favouritism, akin to job reservation under apartheid, and that around the world most other countries had long since abandoned such practices. (The United States is a partial exception, but even there affirmative action is under attack almost everywhere.) South Africa, it would be pointed out, wished to adopt the same rules as others not only because it had to live and compete with that modern world but also because it wanted to be fully part of that modern world. This should be seen as the completion of the process of liberation begun in 1990.

It would also need to be explained that companies and individual employers alike had seen the benefits of having more representative workforces and stakeholders and would not wish to abandon these features. But, above all, affirmative action no longer makes sense now that there is a huge and growing African electoral preponderance in the polity. Provided that the education system is reformed, there would also be an increasingly educated African middle class. No one can be in any doubt that South Africa is, and will increasingly be, an African-dominated country. This enormous (and growing) African preponderance will make itself felt quite naturally in the labour market, with no need for legislation. But South Africa must treasure the fact that it has been Africa's most developed country. This means placing great value on keeping skilled South Africans of all races and encouraging the unfettered immigration of highly skilled folk from elsewhere.

The necessity of immigration control

At the same, however, South Africa needs to impose strict immigration controls (and border controls) over the inflow of unskilled labour. At present, almost no control exists and the result has been large inflows of illegal immigrants not only from all over Africa but even from Pakistan, India and China. Inevitably, given South Africa's high unemployment, this has caused great popular resentment and even xenophobic violence. This inflow has also produced a mushrooming population – it has doubled in 30 years – despite a local birth rate that is low by African standards.

The fact has to be faced that Africa is going through an unprecedented population explosion, adding a further billion people over the next generation, and that this will inevitably produce huge migratory flows towards Europe – and to the more developed south. And South Africa cannot cope with that. Already its population is pushing up against water scarcity and there is a huge housing shortage. South Africa is a dry country, even if its water resources are well managed. But its water resources have been lamentably managed, so a limit has been reached.

In March 2018 South Africa signed the African Continental Free Trade Agreement, which calls for the free movement of goods, capital and labour throughout the continent, a clear attempt to emulate the formula that has made the EU a success. No one can doubt that freer trade and investment across borders would be beneficial, but for South Africa any agreement to the free movement of labour would constitute an almost suicidal triumph of ideology over common sense.

There is no doubt that the liberalisation of the South African economy would produce much higher growth and a rising standard of living. But the danger is that this would then suck in ever larger migratory flows from elsewhere in the continent, which South Africa could simply not cope with. In any case, if one does nothing, immigration control will be forced in the end through the explosion of xenophobic violence. Far better to do it in time, formally and humanely.

Reducing corruption

It goes without saying that there would have to be a determined effort to throttle back corruption. The fact has to be faced that South Africa under ANC rule has become a criminal Mecca. On the one hand, it is easy to bribe police and officialdom – and for very little. On the other hand, the country has good communications to the rest of the world, a good banking system and all the fleshpots one may desire. It's an ideal combination. The Guptas seem typical of many criminals before them, but their novelty lay in the realisation that this was a country in which it was simple to buy the president and as many cabinet ministers as you like. It must be realised that simply getting rid of the Guptas will not stop the rot. Indeed, the lesson of history is that corruption of this kind is very difficult, if not impossible, to root out. All one can do is to raise the price for such behaviour.

This effort would need to begin with a cleansing and upgrading of the police and the judicial and prosecutorial system. Crucially, the metropoles should all be given greater autonomy to develop their economies, including the power to recruit their own police forces and to control local rail systems. There would have to be stiff and exemplary sentences for those found guilty of corruption and the sequestration of whatever they had stolen.

There would also need to be quasi-military measures taken against

167

urban gangs. There is no point in being squeamish about this. The gangs have been in place for many decades and will doubtless fight back with all they have. The situation could develop into a war of extermination, one that the state had to win – rather like the FBI drives against Al Capone and other gangsters in the America of the 1930s. A similarly tough line needs to be taken to stop political assassinations. Indeed, there is something to be said for shock measures. No one wants to emulate Jerry Rawlings, but he is still held up as the only politician who was really serious about fighting corruption in Ghana. When he came to power he began by executing three former presidents and then whenever he found corrupt ministers or generals he would simply march them down to the beach for public execution. He termed this 'house-cleaning'. While this is hardly a method one can recommend, any casual visitor to Accra will note that Rawlings (now retired) is still held in great popular esteem. This is an index of just how desperately the poor – the little people, if you like – want law, order and security. In South Africa, if the current laxness were to continue it would mean that crime reaches such a point that vigilantism and lynchings become the norm, and law and order disappears.

The conundrum of local government

Local government would need to be reorganised. It would have to be recognised that in large areas of South Africa local government has failed: the councils in these areas are chronically bankrupt, irremediably corrupt and simply lack either a sufficient rating base or enough honest, competent and qualified personnel to make them work. In effect, the only barrier to runaway corruption has been the reports of the auditor-general, bringing to light every year just how much unauthorised, irregular or wasteful spending there is. By 2018 this had resulted – rationally enough – in growing physical threats to auditors attempting to do their jobs. Kimi Makwetu, the auditor-general, reported that he and his staff had for years tried to 'advise' local authorities on how to avoid being cited for irregular expenditure – but found that it made not the slightest difference. What the staff wanted was not advice but money. Ultimately auditors received death threats, had their laptops stolen, were taken hostage, and were even shot at.[7]

By 2018 only 13 per cent of municipalities were getting a clean audit – and not one municipality in the North West, Free State or Limpopo managed to achieve this.[8] The worst cases tended to be in poor small towns and rural areas, where typically councils were corrupt, incompetent and heavily in debt. This was, in fact, predictable from the start, and they were only endowed with elected councils in a fit of ideological rectitude.[9] Worse still, the local government boundaries were drawn up in a highly partisan fashion with little regard for practicality.[10] They need changing.

The bankrupt councils need to be replaced by a system of prefects appointed by the provincial government, with powers to appoint engineers, surveyors and so on, as required. The prefects could be assisted by (small) elected advisory councils. This would be a more viable and far cheaper system. Small towns would all be informed that should they be adjudged corrupt they would be placed under administration, and those individuals found guilty of corruption would be forbidden to play any further part in government at any level. At the same time, the system of national salary scales for municipal workers should be ended so that poorer communities would not be forced into bankruptcy by having to pay what rich ones can afford.

As Crispian Olver's *How to Steal a City* made clear, municipal corruption is endemic even in the metropoles; indeed, because they have larger budgets, the scope for corruption there is much greater. Here too one may have to consider putting hopeless cases under administration; it is clear from Olver's account that this should have happened in Nelson Mandela Bay (Port Elizabeth) long ago.[11]

Water, water

A determined effort should be made to stamp out corruption in the various water boards, which, in future, would be privatised and monitored by their provincial governments. With World Bank assistance, a programme would be launched to recycle water in all the major cities, to halt the pumping of raw sewage into the sea, rivers or lagoons, and to bring irrigation to more rural areas. It must be realised that the whole department of water and sanitation is rotten. In 2018 the new minister, Gugile Nkwinti, pointed out that under his predecessor, Nomvula Mokonyane, the whole department had effectively collapsed, was now in debt to the tune of R11.4 billion and was quite unable to discharge its responsibilities. Nkwinti pointed out that while this devastation had been going on – and doubtless most of the money was stolen – the department's internal audit committee had said not a word.[12] The entire department should be the subject of criminal proceedings. This is the awful lesson of what the public management of the water industry has led to in practice. The need to privatise the water industry could hardly be more eloquently stated.

However, far more than this is required. South Africa is a seriously water-stressed country, and the decision to include in the Constitution the right to 'sufficient food and water' – in other words, water as a human right – was irresponsible and hazardous in the extreme. The key to the future has to lie in realistic water pricing. However, once one re-looks at the country through that lens, one realises that many of its cities are in the wrong place. Johannesburg and Pretoria can only exist because they do not pay the economic price for water. If they did – and in the end they are bound to – then the only things there would be activities (like mines) that cannot be anywhere else. The logic would be the same as for Australia, which is also water-stressed. All Australia's main cities lie on the coast, and so should South Africa's. It would be best to plan for this immense task of relocation, which is inevitable in any case. If South Africans become reliant on desalinated water, the logic of such a move will become inescapable.

New farmers

A programme would begin of granting individual freehold property rights to residents of the former Bantustans. This could usefully begin in the Transkei, which has good rainfall and, with the right agricultural extension service, could see a large class of small farmers and market gardeners take root. This would cut unemployment, increase food supplies, make continued residence in the Transkei far more attractive, and slow the population flow to the cities, while the small farmers would be encouraged to set up cooperatives to sell their produce to the towns and cities. Such a programme could then be extended progressively to all the other ex-Bantustan areas. It is essential to rescue these areas from subsistence cultivation, which means growing desertification, soil erosion and, often, near-starvation.

Such a programme would necessarily mean cutting back the power of the chiefs to grant land. Their development into a parasitic rentier class should be halted. If they truly enjoy prestige as community leaders, their social status need not be threatened. If they don't, there is no argument for artificially bolstering their position.

The eastern seaboard

The eastern seaboard has to be recognised as a major natural asset, potentially South Africa's Costa Brava or Costa del Sol, producing a huge annual income. It needs to be made the subject of a separate development programme. The coast from the Mozambique border down to, say, Buffalo City (East London) offers year-round sun and swimming – and it is in the same time zone as Europe. Spain's coastal belt brings in 82 million tourists a year and provides 11 per cent of

Spain's GDP.[13] What is needed is a comprehensive programme to develop the eastern seaboard.

Currently, large parts of this coastline are devoted to traditional low-income settlement. Much of this needs to be relocated. Residents should be offered much better and more modern housing in a more inland location and promised first place in the queue for the large number of jobs that would result from tourist development. This would involve the construction, maintenance and servicing of large numbers of hotels, apartment blocks, game reserves, recreational facilities, restaurants and new airports to feed the resorts with cheap, direct flights from Europe. It would be essential that this development be sensitively planned on both environmental and architectural grounds, thus avoiding the hideous developmental and architectural errors one currently sees on the KwaZulu-Natal North and South coasts.

It should be recognised that South Africa is the world's number-one country in the preservation of African wildlife, and this unique selling point has to be capitalised on to a far greater degree. Naturally, this makes anti-poaching measures a top national priority. These could usefully begin with the construction of a secure border fence with Mozambique, where most of the poachers originate. The World Wildlife Fund reports that since 1970 mammal, reptile, bird and fish populations have fallen by 60 per cent worldwide.[14] This merely emphasises how precious South Africa's wildlife is – and that it is a fast-appreciating asset. The strongest possible conservation measures should be put in place immediately both for marine and land-based life.

Education, the engine of growth

It would be essential to effect a root-and-branch reform of the educational system. Perhaps the greatest of all the ANC's failures has been the steadily deteriorating state of education, a situation that betrays future generations and the country. The state would have to begin by ensuring that there is a basic provision of acceptable school buildings: no more children sitting under trees, no more pit latrines, a completely regular and reliable supply of schoolbooks. It is a disgrace that any of these things should still be lacking in 2019. However, wherever possible cheap private schools should be encouraged to set up in competition with state schools at every level.

There would, at an early stage, have to be a confrontation with the teachers' unions, especially Sadtu, and that battle would have to be won. It is a sad fact that sometimes progress cannot be achieved except by breaking a union determined to retain restrictive practices: one thinks of Rupert Murdoch's battle with the print unions or Margaret Thatcher's with Scargill's miners. The battle with Sadtu is of that ilk. There have to be regular school inspections, regular tests of teachers' competence and a regular weeding out of teachers who fail such tests or who do not spend adequate time in the classroom. The entire current corps of teachers would need to be tested and where necessary retrained or discarded, with a systematic and deliberate raising of standards first at primary and then at secondary and tertiary level. Exam standards need to be raised back to at least the levels they were before the ANC's repeated downgrading.

It would also be important to insist on higher standards of admission to tertiary institutions. At present, these are being flooded with many students who are quite incapable of coping with even a downgraded university education. The result is a huge and wasteful drop-out rate. But in addition all too many very poorly educated students end up with scrape-through degrees. Typically they then either become schoolteachers – thus keeping school standards low – or they get added to the already overstaffed public service, where they can only increase its dysfunctionality. There has to be a firm upward revision of entrance standards and, indeed, of degree standards. This upward revision of both entrance and exit levels would probably be met with student protests at first, but there is simply no other way.

In recent years the standard of South African universities has fallen. This is evident in the fact that most of their remaining research output derives from a relatively small number of senior (and even retired) faculty members, an extremely dangerous situation for it implies a systematic de-skilling of these institutions. It is essential that this process be halted and reversed, using the same testing and weeding-out procedures as will be used elsewhere in the education system. The assumption has to be one of steadily rising standards, as is the case in the developed world.

Transformation

Ever since 1994 the great objective of the ANC regime has been 'transformation'. This term is never defined. Principally it seems to mean what is elsewhere called Africanisation, but sometimes it seems to refer to the necessity for everyone (particularly whites) to adopt new attitudes. What is certain is that if one carries out the structural reforms above, one will be accused of damaging or even abandoning transformation.

This charge needs to be faced head on. The fact is that the transformation that the ANC has been seeking since 1994 is a chimera. It can hardly be otherwise in a society that is constantly de-skilling, where real per capita incomes have been falling for years on end, and unemployment and inequality have been steadily increasing. Moreover, unless radical structural reforms intervene, such trends are set to continue indefinitely. At the end of such a process everyone will have been 'transformed' into jobless paupers and illiterates. The fact that a small privileged elite skates on the top of such a society, delighting in its privileged 'transformation', should be of no satisfaction to anyone.

Much of this disaster derives from preferring redistribution to growth, and even more it is due to the shameful way in which the needs and appetites of the bureaucratic bourgeoisie and their BEE counterparts have been given priority over all other social groups. To be sure, South Africa will always need a civil service and it will need more black businessmen than ever, but there is no need to pamper these groups. The present result of doing so is the gradual immiseration of the whole society. The governing group likes to point to successful images of transformation – the wealthy black businessman, the black woman executive or minister – but such figures are more and more remote from the reality of nearly 10 million unemployed living in shacks.

A much truer form of transformation would be found by prioritising rapid economic growth over redistribution. An economy that grows at six per cent per annum doubles in size every 11 years. That produces real transformation with more and more jobs, and more and more prosperous businessmen and female role models. This is the sort of transformation the government should have been pursuing since 1994. Instead it has been backing the wrong horse in the wrong race – for purely ideological reasons. The only true transformation is that achieved through better education, increasing skills, higher investment, growth and fuller employment.

If such a course were followed, rapid growth would follow, with a rapid shrinkage in the numbers of the unemployed and thus a large reduction in inequality. This would be further enhanced by keeping tight controls over both the numbers and the salary levels of the (currently overpaid) public-service workers. As society moves towards fuller employment it would then begin to be possible to envisage schemes for universal health care, though this and much else besides would depend on whether South Africa could first halt and then reverse the continuous loss of skills that has been bleeding the country dry since 1994.

Completing the promise

To sum up, this sweeping liberalisation of society should be seen as the completion of the promise of 1990–1994. In those years it was finally agreed that there would be no more bannings of people or organisations, no more house arrests, no more one-way exit visas, and no more political censorship. Moreover, everyone would have the vote, would have the right to live by whatever sexual orientation they chose, and would be free to marry or associate with whoever they wished. There would be no racial segregation in any sphere of life and all individuals would have equal rights.

In fact, as we have seen, no sooner had these changes been made than the ANC began to construct its own version of apartheid. In effect, job reservation was reintroduced in a new form and race was once again made the basis of economic life, of procurement, of appointments and promotions. Anti-white, anti-Indian and sometimes anti-coloured racism in public life proliferated and went unpunished. Sure enough, there has been anti-black racism as well but this has been immediately (and rightly) stamped upon. Even so, South Africans have achieved a lot in terms of political equality and in making racial and social equality the norm. What is needed now is prosperity, much more of it and more widely spread.

All that needs to happen is for the process of liberalisation to begin and to be carried through. This is the obvious manifesto for any liberal party, but it should be realised that what any party that adopts such a manifesto is doing is to take the side of the vast mass of ordinary black people against the absurdly pampered and overprivileged black elite. In other words, any party that truly has the interests of the working class at heart would adopt a programme like this, which prioritises growth and employment. So this could quite equally be the programme for a workers' party.

Thus, while such a programme might seem most appropriate for the DA (which currently has a far more muddled and muddy programme), it would be equally appropriate for Ramaphosa and the ANC. If they really mean what they say about wanting the best for 'our people', of wanting growth and jobs, here is the way to achieve those things.

While this is an altogether happier vision of the future than many currently have for South Africa, it is not an easy one. Shock therapy was tough in Eastern Europe for some years, though almost everywhere it has succeeded in producing more prosperous and dynamic societies. What it has going for it is that the whole force of the international political economy is pushing South Africa in that direction. In a sense, the IMF is merely the institutional expression of that economy. Undoubtedly, if South Africa turns to the IMF for a bail-out it will push the country towards a more liberal settlement, one more at ease with a globalised world. But even if such a bail-out were avoided, the pressure of the system would, more diffusely, still be felt in the same direction.

Sometimes programmes for structural reform/adjustment in the Third World have been strikingly successful; in other cases not at all. What explains the difference is simply the degree to which the host government welcomes the changes and does its best to back them. If (as in Zimbabwe) the local government hates the changes and does its best to sabotage them, the programme is bound to fail. So the best results are achieved when the government embarks on the reforms wholeheartedly.

The programme mapped out above is a best-case scenario. But any government that claims to prioritise growth and is truly determined to reduce unemployment should be judged against that. It would be idle to deny that there are major political obstacles that stand in the way of Ramaphosa's taking such a course, assuming he wanted to. But are those obstacles really insuperable? What would need to happen to make this vision real?

Chapter Twelve

The path ahead

If Cyril Ramaphosa is to escape from the very difficult situation that he has inherited, he needs several things, starting with a proper plan. One thing he has to realise is that although South Africa is in a great mess, it still has enormous potential. He should never believe anyone who tells him that the damage is too great, that things can't be turned round. This is never true of societies. Think of Germany in 1945: rubble everywhere, huge human losses, the country in deep disgrace, the polecat of the world, no production of anything – and divided into occupation zones. A hopeless situation? Don't just think of Germany today: even by the late 1950s the West German economy had overtaken the British. Or take Rwanda after the 1994 genocide. A small country with 800 000 dead, including most of the better educated. Unbelievable ethnic tension. Few resources of any kind. Today? Probably the most effective and productive little country in Africa. South Africa may be in a mess, but it is nothing compared to the dire situations faced by those societies. The greater danger is the exact opposite, that Ramaphosa will be soothed by assurances that all that is required is glad talk, a bit more confidence, an easy return to business as usual. It's a complete mirage.

The state of planlessness

Planning has never been the ANC's strong point. Despite its proclaimed goals and the firm belief of some, the party as a whole never expected to come to power: 1990 was a happy surprise. The changeover four years later found the party still with no real plan as to how to govern South Africa. The heritage of the struggle was merely a set of slogans and rallying cries. The SACP had bequeathed the party a set of socialist goals and Mandela came out of jail preaching this rhetoric, but sweeping nationalisation was hurriedly ruled out soon after 1994.

What remained was a general belief in a two-stage revolution, the first being a national capitalist period with some socialist reforms but the main structure of the economy left untouched, followed by a full-scale transition to socialism. This set of ideas was handily summarised as the NDR, though that was also vague. This is not surprising – it had been drawn up in Moscow as a general prescription for developing countries in general – and it was detached from the realities of the country. It included no precise programme of what exactly was to be done or by when. Moreover, belief in the NDR's socialism coexisted quite happily with the incompatible fact that nationalisation had been ruled out – or at least deferred to a later stage.

This vagueness over policy reflects the fact that the ANC is, above all, a communitarian party. None of its programmes has involved planning. Indeed, none of them has been a proper programme. The Freedom Charter[1] was simply a wish list about what a future South Africa might look like. Most of its goals were sweeping, naive and sometimes impossible:

'The people shall govern!' *(But through what means?)*

'All shall have the right to occupy land wherever they choose.' *(And what if their choices conflict? Can squatters be allowed to occupy productive farms?)*

179

'There shall be work and security!' *(How is this to be achieved?)*

'All people shall have the right to live where they choose.' *(Again, so what if their choices conflict?)*

'The doors of learning and culture shall be opened!' *(How will this be paid for?)*

'No one shall go hungry.' *(Who will produce the food?)*

Clearly, there was no guide for governance there. Something of the same was true of South Africa's 1996 Constitution. In general it was drawn up so as to suit an advanced liberal society, not the rough-and-tumble reality of modern South Africa. It included provision for second- and even third-generation rights that had absolutely no chance of being realised. Nonsensically, it guaranteed equality for 11 different official languages. It was interpreted to guarantee the abolition of the death penalty, abortion on demand and gay rights, all of which were opposed by large popular majorities. Again, it reads mainly as a wish list, its main wish being that South Africa could become Sweden.

In power, the ANC government launched the RDP, a large unbudgeted wish list. Although this 'plan' went through many iterations before being presented, it failed every requirement of a proper plan. No attempt was made to gauge the affordability of its projects or how they would fit into the government's economic policy as a whole. Most RDP projects lacked timelines. And there was no allowance made for the fact that the RDP cut across the remit of almost every ministry. Mainly what it suggested was that the ANC had little idea of how to plan or implement policy. The predictable result was an uncontrollable spending splurge and a budget deficit of over eight per cent of GDP. Inevitably, the programme was short-lived.[2]

It became obvious that the ANC government had no economic policy, so the business community (somewhat naively) devised one for it. Thabo Mbeki saw this as his terrain and was furious at their presumption.[3] The result was Gear, introduced in 1996 – the only proper plan ever produced by the ANC. Gear envisaged a five-year period in which inflation would be reduced, debt lowered, and public spending cut so as to bring the budget into balance, privatise the SOEs and liberalise capital flows. By no mean all these goals were met, but nonetheless the plan succeeded in steering South Africa away from an IMF bail-out.

Gear was hugely unpopular with Cosatu, the SACP and the ANC left. No doubt this was the reason why Mbeki tended to let Mandela and Trevor Manuel, the finance minister, defend it in public – though no one doubted that it was Mbeki's work. In addition, Mbeki sought to justify it using Marxist language in his bulletins on the ANC website, *ANC Today*. This was simply an effort to muddy the waters. It was also a crucial failure of leadership: Mbeki really needed to go out front and explain on TV exactly why Gear was necessary. As it was, the unpopularity of Gear dissuaded any of his successors from embarking on any similar plan.

Instead, the ANC reverted to its habit of wish lists of every kind. There were industry charters setting out racial targets for each sector in terms of shareholdings, employment and procurement, and there were endless codes of conduct. These were taken seriously by the business world, which actually did most of the government's work for it, enforcing affirmative action, BEE shareholding and procurement from black suppliers. The black elite in business often cheerfully ignored such rules and even the laws governing such matters. Most striking of all there was the NDP, another huge, uncosted wish list unveiled in 2012. When it was debated in Parliament, the Cope leader, Mosiuoa Lekota, asked who exactly would be responsible for the plan's implementation.[4] There was hearty laughter on all sides, the ANC included, for everyone knew from the first that the NDP was not to be taken seriously. It wasn't.

Why this aversion to proper plans? The reason lies in the original vacuity of the ANC as a populist alliance of the whole African community. Once the black elite was in power, the movement's fundamental goal had been achieved. The elite wants power not in order to use it to achieve various policy goals but simply in order to possess it, to be in charge, to get rich and enjoy the perquisites of office. This is the only way to make sense of the way the ANC actually behaves.

Thus, for example, the ANC claims to be passionate about land reform, but after a quarter of a century in office it has repeatedly failed to make adequate financial provision for it, many farms have corruptly ended up in the wrong hands, and most redistributed farms have gone out of production.[5] The evidence suggests that the ANC is not serious about land reform but regards it as merely an issue that can be wheeled out to mobilise support.

The ANC approach to the greatest problem – mass unemployment – has been the same. While the party deplores the phenomenon and repeatedly makes promises of large-scale job creation, in practice it does nothing and has watched unemployment triple on its watch. Trevor Manuel recounts how he met with a foreign prime minister who showed great interest in his ideas but then asked him what the greatest problem was that South Africa faced. Manuel said mass unemployment. But why then, he was asked, do none of your plans or ideas address that problem?[6] The same question could have been posed to all his successors.

Once, the ANC allowed the SACP to make its policies for it, but latterly it has let the EFF take over this role. The ANC itself is torn between its various factions, who fight wars of position and manoeuvre in which the stakes are patronage, power, rents and jobs: policies are unimportant. The party sways this way and that, trying to accommodate each transient priority in turn. Similarly, it has moved seamlessly from Mandela worship to supporting Mbeki in his Aids denialism and then to defending Zuma over Nkandla. There is simply no fixed point, no set of principles here.

A man with no plan

In line with this tradition, President Ramaphosa has elected to fly by the seat of his pants. He supports EWC and NHI, free higher education and a programme to create black industrialists – although none of these policies is costed, there is no attempt to fit them together into a budget, and no attempt is made to estimate their impact. This is policy-making for the blind.

Moreover, the government has no broader economic strategy. Ramaphosa makes occasional reference to the NDP, perhaps partly because he helped draw it up, but this is not really a plan at all. Costing aside, all its targets – which were extremely wishful in the first place – have since receded into impossibility. Thus, in a very real sense, neither Ramaphosa nor the country knows where he or it is going. Everything is done on a day-to-day basis, and not only is there no plan but also no thought of acquiring one.

The result is mere blundering, very much in the pattern established under Zuma. Take, for example, the commitment made at the jobs summit in October 2018 that there would be no retrenchments at all anywhere in the public sector. Did anyone cost that commitment, with its dire implications for the many loss-making SOEs? If this results in a major SOE going bankrupt, then cross-default clauses in their loan agreements will mean that all the other SOEs follow, like so many dominoes.[7] To prevent that, the government would need to step in with a bail-out – with the already-mentioned result of a final ratings downgrade by Moody's, and the dumping into the market of R100 billion of the government's bonds. All these results are foreseeable and can be costed. But, of course, this work was not done, meaning that rational decisions could not be taken. The result, inevitably, was that barely was the jobs summit over than the finance minister, Tito Mboweni, was making it clear that there was no money either to pay for public-service salary increases or to keep bailing out SOEs[8] – which, in both cases quite clearly, foreshadowed job losses in the public sector. Ramaphosa's promise had lasted barely a week.

Ramaphosa's lack of planning is not an accident. His office contains just a single economic adviser, Trudi Makhaya. With all due respect to Ms Makhaya, a personable and intelligent woman, she is far from being the country's top economist and in any case there is only one of her. And while there is more expertise in the National Treasury and the Reserve Bank, economic planning is outside their remit and they are hard-pressed as it is. The nearest thing to economic planning carried out by anyone in government is done by the minister of trade and industry, Rob Davies, and the minister of economic development, Ebrahim Patel. Both men are communists and it shows. Davies seems mainly concerned to disconnect South Africa from the rest of the world economy, presumably so that it can build 'socialism in one country'. Patel is a trade union activist with no formal economics training. His ministry, which was responsible for producing the vacuous NDP, was only created by President Zuma as part of the continuous game of musical chairs he played with his cabinet. The ministry should be scrapped.

Clearly, a proper economic-planning unit needs to be created with, say, 20 good economists and a support staff of perhaps a hundred, and preferably this should be situated within the presidential office. Its job would be one of continuous evaluation of proposed and actual government programmes, the setting of realistic targets in the various policy areas and the devising of strategies in order to reach them. This is just a matter of entering the 20th century, not the 21st. There has to be an end to situations like that of Ramaphosa's embracing NHI without knowing how many hundreds of billions it will cost or how that enormous expense will be funded – and what the knock-on effects of it will be. After all, as Ramaphosa knows full well, no one in the corporate world would accept anything 'planned' like that.

However, this is hardly enough. For Ramaphosa, the ANC and the country to escape from the present situation, several other factors need to come together.

An assertion of presidential power

Ramaphosa faces an almost desperate situation. There is huge social discontent, negative growth and nearly 10 million unemployed. The country is slipping towards the bottom of all the ratings – educational, competitiveness, crime, in how it treats key industries such as mining, and so on. The ANC secretary-general, Ace Magashule, openly denounces government policies.[9] He and the Zuma faction continue with their own brand of populist economics with which they masked their looting in the past. But even apart from that major split, ministers casually contradict each other over major economic questions from day to day. Many ministers have much to fear from the inquiry into state capture chaired by Deputy Chief Justice Raymond Zondo. Meanwhile, Ramaphosa has no control over Luthuli House, the ANC's headquarters office, and also is at the mercy of shifting majorities at the party's NEC meetings.

This is a picture of a political movement that is morally and politically exhausted. Moreover, when South Africa's traditional chiefs came forward to found the ANC in 1912 they did so out of a wish to end acute division and tribalism and in order to take a common stand. Until 1994 the party was held together by the unifying force of the liberation struggle. With that over, its continuing unity is an open question.

If Ramaphosa continues to act within the confines of the ANC he will get caught up in its endless factional warfare. If he is not to fail, he needs to escape from these constraints. The ANC wishes to govern itself – through its NEC, through Luthuli House, through its top six. Cosatu and the SACP also continuously demand a place at the top table. But none of these bodies has any remit under the Constitution, the ANC machine is now run by a notorious Gupta-ite, and both Cosatu and the SACP are mere shells of what they once were. Ramaphosa needs to rise above all these groups and factions, relying on the fact that the Constitution has given the presidency wide powers and that his oath of office compels him to put the national interest ahead of all such factional considerations.

This is to say that Ramaphosa needs to make a major assertion of presidential power. The size of his winning majority at the Nasrec conference is no longer important: he has the authority and legitimacy of office and he can also rely on a far greater popularity in the country than his predecessor or any of his opponents. His Nasrec majority was narrow only because of Zuma's manipulation. That factor is far weaker now. And, as president, Ramaphosa has the power to appoint and sack cabinet ministers, as well as far-reaching powers of patronage throughout the state. Setting up an economic planning unit within the presidency would thus be part of a strategy to make the South African presidency more like the French or American presidency – the key initiator of policy, the leader of opinion and the real driving force behind the government's legislative programme.

Escape from populism

It is vital that Ramaphosa understand his own situation. He stands at a crossroads where there are only three options. He can approach the IMF for a bail-out, either now or, presumably, soon after the 2019 election *or* he can opt instead for his own programme of economic reform – his own version of Gear – aimed at heading off recourse to the IMF, *or* he can do neither of those things, in which case he is bound to stay trapped within a populist downward spiral – and his presidency is doomed. And since his presidency represents the last chance to save the dream of a successful and democratic rainbow nation, that would be lost too.

In fact, a moment's consideration suggests that those three options collapse into two, for option two can surely be ruled out. In order to rescue the current economic situation, far greater austerity would be required than Gear demanded in 1996 – and even so Gear was so unpopular that it undermined Mbeki's presidency. So it would be sheer folly for Ramaphosa to attempt such a programme on his own. Far better to approach the IMF, secure a large loan that cushions the transition and then be able to blame the IMF for the unpopular measures that would need to accompany it.

It is apparent that Ramaphosa cannot hope to muster the support of the diverse coalition that is the ANC either to carry out the needed reforms or to approach the IMF for a loan. But nor can he afford to remain at the mercy of an ANC that is continually hijacked by Julius Malema's economic populism.

Malema has been extraordinarily successful so far in controlling the ANC's agenda; indeed, he openly boasts that he is effectively leading the organisation.[10] He owes this success to three factors. First, Malema more or less grew up in the ANC and observed all its twists and turns. He is extremely shrewd and understands the ANC and its dynamics better than most. Second, the obvious failure of so many ANC policies has left the movement adrift and uncertain, an easy target for an operator like Malema who knows exactly what he wants and is ruthless in its pursuit.

The third reason for Malema's success is that the ANC is habitually enslaved to the fear of the 'sell-out'. Throughout the struggle, the worst thing that could be alleged against any fellow-struggler was that he or she had 'sold out', perhaps even becoming an *impimpi* (informer) or a witness for the state prosecutors. But 'selling out' also just meant failing to stand by one's revolutionary commitments, adopting any position that could be termed reformist.

In a movement that was naturally quite paranoid about police spies and informers, these fears were manipulated to telling effect by the SACP, for the communists set the standard for what was revolutionary and they alone had a coherent ideology in which revolution not only played a central part but also had a definable shape and form. Indeed, this threat that one might be accused of 'selling out' was a potent means by which the SACP exercised hegemony over the ANC in exile.[11]

This was powerfully backed up by physical threat. Any ANC cadre in exile who was accused of selling out or, worse, of being an informer could expect no mercy. They would be excluded in disgrace from the movement, cut off from all sources of patronage, imprisoned, tortured and perhaps killed. In the 1980s, in the townships, any accusation that one was a sell-out or an *impimpi* might soon lead to assassination or 'necklacing'.

This dreadful history has left a deep mark on the ANC and has been sufficient to make ANC members extremely nervous at the thought of being denounced from the left. Malema, knowing this, has been shrewd enough to launch populist demands with some real popular appeal. Repeatedly, this has been enough to stampede ANC activists and MPs towards his agenda.

If Ramaphosa is to escape from the tight corner that he is in, he has to stand up against all these pressures and populist demands and chart his own course. But how to do that? An initial part of the answer has to be to strengthen the police and army. For it is quite certain that as the necessary – and painful – steps are taken to turn the ship around, populist forces of one sort or another will attempt to veto these steps by the use of main force. This cannot be allowed. However, Ramaphosa also needs to exert his symbolic authority.

Ramaphosa and the Mandela myth

Ramaphosa's key advantage is that he is popular far beyond the bounds of the ANC. This was evident in the eNCA pre-Nasrec survey of October 2017. At that stage, opinion was less than fully formed but the relevant figures were as follows:[12]

Table 1: Choice of president by race (%)

	Africans	Coloureds	Indians	Whites
Ramaphosa	44.2	38.5	28.6	31.6
Other six candidates	36.0	9.6	12.3	11.5
Don't know/won't say	19.8	43.3	48.3	52.6
None of the above	0	8.6	10.8	4.3

Moreover, something similar was apparent among the different African language groups:

Table 2: Support for Ramaphosa and Dlamini-Zuma by African language

African language group	Ramaphosa	Dlamini-Zuma
isiZulu	32.8	37.5
isiXhosa	47.6	21.9
Sepedi	68.9	9.3
Setswana	44.6	9.1
Sesotho	53.4	18.4
Minority language groups	63.8	8.5

As may be seen from Table 1, Ramaphosa not only had several times as much support among the three racial minorities as the other six candidates put together, but large numbers of voters were also, at that stage, undecided or refused a choice, generally indicating indifference or caution. That is to say, opinion for Ramaphosa among the minorities may well have continued to crystallise in the way that we know African opinion overall did, with well over 60 per cent favouring Ramaphosa by mid-November. Even without making that assumption, given South Africa's racially polarised political system, these are impressive numbers.

Similarly, Ramaphosa's support among the various African language groups was everywhere substantial and widely spread (see Table 2). Only among isiZulu-speakers did his opponent lead, and even then not by much. Dlamini-Zuma was essentially a Zulu candidate, Ramaphosa a national one.

Why does Ramaphosa enjoy such broad popularity? In large measure, of course, voting for him was an expression of revulsion of Zuma. But Ramaphosa is also part of the foundation myth of the New South Africa. He held the microphone for Mandela to speak when Mandela came out of jail; he was the ANC's secretary-general in that heroic period; and he helped to negotiate the Constitution. Ramaphosa thus has a strong connection, which other politicians lack, to the golden era of the rainbow nation, Mandela's South Africa.

What this means is that Ramaphosa is uniquely well positioned to draw upon the Mandela myth in support of his mission to 'save the dream'. As we have seen, most ANC voters – and probably most voters in general – wish above all to return to the happy period of Mandela, of optimism, growth and reconciliation. That was when the dream seemed to be working.

The Mandela myth

It is important to understand the power of the Mandela myth. In his own person Mandela incorporated the notion of a party of all Africans and a nation of all colours and races. He also symbolised the great virtues of the historic ANC: he was dedicated, committed, self-sacrificing and ready to risk death in order to stand up for the rights of Africans. Then he kept the faith in jail through several decades and refused all efforts to make him compromise his cause. On top of that he re-emerged as a lovable figure preaching tolerance and reconciliation.

This gave Mandela a unique moral authority. When the Mirage jets of the South African Air Force saluted him at his inauguration on 10 May 1994, it seemed that that authority was acknowledged even by the most advanced elements of white power. At the same time it was also accepted by the whole ANC coalition, from conservative chiefs to the SACP. In 1995, when South Africa won the Rugby World Cup, with Mandela appearing in a No 6 rugby jersey to congratulate the Springbok captain, Francois Pienaar, there was pandemonium, with burly white Afrikaners almost crying, shouting, 'My president, that's my president!' It was a moment of complete national unity, something that South Africa had never experienced before.

As the years went by, various radical elements worked to construct an anti-Mandela myth, according to which the chance of a socialist revolution had been lost in the early 1990s because Mandela had opted instead for a deal with white corporate power. This had led to a secret agreement whereby political power would change hands but white capitalism would continue to hold sway. It had been a sell-out and all the later corruption and difficulties were the result of that.[13]

This new myth was useful to some communists and many more populists, who used it to explain why the revolution they had worked for all their lives had been such a thunderous disappointment. And, of course, to suggest that a proper revolution was still possible. The myth has been equally useful to the EFF, but more generally it penetrated to a younger generation that was seeking to understand why 25 years of ANC rule had been such a failure.

Part of the problem was that the ANC had massively over-promised, so that popular expectations had been raised to an absurd level. The general impression had been given that after 1994 blacks would enjoy exactly the same lifestyle as the majority of whites. In a legal sense blacks were equal before the law, with all apartheid legislation repealed, and everyone had the vote. But that still left a huge gap. As young, uneducated and jobless blacks looked at whites who had jobs, houses, cars and much else besides, they would angrily ask whether anything had really changed.

Quite apart from the way this critique ignored the role of social capital in creating such differences, this tendency to see 'white privilege' as the counterpoint to 'black poverty' (as even the DA leader, Mmusi Maimane was wont to do[14]) was to miss the fact that it was the speedy rise of the bloated bureaucratic elite that had really increased inequality. Punitive taxation of the whites, together with sky-high salaries for public-sector workers, meant that inequality was less and less a race issue.

But such a critique could not really dent the Mandela myth. The world had been waiting for a black hero it could justly celebrate and Mandela fitted the bill so perfectly that the Mandela myth, almost the cult of Mandela, became an immense international phenomenon. Celebrities worldwide queued up to meet the man, and long after he was dead visitors to South Africa continually invoked and celebrated the Mandela name as if the country was always reliving 1994. For that is what a myth does – it goes on, it is always there, it didn't die with Mandela.

As the ANC declined in public esteem, from 'holding the moral high ground' in 1994 to an organisation mainly associated with corruption and thuggery, the Mandela myth became ever more precious to it, its main claim to represent something more than greed and graft. Accordingly, the party was mightily nervous when Mandela entered his final bout of illness in 2013, for this meant that the party was about to lose its last great remaining asset. The hospital where he was being treated was firmly bracketed off and the ANC took complete control of the situation, keeping a tight gag on information coming out and deciding who could see him and when.[15] The party desperately didn't want Mandela to die, but if die he must, the party would take charge of the matter.

It gradually emerged that Mandela was in a coma, being kept alive on a life-support system, with the party, not the family, having the power of decision over when the life-support system would be switched off. In the end the order to switch off the system came on 5 December. That is to say, Mandela's death was timed by the ANC so that, after a period of lying in state, his funeral could take place the day before the great symbolic day of 16 December – the anniversary of the battle of Blood River and the day on which Mandela, as leader of MK, had launched the armed struggle. Now it was the Day of Reconciliation, an even more fitting day for the funeral of the Great Reconciler. This strange death, seemingly timed – in classic Soviet style – to suit the public-relations requirements of a political party, was made stranger still by a eulogy that insulted several of the major international guests who attended. But it helped the Mandela myth go on, more powerfully than ever.

The ANC realises that the Mandela myth is now its chief possession. This is surely why the theft/abuse of money voted for his funeral remains such a sensitive issue, even in a party used to a culture of looting and impunity. Even several years later the Eastern Cape ANC was still trying to have those guilty sacked and criminally charged,[16] though, of course, without result.

What to do

So, in terms of this analysis, what should Ramaphosa actually do? The first thing is that he would be wise to pay the greatest care and attention to the selection of candidates for the ANC electoral lists in 2019. The Zuma faction will undoubtedly attempt to ensure that its people remain in place, and Zuma is a much more skilful player of such games than Ramaphosa. In the election campaign itself, Ramaphosa needs to avoid making large commitments other than to clean government. Then, assuming he is able to win a majority in 2019, soon after the election he will need to level with the electorate, preferably on prime-time TV. It would be a moment of great drama and it is important that it not be wasted. It would be the most important speech of Ramaphosa's life.

What Ramaphosa needs to do is to make the equivalent of Churchill's 'blood, toil, tears and sweat' speech of May 1940, saying that only now, after 18 months in office, does he fully understand just what an appalling situation he has inherited. He will need to restate the promise of the Mandela era as eloquently as possible and say that he and those like him are not prepared to surrender that dream, but that to get out of the present situation the country will need to make substantial sacrifices. It would be best if he were quite blunt and said that the attempt to create an NDR has been followed for quarter of a century and, quite obviously, has failed completely. The NDR has to be discarded quite publicly and explicitly. The double-speak of the Mbeki period has to be avoided at all costs.

With the NDR discarded, the country must go all-out for economic growth and creating jobs. Ramaphosa could then announce that he has decided to approach the IMF for a major loan to help turn the country around, the results of that consultation to be placed before Parliament. He would have to acknowledge that this is a major turning point but that he can see no alternative and he is determined to see changes made. He would appeal for support but make it clear that if support is not forthcoming he would step down rather than reverse himself. This would be both essential and only logical, for in effect he would be putting his whole presidency on the line in making such a speech, so he might as well acknowledge that fact.

The whole point of such a speech would be to be as plain and blunt as possible, so that no one is left in any doubt both as to the seriousness of the situation and of Ramaphosa's determination to overcome it.

But he will then need to lift people's spirits; Churchill did it by talking of a war-ravaged world coming through its travails into 'broad, sunlit uplands'. Ramaphosa would need to do the same, this time evoking the country's yearning to rediscover the Mandela spirit, accepting that a false start has been made but reassuring everyone that all is not lost, that a fresh and more productive beginning is possible.

The EFF, the SACP and Cosatu would be affronted by such a speech, but could they really hope to dislodge a man who had just won a fresh electoral majority? In any case, it should be made plain that the choice lies between supporting Ramaphosa or a return to the chaotic netherworld of Jacob Zuma. No one wants that.

The De Gaulle model

It will be seen that this follows the example of French president Charles de Gaulle. When he took power in 1958, in a similarly critical situation, De Gaulle repeatedly put major policy changes to referenda, declaring that if he lost he would resign. This helped him force through deeply unpopular changes, recognising the Algerian rebels, beginning negotiations with them and finally bringing the Algerian war to an end by granting independence to Algeria. Only when this had been done did the electorate fully accept that the changes had been necessary and beneficial. The years that followed saw headlong economic growth. However, De Gaulle realised that if the presidency was to be the driving force for political change in France it was essential that the president had unchallengeable popular legitimacy – and this could only come with direct election for the president. This required a major constitutional change, again rammed through by referendum.[17]

If Ramaphosa were to adopt the path suggested here, the political logic would be the same. He too might wish to use referenda, thus undercutting opposition from parties and factions – and logically he too might opt for direct presidential election.

195

The voters are already beginning to anticipate such a change. In the eNCA survey of October 2017 we asked ANC members how they felt about the party's new presidential election system, with candidates openly competing against each other. Although 29.2 per cent still preferred the old one-candidate-for-one-post election method, 24.2 per cent preferred the new system and no less than 44.5 per cent wanted it made more open still, with either every ANC branch or just every ANC member voting for the president. It was striking that it was in the provinces that had endured the most tyrannical and corrupt ANC rule (North West, Free State, Mpumalanga) that one found the greatest support for a more open and democratic style of election.

Should Ramaphosa opt to cut the Gordian knot in such a manner he would almost certainly split the ANC and find himself supported by a coalition of the DA and a rump ANC. Thus would begin a new political adventure. There is no need for us to pursue that adventure further at the moment. Suffice it to say that if Ramaphosa found it in himself to take these bold political risks he could help refound the New South Africa on a more sustainable and democratic basis. Mandela's promise would be fulfilled – or at least sustained. Indeed, bringing the racial minorities back into government would emphasise the return to a spirit of racial reconciliation. It is true that to behave in this way would put Ramaphosa's popularity at risk. But it is essential that he acts soon while he is still popular. The alternative – waiting until events force him to do this anyway, which would mean acting when his popularity would have eroded – doesn't bear thinking about.

If Ramaphosa were to take this route it would be sensible to create the post of prime minister who would – again on French lines – be responsible for the day-to-day work of cabinet coordination. Ever since 1994 all sense of cabinet coordination has been lost and ministers have all tended to do their own thing. This has to cease, and the cabinet also has to be radically trimmed in size. Clement Attlee was only one of many former British prime ministers to suggest that the maximum viable size of a cabinet was not more than 18 but it is note-worthy that when crises really erupt – for example in wartime – an inner cabinet of, say, five ministers tends to take over. However, for such smaller groups to be viable there needs to be a highly efficient civil service working beneath them.

South Africa lacks an effective civil service and also has few competent cabinet ministers. The only way to remedy this situation is by allowing the private sector to do many of the things that the government now tries, but fails, to do, and by afforcing the upper ranks of the civil service and government by able people drawn from other walks of life. Again, this is what De Gaulle did, with notable success; and it is what American presidents have always done. This is the way in which such outstandingly successful figures as Ernest Bevin, George Marshall, Robert McNamara and Georges Pompidou came into government.

Finally, Ramaphosa needs to understand that his predecessors have steered South Africa into a very vulnerable situation internationally. To some extent, it should be realised, the country has been living in a fool's paradise since 2008, because the world financial crisis caused the Americans and Europeans to reduce interest rates almost to zero. This in turn made it wonderfully easy for emerging markets to sell their bonds and run up debt. That period is now ending and the result is that emerging markets are in a credit squeeze, with rising interest rates and falling currencies. This will create a very unforgiving climate.

At this point it is exceptionally unwise of South Africa's foreign policy-makers to have put South Africa onto the list of countries that consistently vote against the United States at the UN Security Council. The US Africa Growth and Opportunity Act (AGOA) still gives South Africa duty-free and quota-free access to the US market for a whole range of its goods. AGOA's terms state that the US is offering these benefits in return for their African partners' 'commitment to market liberalization'.[19] EWC is a direct threat to that, and this is no time for Pretoria to be provoking Washington. President Donald Trump could renounce AGOA at any time; he has scant regard for Africa anyway, and will take particular umbrage at Pretoria's outspoken hostility to Israel. Policy-makers need to remember that if AGOA is scrapped, so too is the South African motor industry, with a lot of collateral damage in many other industries.[20] Already Trump's tariffs on steel imports have hit the South African steel industry hard: by 2018, demand for steel output was at a ten-year low.[21]

Something rather similar is true of Rob Davies' scrapping of the investment protection treaties on which foreign investors relied. This created a disastrous impression in Europe, the source of most of South Africa's investment. At the very least Ramaphosa should consider sacking Davies, reinstating those treaties, silencing the anti-Israel clamour and reconfiguring the country's foreign policies so as to reflect South Africa's interests. In particular, foreign policy staff should concentrate their minds on the fact that in the period 2008–2018 South Africa lost 300 000 manufacturing jobs – nearly 15 per cent of the total. Moreover, 105 000 manufacturing jobs were lost in the second quarter of 2018 alone as deindustrialisation gathered pace.[22] Instead of indulging student-union politics about solidarity with Cuba and Venezuela, or keeping a tiny Islamist fringe happy by bashing Israel, they might consider their duty to their local working class.

It is time for charity to begin at home.

Chapter Thirteen

On the other hand ...

To break out of the gridlock that now exists, the ANC needs a leadership with a grim determination to force through structural reforms. In the previous two chapters I have attempted to sketch how Cyril Ramaphosa could 'embrace his century' and opt for that decisive change. But, of course, that might not happen. To date he has appeared as a politician trapped within the usual nationalist and leftist platitudes. A strong argument could be made that there is no prospect of an ANC leadership emerging that is willing to take such bold initiatives. Indeed, it is easy to conclude that Ramaphosa has neither the ability nor the character necessary to drive such a programme. And, as we have seen, the DA has also entered a period of weak and incompetent leadership, so nowhere in the political system does democratic leadership now exist capable of facing up to the country's daunting challenges. So what then?

Time for the IMF

Logically, this again pushes the initiative towards external actors (including international market forces, as well as international institutions like the IMF). Indeed, the time to request a bail-out from the IMF has already arrived, but the ANC has a huge reluctance to face this reality for ideological reasons (it means the end of the NDR) and the simpler fact that to go cap in hand to Washington is to admit very publicly that ANC rule has been a failure. On top of this, the party is well aware that such an initiative could well break its fragile unity into two or more pieces.

Accordingly – and very damagingly – the party is likely to opt to drag along the bottom for some while yet, allowing the situation to get worse, with unemployment risinng and with greater and greater social unrest. Probably, as I argued back in 2015, the government will seek help from Brics (Brazil, Russia, India, China, South Africa) – indeed, Ramaphosa has already referred to such a possibility – but, to repeat, that will not provide a solution.[1] South Africa might well require a loan of $50–60 billion, and this cannot come from the Brics New Development Bank. It could only come from China, and China has shown no appetite to make any open-ended loans. (The fact that Ramaphosa has been unwilling to disclose the terms of the Chinese loans to Eskom and Transnet is a major red light. It can only mean that he is nervous about what their public reception would be.[2]) In any case, there is no point in loans on their own; the key lies in the structural reforms that must accompany the loan.

So, rather than face up to that, one can imagine Ramaphosa temporising, coming up with more non-solutions, such as the jobs summit. He should be warned that such PR exercises quickly produce complete cynicism, as they fail to change the situation.

This stubborn unwillingness to change echoes the way in which the government's Afrikaner Nationalist predecessors behaved when faced with the crisis of apartheid. Even as late as 1985, PW Botha decided to frustrate all the international pressures for reform. Yet the result of that was that those pressures then helped to snuff out economic growth, which in turn triggered rising social discontent. So there was no escape. The Botha regime dragged along the bottom for a few more years, but this merely delayed the collapse. And that is what

Ramaphosa should note: refusing necessary changes simply ends in complete collapse.

It is important to realise that no foreign country, then or now, would seek to intervene simply in order to put a stop to such self-destructive stubbornness, any more than they did when Verwoerd began the nonsense of Bantustans, or when Zimbabwe and Venezuela pursued similarly destructive paths. In effect, the developed world simply waits for such situations to collapse under their own weight. This is what happened with apartheid in the end.

Dragging along the bottom

If the ANC pursues this course the result will be growing chaos throughout the country. Already by 2018 this was quite clear, with levels of community protest not seen since the 1980s[3] and a culture of impunity so that looters at every level went unpunished, thus threatening the integrity of the entire legal order. In such a situation the national government becomes steadily weaker. Already it lacks a serious army or police force with which to impose its will, and neither in the cabinet nor in the civil service is there a sufficient determination or competence to deal with its problems.

As we have seen, the Ramaphosa government has, from the word go, been pushed around mercilessly by Eskom workers, traditional chiefs, the EFF, the public-sector unions, the Zulu king and the various ANC factions. Its attempted solution to the problem of rising unemployment has been the jobs summit, a perfect illustration of the inadequacy of Ramaphosa's corporatist approach in dealing with the country's economic crisis.

For, as we have seen, the summit's main 'achievement' was the government guarantee of no public-sector job losses. That is to say, the major thing done for the unemployed was a guarantee of job security to the already employed. On top of this civil servants, who are already in the top ten per cent of the population by income, have just been given an inflation-plus wage settlement. Taken together, what a wage increase plus a promise of job security means in effect is to privilege the high levels of consumption of this bureaucratic elite. To regard that as somehow a contribution to helping the jobless merely shows how completely this government's perspectives are those of this privileged elite. Asked to help others, their first instinct is to help themselves ...

Furthermore, privileging the consumption of these 'haves' reduces the money available for capital expenditure on the nation's infrastructure and its distribution systems, which are decaying. The government says its priorities are increasing investment and helping the poor, but what it actually does is to shrink investment and help the better off. The kindest word for this is incoherent.

No easy way out

One may imagine that as Ramaphosa faces the option of going to the IMF he might feel that this would be an impossibly bold option, that he would choose instead an easier way out. That would be a major mistake, for if the government refuses to grasp the nettle by going to the IMF the prospect is for the ongoing dissolution of national governance. It is tempting to believe that the country might then split back into its old constituent elements (Natal, the Orange Free State, the Transvaal and the Cape) but nothing so neat and tidy is likely. The true socio-economic reality of today's South Africa is the dominance of four big metropoles (Johannesburg, Durban, Pretoria and Cape Town). These are the centres of economic activity. Their populations continue to increase fast. And, despite the depredations of municipal looters, they still all have working administrations.

Outside these big centres municipal government is in a general state of collapse. This is very much the standard African pattern: usually only the biggest cities – Harare, Windhoek, Nairobi – manage to retain working city councils. This is the world as envisaged by Frans Cronje, the chief executive of the SAIRR. He foresees a future in which middle-class life, white and black, continues within a few metropolitan bubbles, with the rest of the country ruled by traditional chiefs in the countryside and, in the rest of the urban world, by gangs or 'big man' bosses/warlords of one kind or another.[4]

In such a scenario, the major metropoles are the main functional area of the nation's life. So the question is really whether the polity could then reshape itself around the dominance of these city-states.

This would be extremely difficult, for two major reasons. First, it would require a wholesale transfer of functions and revenue-raising powers from the centre to the metropoles. The ANC would resist this, for they would see the loss of national control as the end of their project and, just as important, as a reduction in the power, status and perquisites of the current ruling elite. The Cape Town water crisis of 2017–2018 showed just how difficult such a situation would be. On the one hand, the national government completely failed in its duty to provide bulk water to the city, so that Cape Town faced the crisis on its own. But, at the same time, the city lacked both the legal powers and the revenue-raising ability to build its own water infrastructure so as to secure its future.

Second, any city that does manage to emancipate itself from the dead hand of the centre would doubtless experience a spurt of growth, but as soon as it showed any sign of success it would attract even greater flows of rural migrants to join the vast informal settlements on its fringes. It is noticeable that when one talks to enthusiasts for an independent Cape Republic this is the point of greatest difficulty for them to conceptualise. If such a republic was not to be swamped it would have to fence and protect its (enormous) borders and reinstitute controls on inward migration that would resemble those of the apartheid period.

The shrinking tax base

One of the results of South Africa's recession and, particularly, of the prospect of EWC has been a sharp fall in the housing market as many wealthy and foreign residents move offshore. Understandably, many Africans are unfazed by the news of wealthy whites leaving. But this is a very serious mistake, for a vital factor in all the government's calculations has to be the sheer narrowness of the tax base. Only 13 per cent of the population pay income tax, which provides government with 38 per cent of all its revenue. And the wealthiest one per cent of the population pays 61 per cent of all income tax.[5]

This means that the government is unusually dependent on a very small number of mainly white taxpayers: in the USA, for example, the same top one per cent accounts for only 37 per cent of all income tax. Another 18 per cent of all South Africa's tax receipts come from taxes on mainly white-owned companies, and this small group of wealthier whites also pays a high proportion of the other taxes (VAT, customs and excise, dividend withholding tax, etc). Much of the remaining tax revenue is contributed by the white, Indian and coloured middle classes – 80 per cent of all income tax is paid by just three per cent of the population.[6]

It is worth noting that the tax burden has been greatly increased under ANC rule; in all, taxes have increased 25 per cent since 1994, with South Africa now one of the world's most highly taxed countries. It has the sixth-highest ratio of tax revenue to GDP in the world – only the Scandinavian countries rank higher.[7] Yet the Scandinavian countries are some of the richest in the world, while South Africa is very far from that, and Scandinavians get exceptionally good health, social welfare and educational services for their money, while South Africans get the opposite.

In effect, all this heavy taxation in South Africa has a single purpose – the creation and maintenance of a large bureaucratic elite whose salary levels are 30 to 40 per cent above those for comparable jobs in the private sector.[8] Again, the whole fiscus and the whole array of incentives and disincentives throughout the economy have been distorted in order to subsidise the existence of this large, affluent and essentially dysfunctional group.

Thus, if one turns the figures round the other way, one finds that 36 per cent of all government revenue is spent on the public-service wage bill – a quite crazy figure. And another 17 per cent of the budget is spent on the social grants that essentially serve to keep the poorest from starving or rising in revolt.[9]

Putting these figures together, it is evident that the government depends for its very survival on a very small group of middle-class and rich – and still mainly white and Indian – taxpayers, together with the companies they staff and own. If that group were to be subtracted from the fiscus, the government would have to watch both the bureaucratic elite collapse and the poor majority go to the wall. No government could possibly survive such calamities. Yet, of course, it is precisely this small group of taxpayers who have the greatest potential mobility: they have the money (and often even the passports) that would make emigration simple. This is a huge and insufficiently recognised constraint upon government. And the process seems to have begun: between 2013 and 2017 the number of assessed taxpayers fell by 1.3 million.[10]

Put baldly, if Ramaphosa takes 'the easy way out' and elects to drag along the bottom rather than go to the IMF, the more likely it is that he will have to watch the country's tax base erode away as the most crucial taxpayers pick up sticks and leave. Moreover, past experience suggests this is mainly a one-way process: most of those who leave establish themselves in other countries and do not return. This makes this constraint even more important; once the government's tax base has been run down, causing the collapse of its key programmes and projects, it will be extremely difficult, perhaps even impossible, to reverse matters.

The Zimbabwean descent

When Zimbabwe gained its independence in 1980, Samora Machel of Mozambique warned Robert Mugabe, 'Whatever you do, Robert, do not lose your whites'.[11] This was the voice of experience – Mozambique had been crippled by the loss of its white population – yet Mugabe ignored this advice, to his country's huge cost. It is not clear that South Africa's black elite has fully understood that this warning applies even more to their own country.

Ramaphosa's government needs to reflect on Zimbabwe's experience for another reason. Like South Africa, Zimbabwe is ruled by a bureaucratic elite. As Zimbabwean whites fled after 2000, when Mugabe's farm seizures began, the tax base shrank along with the economy. Logically, this should have led the government to cut back its expenditure – the obvious way would have been to cut back its own size. But cutting back the public service was politically too difficult, so it wasn't done. The result was a growing budget deficit that could be met only by printing more money, which soon produced hyper-inflation and the collapse and withdrawal of the Zimbabwe dollar.

Seventeen years later, Zimbabwe is still stuck with this problem. In 2017 the budget deficit was a thunderous 16.6 per cent of the country's real GDP. This could not be financed by inflows of aid or investment because the land seizures made Zimbabwe a pariah state in those terms. The cost of government employment more than accounted for the size of the deficit; it was an extraordinary 21.6 per cent of GDP[12] (even South Africa's bloated public service costs 'only' 14 per cent of GDP). So, once again, to meet this yawning gap, the Harare government created its own funny money – this time, bond notes. The result was again economic crisis; with no one willing to accept the bond notes, all goods vanished from the shelves and there was no petrol in the pumps.

The most tragic thing about the Zimbabwean situation is that it is now very difficult to see how the country can recover. Its skilled and educated people, black and white, were absolutely crucial citizens, and chasing almost all of them away has not only done lasting damage to the tax base but has also essentially made it necessary for Zimbabwe to lower its levels of administration, health, employment and education – to take a large developmental step backwards, in other words. Moreover, commercial agriculture was the basis of the Zimbabwean economy, with its farmers greatly admired by the World Bank as perhaps the best on the African continent. Now that those farmers have gone it is difficult to see how the economy can be revived even to the levels of 1980. What radical African nationalism has done is to turn one of Africa's most prosperous countries into one of its poorest.

There is no need to labour the point, which is that if Ramaphosa wishes to avoid economic collapse he has to ensure that South Africa's skilled and educated citizens do not emigrate, which in turn means that he cannot afford either to seize their property or to allow South Africa to become mired in economic misery as a result of 'dragging along the bottom'. The need for structural reform is now extremely urgent. The ANC likes to boast of being a 'revolutionary' government, but in fact it has been too timid even to carry out necessary reforms, let alone throw into jail those who steal from the public purse. Instead it has constantly promised mere 'fiscal consolidation', though it has never delivered it. But failing to grasp the need for major structural reforms now would be ruinously expensive for the country's future.

No time like the present

Finally, if Ramaphosa decides to stick to present policies (ie, avoiding structural reform) where does this 'dragging along the bottom' leave him? He would like to believe that he can engineer an economic recovery on his own – hence his $100-billion investment target. Essentially, Ramaphosa hopes to do this simply by talking the economy up and getting business and labour round the table with government. This seems unlikely to work, not only because the situation is too serious to be solved merely by talking and conferences, but because the need for structural reforms is real and urgent.

As it is, the IMF forecasts South Africa's future growth at 0.8 per cent in 2018 and 1.4 per cent in 2019[13] – a very tepid and insufficient recovery, far below the expected growth rates of most of its African peers. As we have seen, domestic investors have been too burnt to bring their capital back home, so the investment strike goes on. And it is no good government claiming that at last there is 'policy certainty' – not if that certainty involves EWC or a 30 per cent BEE share of any mining investment.

Moreover, it is no good pretending that a continuation of present policies represents a stable equilibrium. It doesn't. Eskom is clearly out of control, particularly now that its vast workforce has been given unaffordable wage increases *and* a promise of no redundancies. To pay for those increases Eskom now plans to increase prices at 15 per cent per annum for the next three years – ten per cent more than inflation. What this translates into is a 58.5 per cent increase in the price of electricity in just three years. As we have seen, this would be ruinous for the economy and would cause many companies and homeowners to go off-grid, leading to a further drop in electricity consumption – and a further crisis for Eskom.

In other words, the strategy chosen to rescue Eskom is one that will inflict terrible damage on the rest of the economy without even solving Eskom's problems. And this damaging policy will be caused simply by a reluctance to impose wage discipline or the right-sizing of employment on 15 000–20 000 unnecessary 'workers' at Eskom.

To date, Ramaphosa has refused all possible solutions to the Eskom crisis because they all seemed too politically difficult. First Eskom's management tried to insist on a zero per cent pay increase for its staff. The government, in the form of Pravin Gordhan, stepped in to insist that an inflation-plus increase must be awarded, even though no one knew where the money would come from to pay for it. Eskom management then said they needed to get rid of one third of their staff. This was checkmated by Ramaphosa's vow to allow no public-sector redundancies. Then Eskom asked whether the government would take over R100 billion of its debt (now up to R420 billion). This too Ramaphosa refused for fear of what it might do to the government's credit rating. Finally, in the 2019 budget the government agreed to cover Eskom's interest charges for the next three years, a classic case of kicking the tin down the road. Neither this nor the splitting of Eskom into three units did anything to solve Eskom's basic problems. This is not so much governance as the refusal of governance, in effect an endless game of pass the parcel.

In the end, debts have to be faced. The problem is that huge black holes of debt have been created by decades of corruption, theft and mismanagement. Eskom is the largest example, but other such black holes exist throughout the public sector, in the other SOEs and in local government. Everywhere one finds quite BEE middlemen taking large cuts and pushing prices up. Moreover, public-sector workers at both local and national level have helped themselves to exorbitant wage increases − and then tried to pass the costs on to others. The results are quite extraordinary. Why, for example, are SAA's costs per seat-kilometre 53 per cent higher than the average of their international competitors?[14] Why does it cost several times as much to build a kilometre of motorway in South Africa as it does in the USA, despite higher American wages? Why are South African port charges and airport charges among the highest in the world? Why are South Africa's educational levels among the worst in the world despite one of the highest proportions of GDP spent on education? One could go on.

Not far behind Eskom lurks the problem of municipal debt. Only 33 out of South Africa's 257 municipalities got a clean audit in 2018, a situation that is, moreover, steadily deteriorating: in that year, the auditor-general reported, 16 municipalities had improved and 45 regressed.[15] No less than 78 per cent of municipalities had submitted financial statements that included 'material mis-statements' and were simply not credible enough to be used.[16] Many of these municipalities were in a dire state, effectively bankrupt. Collectively, they were owed R138 billion by government departments, businesses and private households.[17] Indeed, two-thirds of that debt was owed by private households, often as the result of long-standing failures to pay rates and charges for water, electricity, etc. In effect, Eskom and the water boards are prevented by government from cutting off supplies to those who do not pay, which effectively legitimises these non-payers. However, at the same time, as of March 2018, the municipalities owed R43 billion[18] – and many suppliers were bankrupted by the municipalities' long-standing failure to pay. Inevitably, there is pressure for central government to step in and take over many of these bad debts. And the problem is circular; part of Eskom's problem is that many municipalities do not pay for their electricity, so that debts of R17 billion were outstanding in late 2018.[19]

In large parts of rural and small-town South Africa, corruption and maladministration has already seen a collapse of infrastructure, with roads and water delivery the first things to suffer. This is not a simple problem of poverty; of the top four most indebted municipalities, two were major Free State towns with substantial rating bases, for wholesale municipal corruption was endemic under Ace Magashule's notoriously corrupt provincial administration.[20]

Government's attitude to these growing crises has been to ignore them in the hope that they will go away – thus inevitably making them worse. Ramaphosa has continued with this attitude. Moreover, the ANC manifesto drawn up for the 2019 elections studiously ignores all these problems. Instead, Ramaphosa, in his usual consensus-seeking style, allowed the whole panoply of ANC interest groups a free hand in drawing up the manifesto, a process that exactly imitated the disastrous way in which the British Labour leader, Michael Foot, allowed Labour's 1983 manifesto to be drawn up – producing, famously, 'the longest suicide note in history'.[21] In Ramaphosa's case, the result was a vast, 66-page wish-list that bore almost no relation to reality. One poignant example must do: the manifesto commits South Africa to establish a sovereign wealth fund, as if the state has surplus capital to invest rather than an endless series of unpayable debts.

Clearly, such an irresponsible failure to govern can only end in tears. So, as things stand, the main question is whether an IMF bail-out will be forced on the government as a result of slow economic strangulation or by a sudden collapse. There seems no way to avoid it, even if present policies are maintained.

In other words, what might now appear to Ramaphosa as the easy way out really isn't easy at all. In fact, it's harder than the admittedly bold escape route mapped out in previous chapters – and for no gain at all. The only difference is that if the government takes the bold route, it retains the initiative, whereas if it opts for the 'easy' route, it loses it and ends up going to the IMF anyway, clearly defeated.

A political solution

Politicians being what they are, one can predict that Ramaphosa will play for time, in the first instance just to get through the 2019 elections. What that means is that he will stake everything on the hope that he can achieve an autonomous economic recovery and shore up his support within the ANC. Probably what he hopes to do is simply to talk up the economy – what Larry Summers, the former US treasury secretary, once called 'the cheapest form of economic stimulus'. The hope is that the buoyant talk will inspire confidence. That too may seem a cost-less strategy, but it isn't. First, it means accepting a further year (2019) of falling real incomes, with all that that means in terms of social unrest, falling popularity, skills loss due to emigration and further decline in the tax base. And, second, the longer he leaves it before approaching the IMF, the more he 'owns' the economic crisis, whereas if he acted sooner he could plausibly argue that all his problems derive from the economic mess he inherited from Zuma.

African politicians, often nationalists, greatly underestimate the damage done by their erratic and radical politics. Next door in Zimbabwe, President Emmerson Mnangagwa is also trying to talk up his economy in the hope of restoring confidence. This looks to be a hopeless project. The Mugabe years have sown a very deep distrust among investors and Zimbabweans in general, so deep that even those who have not fled the country altogether may never again really trust *any* African nationalist government, perhaps just any African government. There seems no possibility that confidence can be restored in Zimbabwe unless it gets help from the IMF and carries out the Fund's conditions – and perhaps not even then. (The IMF's involvement in a country is itself a sort of guarantee in the eyes of many investors.)

It seems possible that the Zuma years have done somewhat similar damage in South Africa – and Ramaphosa has continued this damage by pursuing EWC, NHI and the new Mining Charter. Above all, the mere advent of Ramaphosa does not deal with the more profound fact that the ANC has failed to produce a new ruling class capable of taking a properly national view of the task of governance. The procession of corrupt politicians and bureaucrats before the Zondo Commission on State Capture left one in no doubt that bribery and corruption were utterly systemic, going way beyond the Guptas or Jacob Zuma. The ruling group that emerges from this perspective is hardly more than a rabble of self-seeking opportunists. Just occasionally figures emerge like Mcebisi Jonas, who resolutely refused bribes and who had a strong sense of propriety and the national interest. But such figures are quite exceptional. The vast generality not merely took bribes and played the system but eagerly sought to do so. Indeed, this is visible right down to councillor level in the

ANC, where political office is sought as a path to riches and where even the assassination of rival councillors is a standard part of the game.

The *Business Day* journalist Natasha Marrian, surveying the flood of damning evidence emanating from the Zondo Commission, asked, 'How does this impact on the ANC?' Her answer: 'It shows that the government it leads was up for sale long before Jacob Zuma arrived on the scene, although he mastered the game.'[22] This is undoubtedly true; after all, the hugely corrupt arms deal, the first great scam involving systemic corruption at every level, took place under Mandela's presidency, with Thabo Mbeki playing a leading part in it. One has to ask such basic questions as to whether the ANC has ever been capable of a comprehensive South African patriotism. After all, what did all those decades of militant nationalist struggle amount to if, in practice, ANC leaders were willing to sell their country down the river at the bidding of a criminal family of Indian immigrants? It's as if the whole ANC pursuit of power was really a journey powered by individual self-enrichment. Or take the way that the Czech gangster and organised crime boss Radovan Krejčíř was able to buy asylum from Zuma. There was no subtlety to this: Krejčíř claimed in an affidavit to have driven to Nkandla and handed over R2.5 million in notes to Zuma and his son Duduzane.[23] Zuma could not have been ignorant of Krejčíř's multiple convictions for drug-dealing, money laundering and attempted murder. Effectively, it was a matter of one crime boss getting paid off by another. Most of Zuma's ANC colleagues seem to have been the same. There was simply no interest in questions of patriotism or propriety, merely in whether the money was good.

The problem starts with the ANC's striking lack of allegiance to a South African nation. ANC politicians repeatedly refer to 'our people' and like to hypothesise melodramatically about 'the African child'. No attempt is made to hide the fact that in their eyes whites and Indians are still an alien, enemy presence in the country, and coloureds are little better. And in practice many still look to a much narrower community defined by region, tribe or clan. And coloureds, Afrikaners and white English-speakers are often little different in that respect. In that sense there may be no or very few 'real' South Africans.

As one looks back, one realises that for most of the 20th century the white Afrikaners who constituted the ruling class enjoyed certain advantages. True, they were committed to white supremacy and, within that, to Afrikaner domination. But they felt a powerful patriotism towards their country, even if not to all its peoples, and their morale as a solidary group and their Calvinist morality exercised a strong limit on personal corruption. The net result was that they presided over a long period of successful national development in which not just Afrikaners but all the other groups shared: their numbers, per capita income, educational levels and life expectancy all increased. The sins and downside of Afrikaner rule are too well known to require re-enunciation but they nonetheless provide the only benchmark that there is. No Afrikaner leader feathered his nest in the way Jacob Zuma did. Already ANC rule has seen steep falls in African life expectancy (due to Mbeki's Aids denialism) and the last five years have seen a steady fall in per capita income. Moreover, future economic development has already been blighted by the way the ANC has transformed Eskom from having a surplus of cheap electricity to dire shortages of very expensive electricity. The comparison is, indeed, so unflattering for the ANC as to make it clear that it cannot succeed on its own.

What is not in doubt is that any regime that is really determined to pull the country forward must draw upon the energies of all its different races and groups. There is no sign that Ramaphosa has understood this. His first year in office has shown considerable timidity and naivety and a consciousness still unhelpfully bounded by what are now almost antique African nationalist platitudes. Everything has proceeded as if the main objective is simply to tread water and temporise. It is not even clear that Ramaphosa has grasped how great a crisis his country faces.

In general, playing for time means prolonging the economic crisis and thus means falling popularity for the Ramaphosa government. This latter is a key factor: Ramaphosa's popularity is the government's chief asset, and if that frays too badly he might even reach a point where he is not able to force through the necessity of an IMF bail-out, even if he wanted one. That is, he should not delay in the belief that he will always have that fall-back. And why would he delay? For fear of reactions and divisions in his party. Exactly such fears long restrained the ANC's Afrikaner Nationalist predecessors from carrying out necessary reforms. When De Klerk took the plunge, it was too late. The divisions faded away but so did the party itself.

These are harsh calculations and it is unlikely that Ramaphosa ever considered them before embarking on his presidential bid. But that is what fighting for the dream of 1994 now comes down to. And it is a dream worth fighting for. There is no reason why South Africa has to accept a future of high crime, social conflict and economic crisis. The country has reached that point only because of hugely mistaken and fraudulent policies. The world we glimpsed under Mandela – economic progress, multi-racial harmony, tolerance and reconciliation – is still waiting offstage. Whether it is achieved or cast aside is mainly a matter of political will.

And that is the final point. It will take a huge effort of political will and national determination to force through the liberal revolution I have sketched. In order to achieve that, it would be best to return to the *status quo ante* of 1994, that is to say, a GNU. The DA, as we have seen, is not in a happy state but it is the only responsible opposition in sight. It might be desirable to include a few non-political businessmen and managers. There would be no question of including the EFF, which would be bound to oppose liberal reforms and would anyway undermine any chance of consensus government.

The last GNU failed because the ANC was determined to rule alone and because De Klerk's National Party had lost both its own and its electorate's confidence. It would be vital that a future GNU worked as a true consensus-seeking cooperative. Moreover, it would have to represent a genuine change of heart, a determination to present a government and introduce measures that would show South Africans and the world that a fundamentally different sort of regime was in power. Only steps as determined as major structural reforms would have any chance of really restoring confidence.

If the GNU includes real heavyweight figures from all the parties and if they work determinedly together in a cooperative fashion, that regime would reflect the reality of South Africa. If one examines any of the country's successful private-sector companies one will find everybody working together, irrespective of race or party, all pulling on the same rope. They do so because they know that all their futures are linked to the success of their companies. South Africa as a country is really no different. The difference between the first GNU and now is that in 1994 the coalition partners saw themselves as entering a New South Africa of unlimited possibilities. Now they would be getting together because they knew it was their country's last chance to save a dream that they all shared. And that is a large part of the point. In a country split by race, tribe, religion, region and class, only in that vision of the rainbow nation are they all one; only that is inclusive. Fighting for the dream is fighting for the country.

Notes

Chapter One

1 Private source.
2 Bongani Fuzile, 'Cattle diverted from the poor to Jacob Zuma for years', *Sunday Times*, 5 August 2018.
3 Adriaan Basson, *Zuma Exposed* (Jonathan Ball Publishers, 2012), p 5.
4 Ray Hartley, *Ramaphosa: Path to Power* (Jonathan Ball Publishers, 2018), p 136.
5 Nickolaus Bauer, 'ANC expels Malema', *Mail & Guardian*, 29 February 2012.
6 Charles Molele, 'ANC denies claims of purging Zuma dissidents', *Mail & Guardian*, 8 June 2013.
7 *City Press*, 'NPA declines to prosecute Duduzane Zuma', *News24*, 17 July 2014.
8 Erika Gibson, Elaine Swanepoel and Abram Mashego, 'Duduzane Zuma to be charged by NPA', *City Press*, 18 February 2018.
9 Hartley, *Ramaphosa*, p 138.
10 News24, 'We want a consultative conference in September – ANC stalwarts'. Available at www.politicsweb.co.za/news-and-analysis/we-want-a-consultative-conference-in-september--an, accessed 29 June 2017.
11 Hlengiwe Nhlabathi, S'Thembile Cele and Rapule Tabane, 'Cyril: Bring it on!', *City Press*, 22 October 2017.
12 Ranjeni Munusamy, 'News analysis: what is David Mabuza's game?', *Sowetan*, 28 November 2017.
13 Norimitsu Onishi and Selam Gebrekidan, 'South Africa vows to end corruption: are its new leaders part of the problem?', *The New York Times*, 4 August 2018. Available at https://www.nytimes.com/2018/08/04/world/

africa/south-africa-anc-david-mabuza.html, accessed 7 January 2019.

14 Nicki Gules and Sipho Masondo, 'Zuma's Dubai exit plan', *City Press*, 28 May 2017.

15 Iavan Pijoos and Jenna Etheridge, 'Ramaphosa cuts short UK visit to resolve Mahikeng chaos', *News24*, 19 April 2018.

16 Iavan Pijoos, 'More shops looted, building and cars torched overnight in Mahikeng', *News24*, 20 April 2018.

17 Private source.

18 Stephen Grootes, 'Ace Magashule's unstoppable oncoming train, now a few metres closer', *Daily Maverick*, 22 October 2018.

Chapter Two

1 For readers wanting a fuller account of the Mandela-Mbeki period, see RW Johnson, *South Africa's Brave New World: the beloved country since the end of apartheid* (Jonathan Ball Publishers, 2010), and, for the Zuma period, the same author's *How Long Will South Africa Survive?: The crisis continues* (2nd edition, Jonathan Ball Publishers, 2017).

2 Special Court for Sierra Leone, *Prosecutor vs Charles Ghankay Taylor*, Judgment, Case no. SCSL-03-01-A, 26 September 2013.

3 *The Telegraph*, 5 October 2010. Ractliffe later returned the stones, having held them for a number of years, ostensibly to avoid adverse publicity for the Children's Fund. In 2016, he was acquitted of the charge of illegal possession of uncut diamonds.

4 Staff Reporter, 'Mandela gave R1 m to Zuma, court hears', *Mail & Guardian*, 3 December 2004.

5 Centre for Development and Enterprise, *Policy-Making in a New Democracy. South Africa's Challenges for the 21ˢᵗ Century*. Johannesburg, August 1999.

6 Ibid, p 67.

7 Ibid, p 69.

8 Ibid. A reference to the 1997 Asian debt crisis, which had severe repercussions throughout the Third World.

9 Ibid. A reference to the amalgamation of the old public service with those of the ten Bantustans.

10 Ibid, p 72.

11 Ibid, p 73.

12 Stephen Ellis, *External Mission: the ANC in exile* (Jonathan Ball Publishers, 2012), p 159.

13 Matt Radcliffe, 'The effects of the education system on South Africa's economic growth', *African Business*, 18 November 2016.

14 Staff Writer, 'This is who is emigrating from South Africa – and where they are going', *BusinessTech*, 28 July 2016.

15 ANC Department of Education and Training, 'The Character of the ANC', *Umrabulo*, no 3, 1997.

16 ANC, 'Strategy and Tactics as amended at the 50th national conference of the ANC', December 1997, p 13.

17 Sapa, 'Joe Modise benefited from arms deal: former Scopa chair', *TimesLive*, 2 September 2014.

18 Helen Suzman Foundation, 'Arms deal inquiry crushed', *Focus*, issue 21 (first quarter 2001). Available at hsf.org.za/publications/focus/issue-21-first-quarter-2001/arms-deal-inquiry-crushed, accessed on 7 January 2019.

19 Simpiwe Piliso and Buddy Naidu, 'Thabo Mbeki's Shaik-Down', *Sunday Times*, 15 August 2010.

20 Naledi Shange, 'Hitachi settlement proves Medupi is "rotten to the core" – DA', *News24*, 28 September 2015.

21 Carol Paton, 'ANC is technically insolvent', *Business Day*, 20 December 2017.

22 Celia W Dugger, 'Study cites toll of AIDS policy in South Africa', *The New York Times*, 25 November 2008.

23 Yarik Turianskyi, 'Why Africa is losing out by letting the peer review process collapse', *The Conversation*, 23 September 2015. Available at theconversation.com/why-africa-is-losing-out-by-letting-the-peer-review-process-collapse-47955, accessed on 7 January 2019.

24 Jac Laubscher, 'South Africa's growth tragedy', *Fin24*, 28 December 2017.

25 William Mervin Gumede, *Thabo Mbeki and Battle for the Soul of the ANC* (Zebra Press, 2005), pp 179–180.

26 Gareth van Onselen, 'The ANC's all-time top 10 most disturbing quotes', blog post, Inside Politics, 23 April 2012. Available at inside-politics.org/2012/04/23/the-ancs-all-time-top-10-most-disturbing-quotes/, accessed on 7 January 2019.

27 Crispian Olver, *How to Steal a City: the battle for Nelson Mandela Bay – an inside account* (Jonathan Ball Publishers, 2017), pp 232–233.

28 See Johnson, *How Long*, pp 11–17.

29 Ibid.

Chapter Three

1 Susan Njanji, 'ANC "stepping stone to personal gain": Motlanthe', *IOL*, 30 November 2012.

2 Andiswa Makinana, 'Revealed: why Supra Mahumapelo was removed as North West premier', *TimesLive*, 15 June 2018.

3 Mondli Makhanya, 'Sunset for the ANC Premier League', *City Press*, 3 November 2018.

4 In 2018, the South Gauteng High Court ruled that Maphatsoe should be removed from his position as head of the MKMVA for failing to administer

and manage the MK Veterans Trust SA; see Greg Nicholson, 'MK veterans' trust taken out of Kebby Maphatsoe's hands', *Daily Maverick*, 31 May 2018.

5 Ngwako Modjadji, 'Collen Maine ready to tell all about Guptas, state capture', *City Press*, 12 November 2018.

6 For more detail, see Jacques Pauw, *The President's Keepers: those keeping Zuma in power and out of prison* (Tafelberg, 2017).

7 Paddy Harper, 'ANC killings were "hits by a party faction"', *Mail and Guardian*, 22 September 2017. Evidence of SACP provincial secretary Themba Mthembu to the Moerane Commission.

8 Kaveel Singh, 'Former KZN premier outlines "processes of corruption" in local ANC structures', *News24*, 20 September 2017.

9 Gareth van Onselen, 'Blade Nzimande and the idea of respect', politicsweb, 15 January 2013. Available at www.politicsweb.co.za/opinion/blade-nzimande-and-the-idea-of-respect, accessed on 8 January 2019.

10 See Stephen Ellis, *External Mission: the ANC in exile* (Jonathan Ball Publishers, 2012), p 220.

11 See RW Johnson, *How Long Will South Africa Survive?* (2nd edition, Jonathan Ball Publishers, 2017), pp 71–73.

12 For the background to this, see Johnson, *How Long*, pp 68–73.

13 Nathi Olifant and Matthew Savides, 'ANC KZN conference declared invalid, leadership now in question', *TimesLive*, 12 September 2017.

14 For the growth of the hitman phenomenon, including much material on KwaZulu-Natal, see Mark Shaw, *Hitmen for Hire: exposing South Africa's underworld* (Jonathan Ball Publishers, 2017)

15 Harper, 'ANC killings were "hits by a party faction"'. The reporting on these matters by the *M&G*'s correspondent, Paddy Harper, has been consistently invaluable.

16 Ibid.

17 Ibid.

18 After a long hiatus, two suspects were final charged in October 2018; see Clive Ndou, 'Relief at last for Mchunu in 2015 murder case', *The Witness*, 11 October 2018.

19 ANA Reporter, 'Willies Mchunu replaces Senzo as KZN premier', *IOL*, 23 May 2016.

20 Jessica Bezuidenhout, 'Days of Zondo: Ramatlhodi lets rip about Zuma's dangerous liaison with the Guptas', *Daily Maverick*, 28 November 2018.

21 He had valued his house at R29 000 despite the surrounding houses all being valued at more than ten times as much, in order to pay lower rates; see Andisiwe Makinana and Setumo Stone, 'How new mineral resources minister was sneaked in', *City Press*, 27 September 2015.

22 Ibid.

23 The secretary-general, deputy secretary-general, deputy president, treasurer-general and national chairperson.

24 Constitutional Court of South Africa, Judgment, Cases CCT 143/15 and CCT 171/15, 31 March 2016.

25 Greg Nicholson, 'No confidence: ANC wins the vote, but Zuma suffers in battle', *Daily Maverick*, 10 November 2016.

26 Malusi Gigaba, 'Deeper conspiracy behind the anti-Zuma drive – Malusi Gigaba', speech in National Assembly, politicsweb, 10 November 2016. Available at www.politicsweb.co.za/politics/deeper-conspiracy-behind-the-antizuma-drive—malus, accessed on 18 January 2019.

27 TMG Digital, 'Ramaphosa speaks out: Firing of Gordhan is "unacceptable"', *SowetanLive*, 31 March 2017.

28 *TimesLive*, 'Watch: "Zuma is an elite predator", says SACP's Solly Mapaila', *TimesLive*, 26 September 2017.

29 Vhahangwele Nemakonde, 'Malema: SACP must protect Mapaila, the only man Zuma is worried about', *The Citizen*, 30 May 2017.

30 Kaveel Singh, 'SACP activists were among those who had been gunned down in KwaZulu-Natal', *News24*, 21 September 2017.

31 Baldwin Ndaba, 'SACP: Ramaphosa on the warpath', *IOL*, 11 July 2017; Greg Nicholson, 'SACP Congress: "The house is burning" – Ramaphosa', *Daily Maverick*, 12 July 2017.

32 Dineo Bendile, 'Zuma not welcome at SACP congress to avoid Cosatu May Day "fiasco"', *Mail & Guardian*, 12 July 2017.

33 *News24*, 'Zuma like a "tsunami wave"', *News24*, 5 April 2007.

34 Hlengiwe Nhlabathi, 'Nkosazana Dlamini-Zuma: elusive economic transformer', *City Press*, 3 December 2017.

35 Carien du Plessis, 'Unforgiven: the extraordinary tale of Carl Niehaus', *Daily Maverick*, 25 October 2017.

36 See RW Johnson, 'Ramaphosa and the strange workings of ANC democracy', in *@Liberty*, Issue 36, January 2018 (Institute of Race Relations, Johannesburg).

37 Citizen Reporter, '"Plot" to remove Mathabatha causing "war" in ANC', *The Citizen*, 25 September 2016.

38 Tshidi Madia, 'No such thing as white monopoly capital – ANC Gauteng', *News24*, 26 June 2017.

39 Ranjeni Munusamy, 'News analysis: what is David Mabuza's game?', *Sowetan*, 28 November 2017.

40 Carien du Plessis, 'ANC leadership race: Dlamini-Zuma supporters in battle to secure the final prize – the Eastern Cape', *Daily Maverick*, 3 November 2017.

41 Olebogeng Molatlhwa, 'Zamani Saul elected new chairperson of ANC in Northern Cape', *BusinessLive*, 12 May 2017.

42 Nomahlubi Jordaan, 'Violence at ANC conference an attempt to collapse event: Mabuyane', *TimesLive*, 2 October 2017.

Chapter Four

1 Gordhan was removed as finance minister on 30 March 2017, together with his deputy, Mcebisi Jonas.

2 In January 2019, evidence emerged suggesting that elements of the Zuma faction conspired to rig the Nasrec vote. See Marianne Thamm, 'National police commissioner turns to court to flush out info on ANC vote-buying scandal', *Daily Maverick*, 11 January 2019.

3 See, for example, Paddy Harper, '"Ghost" branches, municipal capture "threatens" ANC in Mpumalanga', *Mail & Guardian*, 1 June 2018.

4 Bekezela Phakathi, 'Auditor-General details tender deviation spree under Nomvula Mokonyane', *Business Day*, 28 March 2018.

5 *News24*, 'Mokonyane rubbishes claims of rigging, ANC vote delay', *News 24*, 19 December 2017.

6 Alex Mitchley, 'ANC conference could stop SA from becoming a nation of pigs – Senzo Mchunu', *News 24,* 17 November 2017.

7 Citizen Team, '"Missing" 68 votes belong to Vhembe delegates, Mathabatha says', *The Citizen*, 19 December 2017.

8 *News24*, 'Mokonyane rubbishes claims of rigging, ANC vote delay'.

9 Marianne Merten, 'ANC Policy Conference 2017: "Unity" at the close, now for the pushback', *Daily Maverick*, 5 July 2017.

10 Gareth van Zyl, 'No joke, SA land claims could take 700 years to deal with – Anthea Jeffery', *BizNews*, 4 July 2018.

11 Sobantu Mzwakali, 'Op-Ed: Budget 2018 shows misguided land reform', *Daily Maverick*, 26 February 2018.

12 ANA Reporter, 'ANC needs support to amend Constitution to force land reform', *IOL*, 21 December 2017.

13 The ANC spokesman, Zizi Kodwa, took strong exception to such reports and had berated the journalist Qaanitah Hunter who had tweeted about the scuffles. He claimed the tweets had been a 'mischievous and complete distortion and completely false' – yet video available online clearly showed the scuffles. See *TimesLive*, 20 December 2017.

14 As was often the case, the Cope leader, Mosiuoa Lekota, had the clearest head: 'If you are going to take land and give it to people who don't farm, they'll walk away from it.' This is exactly what has happened in the largest land reform in the country, in the Richtersveld. See Lauren Isaacs, '"ANC's decision on land expropriation without compensation a radical move"', *Eyewitness News*, 20 December 2017.

15 ANA Reporter, 'ANC54: Scuffles during debate on land redistribution without compensation', *IOL*, 21 December 2017.

16 Tehillah Niselow, 'Loud cheers as Ramaphosa says #ANC54 unanimous on land reform', *Fin24*, 21 December 2017.

17 *News24*, 'Taxpayers will keep paying Zuma's legal fees – Cyril Ramaphosa', politicsweb, 14 March 2018. Available at www.politicsweb.co.za/news-and-

analysis/taxpayers-will-keep-paying-zumas-legal-fees—cyril, accessed on 22 January 2019.
18 Mathlatse Mahlase, 'Ramaphosa tells Zulu King Zwelithini that land in Ingonyama Trust is safe', *News24*, 7 July 2018.

Chapter Five

1 Andiswa Makinana, 'Revealed: why Supra Mahumapelo was removed as North West premier', *TimesLive*, 15 June 2018.
2 Iavan Pijoos and Jenna Etheridge, 'Ramaphosa cuts short UK visit to resolve Mahikeng chaos', *News24*, 19 April 2018.
3 Stephen Grootes, 'Ace Magashule's unstoppable oncoming train, now a few metres closer', *Daily Maverick*, 22 October 2018.
4 Setumo Stone, 'Another revolt: ANC's North West woes continue', *City Press*, 20 September 2018.
5 Quinton Mytala, 'Supra Mahumapelo out as North West ANC chair after PEC disbands', *IOL*, 31 August 2018.
6 See RW Johnson, 'Frankenstein and the universities', politicsweb, 7 March 2012. Available at www.politicsweb.co.za/news-and-analysis/frankenstein-and-the-universities, accessed 9 January 2019.
7 Pauli van Wyk, 'SARS Inquiry, Day Two: Tom Moyane accused of costing SARS, and South Africa, at least R142-billion', *Daily Maverick*, 28 June 2018.
8 Correspondent, 'ANC received R2m donation from VBS – report', *News24*, 28 October 2018. The story was first reported by the *Sunday Times*.
9 *TimesLive*, 'In Full: The great bank heist: the damning report on VBS Mutual Bank', *TimesLive*, 10 October 2018. The article includes the full text of the report by Advocate Terry Motau SC, 'The Great Bank Heist: Investigator's Report to the Prudential Authority'.
10 In December 2018, Denel launched proceedings to recover the money paid to Oarabile Mahumapelo, after the board found that the bursary had been awarded illegally. See Thabo Mokone, 'Denel to claw back pilot bursary awarded to Supra Mahumapelo's son', *Sunday Times*, 5 December 2018.
11 Theto Mahlakoana, 'Denel confident it will pay salaries', *Business Day*, 17 January 2018.
12 Emsie Ferreira, 'Pravin Gordhan names interim Transnet board', *IOL*, 14 May 2018.
13 Abram Mashego and Nicki Gules, 'Transnet wants former bosses to pay back the money', *City Press*, 30 September 2018.
14 Bongani Nkosi, 'State-owned bank could soon be a reality', *IOL*, 7 May 2018.
15 Dewald van Rensburg and Sipho Masondo, 'VBS CEO: I knew, heard nothing', *City Press*, 22 July 2018.
16 Pauli van Wyk, 'Scorpio: VBS bank heist: EFF's family ties and moneyed connections', *Daily Maverick*, 21 November 2018.

17 Floyd Shivambu, 'Dismantle the Pravin Gordhan cabal!', politicsweb, 19 October 2018. Available at www.politicsweb.co.za/archive/dismantle-the-pravin-gordhan-cabal--floyd-shivambu, accessed on 9 January 2019.

18 Nomboniso Gasa, '"Indian cabal" narrative is to protect the looting project', *City Press*, 19 November 2018.

19 Dineo Bendile and Paddy Harper, 'We're being purged, say JZ's people', *Mail & Guardian,* 20 April 2018.

20 Loyisa Sidimba et al, 'Going, going, gone: jilted president fights back, warns of crisis after recall', *The Star*, 15 February 2018.

21 Paddy Harper, 'Zuma: They must not provoke me', *Mail & Guardian*, 6 June 2018.

22 See RW Johnson, *South Africa's Brave New World: the Beloved Country since the end of apartheid* (Jonathan Ball Publishers, 2010), especially pp 507–572; and Johnson, *How Long Will South Africa Survive?* (1st edition, Jonathan Ball, 2015), pp 303–334.

23 In November 2018, the NPA announced it had 'temporarily' dropped the Estina case until sufficient evidence could be obtained to secure convictions. See Odwa Mjo, 'NPA drops Estina Dairy charges and South Africans want answers', *Sunday Times*, 29 November 2018.

24 Andiswe Makinana, '"Shocked" Kebby Maphatsoe stripped of military veterans' powers', *Sunday Times*, 10 June 2018.

25 Greg Nicholson, 'MK veterans' trust taken out of Kebby Maphatsoe's hands', *Daily Maverick*, 31 May 2018.

26 Norimitsu Onishi and Selam Gebrekidan, 'South Africa vows to end corruption: are its new leaders part of the problem?', *The New York Times*, 4 August 2018. Available at https://www.nytimes.com/2018/08/04/world/africa/south-africa-anc-david-mabuza.html, accessed 7 January 2019.

27 Mathlatse Mahlase, 'Ramaphosa tells Zulu King Zwelithini that land in Ingonyama Trust is safe', *News24*, 7 July 2018.

28 Jeff Wicks, 'ANC told it cannot hold its KZN elective conference', *Business Day*, 8 June 2018.

29 ANA, 'Political killings becoming a "permanent" feature in KZN politics, says IFP', *The Citizen*, 16 September 2018.

30 Bongani Hans and Zimasa Matiwane, 'Watch: KZN ANC's revolt against Cyril Ramaphosa', *IOL*, 24 April 2018.

31 Sibongakonke Shoba, 'ANC will pay if it cannot unite fractious KZN before elections', *Sunday Times*, 6 May 2018.

32 See, for example, Loyiso Sidimba et al, 'Zuma goes down tjanking', *Cape Times*, 15 February 2018.

33 Ranjeni Munusamy, 'Zuma is the hidden force fomenting ANC breakaway movements', *Sunday Times*, 3 June 2018.

34 Ibid.

35 Tom Head, 'Mazibuye Emasisweni: Could a new pro-Zuma party split the ANC vote?', *The South African*, 31 May 2018.

36 Johnson, *How Long*, pp 18–20.

37 Bongani Mthethwa, 'Mafia-style business forum halts multi-million road project', *TimesLive*, 9 February 2018.

38 SABC News Online, 'Non-black owned funeral companies will not operate in townships', SABC News, 19 January 2018.

39 Bongani Mthethwa, 'I'm not afraid of being convicted: Zuma', *TimesLive*, 1 June 2018.

40 Paddy Harper and Dineo Bendile, 'JZ's apostles to launch new party', *Mail & Guardian*, 1 June 2018.

41 Sibongakonke Shoba and Ranjeni Munusamy, 'Zuma plots – and wrecks ANC deal', *Sunday Times*, 10 June 2018.

42 Zimasa Matiwane, 'KZN vote deals blow to Zuma', *Sunday Times*, 22 July 2018.

43 See, for example, Derrick Spies, 'Political killings in KZN continue, strongly condemned', *News24*, 5 December 2018.

44 Shoba and Munusamy, 'Zuma plots – and wrecks ANC deal'.

45 S'Thembile Cele and Hlengiwe Nhlabathi, 'Zuma fuels ANC war', *City Press*, 10 June 2018.

46 Zimasa Matwane, '"Harsh" media worsened Vusi Zuma's illness, family says', *Sunday Times*, 8 July 2018.

47 Mxolisi Mngadi, '"I've never committed any crime" – Zuma', *News24*, 31 May 2018.

48 Karyn Maughan, 'Zuma uses Khwezi case in his battle against NPA', *Business Day*, 1 October 2018.

49 See Karyn Maughan, 'Court orders Jacob Zuma to pay his own legal fees', *TimesLive*, 13 December 2018.

50 Qaanitah Hunter, 'ANC KZN day of chaos and anger', *Daily Maverick*, 9 June 2018.

51 Hlengiwe Nhlabathi, 'Choose people over chiefs', *City Press*, 20 May 2018.

52 Jeff Wicks and Lwandile Bhengu, 'Zulu king warns of clash of the nations over land', *Business Day*, 5 July 2018.

53 One participant, to whom I am grateful, described the scene to me as 'preparatory to another Zulu War'.

54 Aphiwe de Klerk, 'I was showing the king a book, not kneeling before him – Ramaphosa', *TimesLive*, 14 July 2018.

55 William Saunderson-Meyer, 'Seizing the nettle of bloated bureaucracy', *IOL*, 28 April 2018.

56 Mahlatse Mahlase, '"I am not weak," says Cyril Ramaphosa after signing $20bn in deals', *City Press*, 15 July 2018.

57 Qaanitah Hunter and Jeff Wicks, 'Exposed – Zuma plot to oust Cyril', *Sunday Times*, 9 September 2018.

58 Stephen Grootes, 'Magashule will fight to the bitter end, Zuma too', *Daily Maverick*, 25 September 2018.

59 Dineo Bendile, 'Ramaphosa takes a swipe at ANC members accused of plot to

unseat him', *Mail & Guardian*, 17 September 2018.

60 Mutaba allegedly sent a threatening message to Qaanitah Hunter, one of the journalists involved in breaking the story. She subsequently denied knowledge of the message, but apologised publicly to Hunter.

61 Hlengiwe Nhlabathi and S'Thembile Cele, 'Magashule lashes out at "third force" as court rules ANC Limpopo conference must continue', *City Press*, 24 June 2018.

62 South African Institute of Race Relations, *The Criterion Report*, vol 1, no 1, 28 September 2018. I am grateful to Gareth van Onselen for providing me with a copy of this report.

Chapter Six

1 Irina Filatova and Apollon Davidson, *The Hidden Thread: Russia and South Africa in the Soviet era* (Jonathan Ball Publishers, 2013), pp 390–391.

2 RW Johnson, *How Long Will South Africa Survive? The looming crisis* (1st edition, Jonathan Ball Publishers, 2015), p 107.

3 Jean-François Bayart, *The State in Africa: the politics of the belly* (Polity, 2009).

4 René Dumont, *L'Afrique noire est mal partie* (Éditions du Seuil, 1962).

5 John Campbell, 'Global peacekeeping operations overwhelmingly African and in Africa', blog post, Council on Foreign Relations, 10 July 2018. Available at https://www.cfr.org/blog/global-peacekeeping-operations-overwhelmingly-african-and-africa, accessed on 9 January 2019.

6 Anim van Wyk, 'Does S. Africa really employ more civil servants than the US? The claim is false', *Africa Check*, 19 February 2018. Available at africacheck.org/reports/does-south-africa-really-employ-more-civil-servants-than-the-us-the-claim-is-false/, accessed on 21 January 2019. See also p 123.

7 See, for example, amaBhungane and Scorpio, '#GuptaLeaks: How the Guptas picked up MK vets' conference tab', *News24*, 18 July 2017.

8 Stephan Hofstatter, 'Counting the cost of state capture', *Financial Mail*, 6 September 2018.

9 Staff Writer, 'SA government's R137 billion wage bill vs emerging economies', *BusinessTech*, 14 August 2017.

10 Reuters, 'Public sector: this is best wage deal we could get', *Fin24*, 20 May 2015.

11 P Eric Louw, *The Rise, Fall, and Legacy of Apartheid* (Praeger, 2004), p 82.

12 Hlengiwe Nhlabathi, 'Choose people over chiefs', *City Press*, 20 May 2018.

13 Staff Writer, 'How much South Africa's kings and queens and traditional leaders will get paid in 2018', *Business Tech*, 7 January 2018.

14 Mathlatse Mahlase, 'Ramaphosa tells Zulu King Zwelithini that land in Ingonyama Trust is safe', *News24*, 7 July 2018.

15 United States of America Department of State, 'Voting Practices in the United Nations 2017: Report to Congress Submitted Pursuant to Public

Laws 101-246 and 108-447', March 2018. Available at www.state.gov/documents/organization/281458.pdf, accessed on 14 January 2019.

16 Ruth Hopkins, 'Tortured behind bars', *City Press*, 6 August 2017.

17 Sipho Hlongwane, 'Marikana: Freed miners speak of torture in police cells', *Daily Maverick*, 4 September 2012.

18 Johnson, *How Long*, pp 117–118.

19 The USA is the world's largest food exporter and Africa's chief source of wheat. By 2014 sub-Saharan Africa was importing $48.5 billion of food, a figure predicted to rise to $110 billion by 2025. Africa has the highest food imports/per capita in the world. See US Dept of Agriculture, Foreign Agricultural Service, 'A turning point for agricultural exports to sub-Saharan Africa', International Agricultural Trade Report, 2 November 2015. Available at www.fas.usda.gov/sites/default/files/2015-11/11-2015_sub-saharan_africa_iatr_0.pdf, accessed on 12 February 2019.

20 See Errol Knott Moorcroft, 'Land reform in South Africa – "good times, bad times"', in M Savage (ed), *The Passion for Reason: Essays in Honour of Frederik van Zyl Slabbert* (Jonathan Ball Publishers, 2010), pp 227–252.

21 Bennie van Zyl, 'Farming holds its own in South Africa: Productive farms should not be tampered with', *Harvest SA*, 15 February 2018. Available at www.harvestsa.co.za/articles/farming-holds-its-own-in-south-africa-24809.html, accessed on 21 January 2019.

22 AgriSa, Constitutional Review Committee, Submission on Expropriation without Compensation, 22 May 2018.

23 Mahlatse Mahlase, 'Land expropriation: here's how it could be implemented, says Mantashe', *News24*, 15 August 2018.

24 See RW Johnson, *South Africa's Brave New World* (Jonathan Ball, 2010), p 53.

25 Cyril Ramaphosa, 'How SA can succeed', address to ANC Johannesburg Region Economic Colloquium, politicsweb, 13 November 2017. Available at www.politicsweb.co.za/documents/how-sa-can-succeed--cyril-ramaphosa, accessed on 9 January 2019.

26 Figures from Mike Schussler, economists.co.za.

27 'Editorial: the sad decline of SA's mines', *Business Day*, 20 July 2018.

28 Mills Soko and Mzukisi Qobo, 'SA's cancellation of bilateral investment treaties – strategic or hostile?', *Fin24*, 28 September 2018.

29 Genevieve Quintal, 'Mantashe tells of ANC talks with banks on closure of Gupta accounts', *Business Day*, 27 November 2018.

30 See the public protector's reports, 'Secure in Comfort' and 'State of Capture', on Nkandla and state capture, respectively.

31 News24, 'Nkandla not about Zuma – SACP', *News24*, 12 November 2012.

32 Riana de Lange, 'Government to fund another 100 black industrialists after meeting 1st goal', *City Press*, 3 June 2018.

33 Stephen Ellis, *External Mission: the ANC in exile* (Jonathan Ball, 2012), pp 161–170.

Chapter Seven

1 See II Filatova, 'The Lasting Legacy: the Soviet theory of the National Democratic Revolution and South Africa', *South African Historical Journal*, vol 64, no 3 (2012).

2 Riana de Lange, 'Government to fund another 100 black industrialists after meeting 1st goal', *City Press*, 3 June 2018.

3 Babalo Ndenze, 'Severe job losses in SA mining sector continue to be a threat', *Eyewitness News*, 19 October 2018.

4 Leon Kok, 'State of SA's mining sector raises fundamental questions', *Finweek*, 11 June 2018.

5 William Saunderson-Meyer, 'Seizing the nettle of bloated bureaucracy', *IOL*, 28 April 2018.

6 Andiswe Makinana, 'Prasa on brink of financial collapse, annual report shows', *TimesLive*, 10 September 2018.

7 Gareth van Onselen, 'Political Musical Chairs: Turnover in the National Executive and Administration Since 2009', report, South African Institute of Race Relations, August 2017. Available at irr.org.za/reports/occasional-reports/files/irr-political-musical-chairs.pdf, accessed on 21 January 2019.

8 Gareth van Onselen, 'High turnover rate of MPs tells tale of how an authoritarian party is run', *Business Day*, 13 February 2018.

9 Stephen Ellis, *External Mission: the ANC in exile* (Jonathan Ball Publishers, 2012), p 167.

10 See RW Johnson, *South Africa's Brave New World* (Jonathan Ball Publishers, 2010), pp 30–50.

Chapter Eight

1 Alan Hirsch, 'Did South Africa's investment summit mark a game-changing moment?', *Mail & Guardian*, 31 October 2018.

2 Nick Hedley, 'Trevor Manuel: land issue makes SA a tough sell for Ramaphosa's investment envoys', *Business Day*, 19 July 2018.

3 Mike Schussler, 'Tragic data shows capital fleeing along with jobs', *The Citizen*, 16 January 2019.

4 See RW Johnson, *How Long Will South Africa Survive?* (1st edition, Jonathan Ball Publishers, 2015), pp 11–17.

5 Allan Seccombe, 'New Mining Charter released, with new BEE requirements', *Business Day*, 15 June 2018.

6 Alex Mitcheley, 'Land: the people speak – not every black person who wants land wants to be a farmer', *News24*, 29 June 2018.

7 See JB Peires, *The Dead Will Arise: Nongqawuse and the Great Xhosa Cattle-Killing Movement of 1856–7* (James Currey, 1989).

8 Leon Kok, 'State of SA's mining sector raises fundamental questions', *Finweek*, 11 June 2018.

9 Mahlatse Mahlase and Sibongile Khumalo, 'Mantashe slams job losses, "backward" leadership at Gold Fields', *News24*, 15 August 2018.

10 Mahlatse Mahlase, 'Mantashe's proposal to limit land ownership not practical – black farmers' union', *News24*, 17 August 2018.

11 Katharine Child, 'NHI fund will be mandatory – Motsoaledi', *TimesLive*, 21 June 2018.

12 Johnson, *How Long*, pp 146–174.

13 Anim van Wyk, 'Does S. Africa really employ more civil servants than the US? The claim is false', *AfricaCheck*, 16 October 2014. See also Njabulo Mhlambi, 'Government wage bill – overbloated and underwhelming', *BizNews* 17 October 2018; and *The South African*, 22 March 2018.

14 Chantall Presence, 'MTBPS: No money to fund shortfalls due to higher public sector wages', *IOL*, 24 October 2018.

15 Tebogo Tshwane, 'Govt "no" to public service wage hikes', *Mail and Guardian*, 26 October 2018.

16 Bekezela Phakathi and Linda Ensor, 'Mboweni left in the cold over plans for SAA', *Business Day*, 7 November 2018.

17 See, for example, World Bank Group, 'An Incomplete Transition: Overcoming the Legacy of Exclusion in South Africa', Systematic Country Diagnostic, 30 April 2018. Available at openknowledge.worldbank.org/handle/10986/29793, accessed on 21 January 2019.

Chapter Nine

1 Athandiwe Saba, 'The DA's long game: Dreaming the impossible dream – clinching it – finally pays off', *Mail & Guardian*, 19 August 2016.

2 See, for example, 'Lindiwe Mazibuko owns her future', *Northcliff Melville Times*, 23 January 2014.

3 *News24*, 'Knives out for DA's Mazibuko', *News24*, 21 July 2013.

4 Mamphela Ramphele, 'Ramphele: Speaking truth to power, from the World Bank to Thabo Mbeki', extract from autobiography, *Mail & Guardian*, 8 November 2013.

5 *Sunday Times*, 'Homo naledi: unearthing SA's great hour of science, and failure of logic', *Sunday Times*, 20 September 2015.

6 Nico Gous, 'Solly Msimanga named as DA's candidate for Gauteng premier', *TimesLive*, 19 August 2018.

7 S'thembile Cele, 'Maimane wants diversity on DA benches', *City Press*, 12 May 2018.

8 GroundUp Editors, 'Day Zero and Cape Town's cacophony of chaos', *GroundUp*, 24 January 2018.

9 Dominic Adriaanse and Francesca Villette, 'Maimane says sorry, sort of', *Cape Times*, 30 October 2018.

10 Claudi Mailovich, 'Why Mmusi Maimane opted out of race for Western Cape premier', *Business Day*, 19 September 2018.

11 Hlengiwe Nhlabathi and S'Thembile Cele, 'DA split looms amid serious tensions over race, transformation and policy', *City Press*, 27 May 2018.

Chapter Ten

1 See Cyril Ramaphosa 2017, 'A New Deal for Jobs, Growth & Transformation', no date, available at ramaphosa.org.za/new-deal-for-jobs-growth-transformation/, accessed on 10 January 2019.

2 Cyril Ramphosa, 'How SA can succeed', address to ANC Johannesburg Region Economic Colloquium 2017, politicsweb, 13 November 2017. Available at http://politicsweb.co.za/documents/how-sa-can-succeed--cyril-ramaphosa, accessed on 9 January 2019.

3 Patrick Bond, 'Is Tito preparing an IMF financial parachute, now a $171bn foreign debt cliff looms?', *Mail & Guardian*, 18 December 2018.

4 Carin Smith, 'RW Johnson: Four things the World Bank and IMF want SA to do', *Fin24*, 7 September 2017.

5 International Monetary Fund, Staff Report for the 2018 Article IV Consultation, 21 June 2018.

6 Ibid, p 1.

7 Ibid, p 21.

8 Ibid, p 27.

9 Ibid, p 28.

10 Ibid, p 38.

11 This was when the first edition of *How Long Will South Africa Survive?* was published, though I had actually written it in late 2014.

12 For a typical example of this sort of alarmism, see Magda Wierzycka, 'Beware of the IMF dragons', *Business Day*, 10 October 2018.

13 Stephen Grootes, 'Mbeki: GEAR programme was meant to save SA from debt', *Eyewitness News*, 21 March 2016.

14 Lisa Steyn, 'Eskom has no idea how it will fund wage increases', *Business Day*, 31 August 2018.

15 Penelope Mashego and Pericles Anetos, 'Ramaphosa takes charge of NHI', *Sunday Times*, 26 August 2018.

16 Lameez Omarjee, 'Fitch says Ramaphosa's stimulus plan unlikely to boost growth significantly', *News24*, 25 September 2018.

17 Allan Seccombe, 'New Mining Charter released, with new BEE requirements', *Business Day*, 15 June 2018.

18 'Time for take-off', *Financial Mail*, 11 October 2018.

19 Govan Whittles, 'Labour regroups after damp-squib jobs summit', *Mail & Guardian*, 8 October 2018.

20 Theto Mahlakoana, 'Government foresees period of huge employment creation', *Business Day*, 2 October 2018.

21 Katharine Child, 'NHI fund will be mandatory – Motsoaledi', *TimesLive*, 21 June 2018.

22 Pieter du Toit, 'AgriSA's Dan Kriek: "We don't have time; we need results"', *News24*, 9 October 2018.

23 Norimitsu Onishi and Selam Gebrekidan, 'South Africa vows to end corruption: are its new leaders part of the problem?', *The New York Times*, 4 August 2018. Available at www.nytimes.com/2018/08/04/world/africa/ south-africa-anc-david-mabuza.html, accessed 7 January 2019.

24 US Department of Agriculture, *Census of Agriculture: 2012 Census Highlights – Farm Demographics* (ACH 12-3, May 2014).

25 Carol Paton, 'Only bold risk-taking will stop us bundu-bashing to the precipice', *Business Day*, 28 August 2018.

26 See, for example, 'Ramaphosa rules out IMF assistance for Eskom', eNCA, 1 December 2017.

27 Drazen Jorgic, 'Pakistan, IMF extend bailout talks after failing to reach agreement', *Reuters*, 20 November 2018.

28 Rene Vollgraaff, 'Land Bank warns expropriation could trigger default', *Fin24*, 21 August 2018.

29 Yolandi Groenewald, 'Could banks be the biggest losers in expropriation without compensation?', *Fin24*, 1 March 2018.

30 Ana Monteiro/Bloomberg, 'SA land prices drop 32% on land reform change, drought', *News24*, 10 September 2018.

31 Alistair Anderson, 'Listed property unlikely to shake off doldrums in 2018', *Business Day*, 12 June 2018.

32 Bekezela Phakathi, 'ANC's land plan could trigger "classical banking crisis"', *Business Day*, 10 September 2018.

33 Carol Paton, 'Eskom applies for 15% tariff increase', *Business Day*, 22 October 2018.

34 Lisa Steyn, 'Eskom adds R1bn to diesel bill to keep the lights on', *Business Day*, 16 November 2018.

35 Carol Paton, 'Eskom retreats from debt-exchange plan', *Business Day*, 29 August 2018.

36 Antoinette Slabbert, 'Eskom needs a bailout: heading for a full-year loss of R15bn', *Moneyweb*, 29 November 2018.

37 Theto Mahlakoana, 'Eskom unions accept 7.5% pay increase', *Business Day*, 30 August 2018.

38 Steyn, 'Eskom has no idea how it will fund wage increases'.

39 *Business Day*, 'Get Eskom right or we all go down', *Business Day*, 21 November 2018.

40 *The Economist*, 'The IMF agrees to beef up Argentina's bailout', *The Economist*, 8 September 2018, pp 57–58.

41 Associated Press, 'Argentina seeks emergency release of $50bn in IMF funds amid financial crisis', *The Guardian*, 29 August 2018.

42 Claudi Mailovich, 'VBS report details greed of officials', *Business Day*, 11 October 2018.

43 Gemma Ritchie, 'Pattern of wasteful expenditure as audit regression increases', *Mail & Guardian*, 21 November 2018.

44 Bekezela Phakathi, 'Kimi Makwetu decries lack of consequences for wasteful, irregular spending', *Business Day*, 11 October 2018.

Chapter Eleven

1 See Charles Feinstein, *An Economic History of South Africa: Conquest, Discrimination and Development* (Cambridge University Press, 2005).

2 Dieter von Fintel and Marlies Piek, 'South Africa's national minimum wage could hurt small firms and rural workers', *The Conversation*, 27 April 2017. Available at theconversation.com/south-africas-national-minimum-wage-could-hurt-small-firms-and-rural-workers-76474, accessed on 11 January 2019.

3 All data from tradingeconomics.com, 'China Average Yearly Wages', 1952–2018.

4 Nicoli Nattrass and Jeremy Seekings have published widely on this theme; see, most recently 'Labour market reform is needed for inclusive growth', *Viewpoints*, no 4 (October 2018).

5 Joan Robinson, *Economic Philosophy* (Transaction Publishers, 1962), p 45.

6 James-Brent Styan, 'Inside the Eskom crisis – a critical analysis', *Moneyweb*, 6 December 2018.

7 See Claudi Mailovich, 'Auditor-general Kimi Makwetu's personnel terrorised at municipalities', *Business Day*, 22 October 2018.

8 Natasha Marrian, 'Ramaphosa "deeply concerned" about dysfunctional municipalities', *Business Day*, 24 May 2018.

9 Lukhona Mnguni, 'Why SA's municipalities are failing and how to fix them', *Business Day*, 3 March 2016.

10 Malachia Mathoho, 'Examining the politics of municipal demarcation', *NGO Pulse*, 9 April 2015.

11 See Crispian Olver, *How to Steal a City: the battle for Nelson Mandela Bay – a personal account* (Jonathan Ball Publishers, 2017).

12 Andiswiwe Makinana, 'Nkwinti lays bare the broke, broken mess at water affairs', *Sunday Times*, 27 May 2028.

13 With jobs created indirectly, the figure rises to 16 per cent of GDP; see CaixaBank, 'Tourism accounts for 16% of Spain's Gross Domestic Product, according to CaixaBank Research', 7 June 2017.

14 Flora Graham, 'Daily Briefing: Within two years, we must commit to saving the web of life', *Nature Briefing*, 30 October 2018. Available at www.nature.com/articles/d41586-018-07250-y, accessed on 11 January 2019.

Chapter Twelve

1 The Freedom Charter, 25–26 June 1955. Available at www.historicalpapers. wits.ac.za/inventories/inv_pdfo/AD1137/AD1137-Ea6-1-001-jpeg.pdf, accessed on 9 January 2019.

2 See RW Johnson, *South Africa's Brave New World* (Jonathan Ball Publishers, 2010), pp 71–73.

3 Ibid, pp 73–76.

4 *Business Report*, 'Lekota takes the spoils in hot debate on NDP plan', *Business Report*, 17 August 2012.

5 Mzingaye Brilliant Xaba and Monty J Roodt, 'South Africa's land reform efforts lack a focus on struggling farmers', *Mail & Guardian*, 6 December 2016.

6 Interview, SABC-TV, 15 September 2018.

7 Hilary Joffe, 'Teetering dominoes of SA's state entities', *Business Day*, 2 August 2017.

8 Tim Cohen and Asha Speckman, 'No more money for the public-sector wages, according to the medium-term budget', *Business Day*, 24 October 2018.

9 See, for example, Carien du Plessis, 'Ramaphosa and Magashule contradict each other on Reserve Bank nationalisation', *Daily Maverick*, 16 January 2019.

10 Chester Makana, 'ANC isn't leading, it's following the EFF, Says Malema', *HuffPost*, 14 January 2018.

11 Stephen Ellis, *External Mission: the ANC in exile* (Jonathan Ball Publishers, 2012), pp 307–308.

12 The data in Tables 1 and 2 are drawn from the eNCA national survey of October 2017, conducted by MarkData.

13 J Brooks Spector, 'Op-Ed: Mandela's footprint and the great sell-out myth', *Daily Maverick*, 7 December 2015.

14 S'thembile Cele, 'Mmusi Maimane feels pressure as "white privilege" race row rocks DA', *City Press*, 5 June 2018.

15 Genevieve Quintal, Jonisayi Maromo, and Mpho Raborife, Sapa, 'ANC: Stop speculating about Mandela', *News24*, 10 June 2013.

16 Jan Gerber, 'Eastern Cape fraud surrounding Mandela's funeral to be probed after Ramaphosa signs SIU proclamations', *News24*, 25 May 2018.

17 See Julian Jackson, *A Certain Idea of France: the life of Charles de Gaulle* (Allen Lane, 2018).

18 Jerry H Brookshire, *Clement Attlee* (Manchester University Press, 1995), p 25.

19 See Agoa.info, accessed on 11 January 2019.

20 Linda Ensor, 'US duties to knock SA's Agoa exports', *Business Day*, 18 July 2018; Geoffrey Allen Pigman, 'AGOA-IV and the trade prospects of sub-Saharan Africa', Tralac (Trade Law Centre) News, 29 March 2016. Available at www.tralac.org/news/article/9343-agoa-iv-and-the-trade-

prospects-of-sub-saharan-africa.html, accessed on 22 January 2019.

21 Siseko Njobeni, 'ArcelorMittal pins its hopes on exports: low steel demand in SA prompts search for opportunities elsewhere', *Business Day*, 11 October 2018.

22 Dean Macpherson, 'South Africa's manufacturing sector needs a rescue plan', *Daily Maverick*, 10 August 2018; Statistics South Africa, 'Quarterly Labour Force Survey, Quarter 2: 2018'. Available at www.statssa.gov.za/publications/ P0211/P02112ndQuarter2018.pdf, accessed on 12 February 2019.

Chapter Thirteen

1 RW Johnson, *How Long Will South Africa Survive?* (1st edition, Jonathan Ball, 2015), pp 211–220.

2 *Fin24*, 'DA demands details of R370bn Chinese loan, warns of "debt trap"', *Fin24*, 16 September 2018.

3 See Karen Heese and Kevin Allan, 'Communities hurt by more frequent and more violent protests', *Business Day*, 29 August 2018. By that stage the number of protests had reached a new record since statistics on such matters began to be collected again in 2004.

4 Frans Cronje, *A Time Traveller's Guide to South Africa in 2030* (Tafelberg, 2017).

5 Staff Writer, 'This is who is paying South Africa's tax', *BusinessTech*, 26 October 2017.

6 Golopang Makou, 'Do 1.7 million people pay 80% of SA's income tax?', *Africa Check*, 10 May 2017. Available at africacheck.org/reports/1-7-million-people-pay-80-sas-income-tax/, accessed on 22 January 2019.

7 Mike Schussler has devised figures for countries of over 1 million population that are non-oil exporters. South Africa levies 27.3 per cent of GDP in tax – compared to a global average of 15 per cent and the Eurozone average of 19 per cent. Overall, Schussler says South Africa is the seventh most highly taxed country, though once payments to the surrounding SACU countries (Southern African Customs Union) are taken into account, this rises to fourth. See Staff Writer, 'The highest income tax rates in the world – including South Africa', BusinessTech 22 March 2018.

8 Mike Schussler, 'Tax: the burden killing South Africa', *The Cape Messenger*, 1 July 2018.

9 Staff Writer, 'This is who is paying South Africa's tax'.

10 Claire Bisseker, 'Mini-budget: Tito's first test of boldness', *Financial Mail*, 18 October 2018.

11 The quotation comes from a 1981 biography of Mugabe by David Smith and Collin Simpson. See also 'Samora Machel 1980 warning to Mugabe: chasing white Rhodesians will ruin Zimbabwe', *Zimbabwe Today*, 6 February 2017.

12 Brett Chulu, 'US$2.52bn 2017 budget deficit unprecedented', *Zimbabwe Independent*, 13 July 2018.

13 Jan Cronje, 'IMF downgrades SA's 2018 growth forecast to 0.8%', *Fin24*, 9 October 2018.
14 Tim Cohen, 'What if we just shut down SAA?', *Financial Mail*, 17 January 2019.
15 Penwell Dlamini, 'Municipal audit outcomes deteriorating – AG', *TimesLive*, 23 May 2018.
16 Ibid.
17 Simone Liedtke, 'Municipal debt a threat to viability of municipalities – Parliament', *Engineering News*, 11 May 2018.
18 *Municipal Focus*, 'Municipalities drown in debt of R43bn – Parliament hears', *Municipal Focus*, 19 March 2018.
19 Chantall Presence, 'Municipal debt owed to Eskom is at a staggering R17bn', *IOL*, 13 November 2018.
20 Amil Umraw, 'This is how Ace Magashule captured the Free State', *HuffPost*, 24 January 2018.
21 The phrase was coined by Gerald Kaufman, a member of the Labour shadow cabinet.
22 Natasha Marrian, 'Bosasa corruption scandal exposes rot in ANC', *Business Day*, 18 January 2019.
23 Abram Mashego, '"I paid Zuma R2.5 million for asylum" – Radovan Krejcír', *City Press*, 13 January 2019.

Index

236

CPSIA information can be obtained
at www.ICGtesting.com
Printed in the USA
BVHW091638200519
548791BV00008B/1183/P